HAYNES **MAX** **Ford**
POWER

focus

The definitive guide to **modifying**
by **Bob Jex** and **Em Willmott**

HAYNES MAX POWER Ford

focus

The definitive guide to modifying
by **Bob Jex** and **Em Willmott**

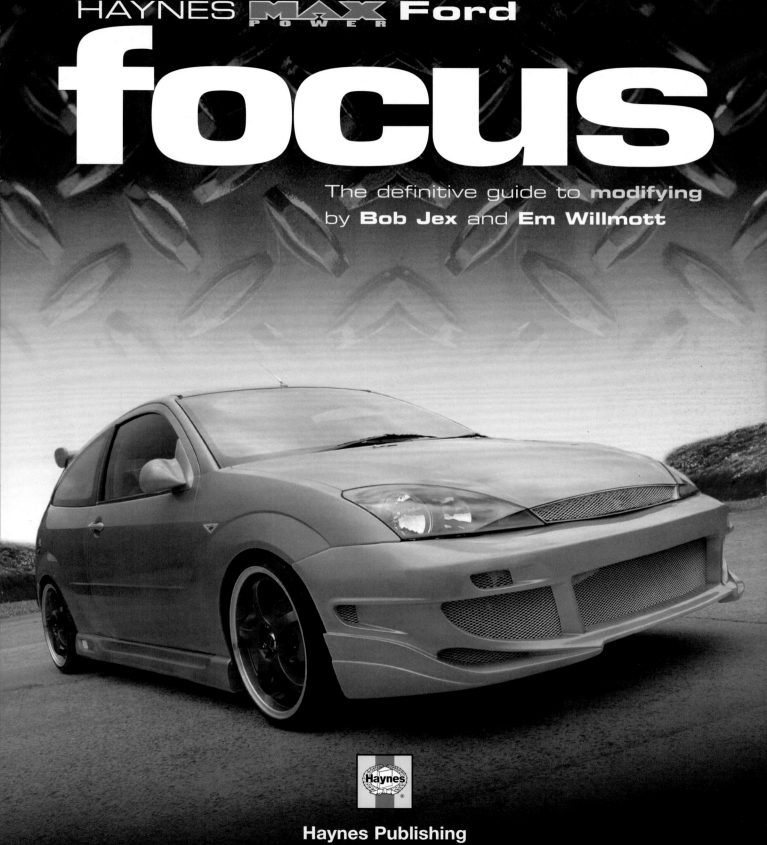

Haynes

Haynes Publishing

First published 2004
Updated and reprinted 2006

ISBN 1 84425 600 6

Printed by **J H Haynes & Co Ltd,**
Sparkford, Yeovil, Somerset BA22 7JJ, UK.

Tel: 01963 442030 Fax: 01963 440001
Int. tel: +44 1963 442030 Fax: +44 1963 440001
E-mail: sales@haynes.co.uk
Web site: www.haynes.co.uk

Haynes North America, Inc
861 Lawrence Drive, Newbury Park, California
91320, USA

Editions Haynes
4, Rue de l'Abreuvoir
92415 COURBEVOIE CEDEX, France

Haynes Publishing Nordiska AB
Box 1504, 751 45 UPPSALA, Sweden

(4085-3AH1)

It wasn't my idea guv'nor!

1 Advice on safety procedures and precautions is contained throughout this manual, and more specifically on page 186. You are strongly recommended to note these comments, and to pay close attention to any instructions that may be given by the parts supplier.

2 J H Haynes recommends that vehicle customisation should only be undertaken by individuals with experience of vehicle mechanics; if you are unsure as to how to go about the customisation, advice should be sought from a competent and experienced individual. Any queries regarding customisation should be addressed to the product manufacturer concerned, and not to J H Haynes, nor the vehicle manufacturer.

3 The instructions in this manual are followed at the risk of the reader who remains fully and solely responsible for the safety, roadworthiness and legality of his/her vehicle. Thus J H Haynes are giving only non-specific advice in this respect.

4 When modifying a car it is important to bear in mind the legal responsibilities placed on the owners, driver and modifiers of cars, including, but not limited to, the Road Traffic Act 1988. IN PARTICULAR, IT IS AN OFFENCE TO DRIVE ON A PUBLIC ROAD A VEHICLE WHICH IS NOT INSURED OR WHICH DOES NOT COMPLY WITH THE CONSTRUCTION AND USE REGULATIONS, OR WHICH IS DANGEROUS AND MAY CAUSE INJURY TO ANY PERSON, OR WHICH DOES NOT HOLD A CURRENT MOT CERTIFICATE OR DISPLAY A VALID TAX DISC.

5 The safety of any alteration and its compliance with construction and use regulations should be checked before a modified vehicle is sold as it may be an offence to sell a vehicle which is not roadworthy.

6 Any advice provided is correct to the best of our knowledge at the time of publication, but the reader should pay particular attention to any changes of specification to the vehicles, or parts, which can occur without notice.

7 Alterations to vehicles should be disclosed to insurers and licensing authorities, and legal advice taken from the police, vehicle testing centres, or appropriate regulatory bodies.

8 The vehicle has been chosen for this project as it is one of those most widely customised by its owners, and readers should not assume that the vehicle manufacturers have given their approval to the modifications.

9 Neither J H Haynes nor the manufacturers give any warranty as to the safety of a vehicle after alterations, such as those contained in this book, have been made. J H Haynes will not accept liability for any economic loss, damage to property or death and personal injury arising from use of this manual other than in respect of injury or death resulting directly from J H Haynes' negligence.

Contents

Haynes
Max Power

01

Buyer's guide

02

Insurance &
The Law

03

08

Suspension

09

Brakes

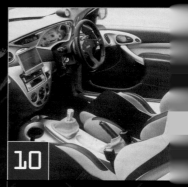

10

Interiors

Security

04

Body styling

05

Lights & bulbs

06

Wheels & tyres

07

11

ICE

12

Engines

13

Exhausts

14

Reference

Haynes
Max Power

What's that then?

Haynes Publishing have, for more than forty years, been helping people keep their cars on the roads in countries all over the world by publishing maintenance manuals. Chances are you've either got one of them yourself or you know somebody who has.

"Lights & bulbs" includes fitting smoked lights, clear side repeaters, etc.

Before

After

Remember what it feels like on your birthday, or at Christmas, when you're faced by a pile of pressies? So do we, that gnawing feeling in your gut, what's in them? What did I get? Take that feeling and multiply it by twelve, that's how we felt when we started this project. When we decided that it was time to try something new, we couldn't wait. Because the same theories apply to modifying your car as servicing it, we reckoned we'd better get on and do it ourselves. We don't pay other people to do it for us, and we get the same dodgy instructions with kit as everybody else.

So if you've ever wondered how to fit a universal door mirror properly, smooth a tailgate or just bolt a seat in, this book is for you.

We've picked up a skip full of tips along the way, and they're all here for you to use. We haven't tried to set any trends, but we've covered every possible process we think you'll need. So where we've tinted a front door window, the same rules apply to a rear one, job done.

If you look in the magazines and want some of that, join us, 'cos so do we, and we'll show you how to get it.

Keeping it real

Modifying a car is not without its problems in the 'real world', as opposed to the seemingly fantasy world of the glossy mags. For instance, it's pretty silly to spend hours fitting illegal window tints or smoked lights if you get pulled the first time you're out

afterwards. Of course, you can get pulled for all sorts of reasons (and just driving a modified car is reason enough sometimes), but keeping the car actually legal is one of the 'hidden' challenges with modifying. Throughout the book, our tips should give all the help you need to at least appear to be on the right side of the law. The annual MOT test is another favourite time for your mods to get panned, and again, we aim to give you all the help necessary to ensure at least that what you've changed doesn't lead to a fail.

Security is another major issue with a tweaked motor, and the perils of insurance cannot be taken lightly, either. We aim to give down-to-earth advice to help you keep the car in the first place, and to help you in not upsetting your insurers too much if the worst happens.

A word about fashion

In producing this book, we're aware that fashions change. What we show being fitted to our car might well be hideously out of date in 6 months time, or might not be your thing in the first place! Also, some of the stuff we've acquired from our various suppliers may no longer be available by the time you read this. We hope that, despite this, our approach of showing you step-by-step how to fit the various parts will mean that, even if the parts change slightly, the procedures we show for fitting will still be valid.

Our main project car was a 1.8 Zetec 3-door, 1999 T reg.

"Wheels & tyres" takes a detailed look at all the options.

"Body styling" shows you how to fit universal mirrors to full body kits.

"Interiors" includes seats, painting trim, gear knobs and loads more.

Don't mention
the Escort

Is this really the car that replaced the Escort? Oh, sorry. No wonder they decided to change the name of Britain's best-selling hatch when this one came along - it didn't just move the goalposts, it took the game to the next stadium. With its radical New Edge styling, not everyone actually liked the Focus when it was first unveiled, but inside a few weeks, there were no worries that Ford had "done another Sierra".

This was a truly modern design, and now, six years later, other car makers are only just catching up. Respect.

One thing they didn't change was the blue oval on the front, meaning it was bound to sell. In big numbers. And also meaning it was bound to be modified lots, resulting in plenty of choice of kit. The Focus ain't bad-looking as standard (always a bonus), and adding a kit only improves things. Want inspiration for a modded look? Well, there's the WRC rally car for starters, plus the almost-a-Cosworth RS, which you could do worse than try to copy. Foci also have some of the roomiest arches out there - monster rims? No problem.

The future's bright for the Focus, especially as it's now within more people's budgets - and the choice of modding parts looks set to grow even larger. Y'see, besides Europe, the car's also been a pretty big success in America (where it's known as - the Ford Focus, strangely), and looks like it could even be as big as the Civic. Now that's big. If it happens, expect to see Wings West kits by the shedload, as well as tons of trick engine bits. There may even be a movie. A sure sign of greatness is when the modding world takes an item from a car, and copies it to death. What are we talking about? The Focus side repeaters, now seen at any cruise, on any car. Style icons from a Ford? When did that last happen? Britain's favourite car just got very good indeed.

Buyer's guide

What to buy

Ford's glossy sales brochure tells us buying a Focus will help you live a *rewarding, purposeful* and *confident* life, and to a degree, Ford have hit the nail right on the head. Designing a new look for your car will give you the *confidence* to trust your opinions. Modifying a car gives you a *purpose* to get out of bed during daylight hours on the weekend, and when the project is completed - *rewards* you with a phat car and admiring friends, and maybe some attention from the opposite sex. Excellent.

So which model should you buy? Well as usual you have to consider your budget and insurance restraints, but then what? Does it have to be a 3-door Focus? They're quite rare, and it's certainly not a crime to have a 5-door - some of the kits actually look better on 5-door versions. Walk away if the words 'Saloon' or 'Estate' are mentioned (unless you're planning an amazing install of bass and TV screens, for which an Estate would be quite sweet!).

One day, **it shall be mine**. Oh yes.

IF (that's a big IF) you have a spare 20,000 squid kicking about somewhere (well, £19,995 to be exact!) and insurance is no consideration, our first choice is the long-time-coming Focus RS. Although the car has the Focus badge, it's actually made up of 70% new RS-only parts, and in Germany, too. The Ford Cosworth Focus concept was inspired by the 1999 Ford WRC, and was finally introduced to the European market in August 2002.

The Cosworth-developed 2.0 litre 4-cylinder 16-valve, turbocharged engine, sports 213 horses and 310 Nm torque - with plenty more tuning possibilities if you have the cash. Group 16 insurance will sting a little, but you're getting a helluva car for the money. The car hosts a range of well-known brands such as Brembo brakes, Eibach suspension and Koni adjustable rate shocks, and sits on 18 inch OZ alloys wrapped in low-profile rubber. The cabin, decked out with Sparco seats and aluminium accessories, only adds to the car's integrity. So where's the four-wheel-drive Cosworth model with a more powerful engine? Don't hold your breath!

Meanwhile, back in the real world...

For all those who aren't loaded don't worry, there are good alternatives. Broadly speaking, the cars are split into 1.4, 1.6, 1.8 and 2.0-litre petrol and 1.8 TDi/TDCi diesel engine categories.

The 1.4 CL/LX hasn't changed too much since it was introduced. The nippy 75bhp 16-valve engine won't go like stink, but it will definitely keep up with the car in front. Insurance group 4E is ridiculously low, and if you can find a 1.4 Zetec, this is the one we'd recommend, however they were discontinued in 2001.

Popular opinion is that the 1.6 or 1.8 litre models are the best. You won't get stung on the insurance (Group 5 or 6), and there's plenty of oomph in them – particularly the 115 horses found under the 1.8 bonnet. The facelift in November 2001 brought revised headlamps and bumpers, plus other interior equipment tweaks and upgrades. The most obvious way to spot the facelift is the front indicators - previously located in the front bumper, now as an integral part of the headlamp. Plenty of special editions with these two engines - the 2002 Zetec MP3 had 17-inch alloys and other cool tricks, and is one of our faves.

Which trim level to go for - CL, LX, Zetec, or Ghia? The CL's the base model, but still has central locking, electric windows and power steering. The LX usually gives you air con, remote locking and tailgate release among other goodies. The Zetec's our modding favourite, with firmer suspension, sporting cues inside, 15-inch alloys and front fogs. And so to the Ghia. Already you're thinking wood-covered dash, cracked grey leather and a tartan rug on the parcel shelf. Old people alert! However, find a Ghia at a good price and it's worth considering - lots of extra toys. But if you're ripping it apart to modify it, is there much point?

2.0 litres - that'll do nicely

The 2.0 litre range includes the RS, ST170, 2.0 Ghia and Zetec ESP. The 2.0 Ghia and Zetec ESP both belong in insurance group 8E (still reasonable) and have 130 equine power each. What's ESP? Simply, it's a system to help stop you losing it on corners. The system works with the traction control and ABS, monitoring the car's attitude, road speed, wheel speed and lateral (sideways) acceleration. If the car starts skidding, the system brings it back in line (applying brakes to individual wheels, reducing engine power etc.) So pulling handbrake turns, or doing doughnuts, might not be on?

The ST170 packs 171bhp (hence the name - ish), having an exclusive variable valve timing engine delivering 33% more power than the existing 2.0 Zetec model, and a 6-speed gearbox. But - group 15A insurance is a huge jump over a normal 2.0 litre, especially against the RS' group 16, and some critics have accused it of being not that quick, not that exciting, and big money. The half-leather bucket seats and alloys are very tasty – but would you choose one instead of an RS? Really?

Fuel economy can be fun

The 1.8 TDi/TDCi direct injection turbo-charged diesel engine cars are certainly not to be scoffed at. Not only do you get superb fuel economy (which is a bonus for the cruising master) but turbo-diesels are also very tuneable and chip-able. Ranging from group 5E to 7E, the insurance is certainly modifier-friendly. They even do a 3-door Zetec, with a choice of 100 bhp or 115 bhp engines. They even sound less like a tractor than older diesels (especially the later TDCi) - give one a try.

Don't buy a dog

Ford used to mean Fix Or Repair Daily, apparently, but the Focus is a modern Ford, meaning it has excellent day-to-day reliability, low running costs - and it doesn't rust, either.

Even the Germans buy them (and they've got the Golf, remember). So nothing ever goes wrong? Er, no, not quite - but they're way better than average. The main problem is they're favourites with companies, and you may find several with big mileages, worn trim, smoky interiors, and a generally 'loose' feel. You might also find these things on a car showing a more-sensible mileage, meaning there's a strong chance it's been clocked.

Check for signs that water's getting into the boot - especially around the rear lights. Clues are (obviously) damp boot carpet/trim, but you may get strange problems with the rear lights themselves, or even a current drain leading to a flat battery. While you're at the back, look in the 'V' at the base of the tailgate window for signs of flaking paint or even rust. The only other spot known to show rust is the bottom edge of the front arches, through stone damage.

Inside, check all electrical equipment with the engine running, especially on the 1.4 and 1.6 models. On the test drive, check that the fuel gauge is behaving itself, as this can cost hundreds to cure. Listen for droning rear wheel bearing noise at 30 to 50 mph (about £50 per side), or for any clonks from the front suspension, which could be worn anti-roll bar drop links. Petrol Foci can suffer from stalling problems, but this is usually curable by having a Ford dealer reset the car's ECU. It's worth buying one with a full Ford history - there's been a few recalls in the car's life, which a dealer would pick up on (even if the owner hasn't).

All Foci have a camshaft drivebelt (cambelt, or timing belt) which is made of reinforced rubber. The belt deteriorates with age, and for safety's sake, a new one should be fitted every 3 years or 36000 miles, especially if the engine gets a regular caning. If the belt snaps, the engine could be wrecked. Finished. Ruined. Knackered. It's not too bad a DIY job if you're confident under the hood, or budget for a garage bill around the £80 mark.

General stuff

Usually, it's far better to buy your Focus privately, as long as you know what you're doing. Dealers charge over the odds for Fords, but sometimes all you'll get for the extra money is a full valet and some degree of comeback if the car's a hound. Buying privately, you get to meet the owner, gaining you valuable clues about how the car's been treated.

Everyone's nervous when buying a car, but don't ignore your 'gut feelings' at first sight, or when meeting the owner. Don't make the mistake of deciding to buy the car *before you've even seen it* - too many people make up their minds before setting out, and blindly ignore all the warning signs. Remember, there *are* other cars, and you *can* walk away! Think of a good excuse before you set out.

Take someone who 'knows a bit about cars' along with you - preferably, try and find someone who's either got a Focus, or who's had one in the past.

Never buy a car in the dark, or when it's raining. If you do have to view any car in these conditions, agree not to hand over any major money until you've seen it in daylight, and when the paintwork's dry (dull, faded paint, or metallic paint that's lost its lacquer, will appear to be shiny in the rain).

Full service history (fsh)

Is there any service history? If so, this is good, but study the service book carefully:

a *Which garage has done the servicing? Is it a proper dealer, or a backstreet bodger? Do you know the garage, and if so, would you use it?*

b *Do the mileages show a nice even progression, or are there huge gaps? Check the dates too.*

c *Does it look as if the stamps are authentic? Do the oldest ones look old, or could this 'service history' have been created last week, to make the car look good?*

d *When was the last service, and what exactly was carried out? When was the cambelt last changed? Has the owner got receipts for any of this servicing work?*

One sign of a genuine car is a good batch of old MOTs, and as many receipts as possible - even if they're for fairly irrelevant things like tyres.

Check the mileages and dates shown on the receipts and MoTs follow a pattern indicating normal use, with no gaps in the dates, and no sudden drop in the mileage between MoTs (which might suggest 'clocking'). If you're presented with a sheaf of paperwork, it's worth going through it - maybe the car's had a history of problems, or maybe it's just had some nice new parts fitted (like a clutch, starter motor or alternator, for instance).

Check the chassis number (VIN number) and engine number on the registration document and on the car. Any sign of welding near one of these numbers is suspicious - to disguise the real number, a thief will run a line of weld over the old number, grind it flat, then stamp in a new number. Other scams include cutting the section of bodywork with the numbers on from another car, then cutting and welding this section into place. The VIN number is stamped into the floor next to the driver's seat (lift the flap in the carpet), on a tag on the dash, and on the VIN plate on the front crossmember.

The engine number is stamped into the front or the side of the engine block, at the transmission end - shouldn't be difficult to spot. If the number's been removed, or if there's anything suspicious about it, you could be buying trouble.

Check the registration document (V5) very carefully - all the details should match the car. Never buy a car without seeing the V5 - accept no excuses on this point. If buying privately, make sure that it's definitely the owner's name and address printed on it - if not, be very

The engine number is stamped into the end of the engine block . . .

. . . and the VIN is stamped into the floor by the driver's seat.

careful! If buying from a dealer, note the name and address, and try to contact the previous owner to confirm mileage, etc, before handing over more than a deposit. Unless the car's very old, it shouldn't have had too many previous owners - if it's into double figures, it may mean the car is trouble, so checking its owner history is more important.

While the trim on a Focus is quite durable, it should still be obvious whether the car's been abused over a long period, or whether the mileage showing is genuine or not (shiny steering wheels, worn carpets and pedals are a good place to start checking if you're suspicious). Okay, so you may be planning to junk most of the interior at some point, but why should you pay over the odds for a tat car which the owner hasn't given a stuff about?

Although you may feel a bit stupid doing it, check simple things too, like making sure the windows and sunroof open and shut, and that all the doors and tailgate can be locked (if a lock's been replaced, ask why). The Focus bonnet opens with a key, behind the blue oval. Check all the basic electrical equipment - lights, front and rear wipers, heated rear window, heater fan; it's amazing how often these things are taken for granted by buyers! If your chosen Focus already has alloys fitted, does it have locking wheel bolts? Where's the key? What about the code and removal tools for the stereo?

Is the catalytic converter ('cat') working? This is a wickedly expensive part to replace - the best way to ensure at least one year's grace is to only buy a car with a full MoT (the cat is checked during the emissions test). Many Focus modifiers remove the cat altogether (by fitting a de-cat pipe), which is great for performance, but means the car's illegal to use on the road.

Look closer

Don't take anything at face value. Even a fully-stamped service book only tells half the story of how your chosen Focus has been treated. Does the owner look bright enough to even know what a dipstick is, never mind how to check the oil level between services? Remember, many Focuses are 'just transport' to their owners.

Check for signs of accident damage, especially at the front end. Ask if it's ever been in a shunt - if the seller says no, but there's paint overspray under the bonnet, what's going on? Also check for paint overspray on the window rubbers, light units and bumpers/trim. Look at the car side-on - are there any mis-matched panels? With the bonnet open, check that the headlight rear shells are the same colour - mis-matched or new-looking ones merit an explanation from the seller. Does the front number plate carry details of the supplying garage, like the back one? If not, why has a new plate been fitted?

Check the glass (and even the head and tail lights) for etched-in registration numbers - are they all the same, and does it match the car's actual registration? A windscreen could've been innocently replaced, but new side glass indicates a break-in at least - is the car a 'stolen/recovered' (joyridden) example? Find the chassis and engine numbers, as described earlier in this Section, and satisfy yourself that they're genuine - check them against the registration document. An HPI check (or similar) is worthwhile, but even this won't tell you everything. If you're in doubt, or if the answers to your questions don't ring true, walk away. Make any excuse you like.

The Focus has a decent immobiliser as standard, but there's no harm fitting a good ultrasonic alarm on top - might even be worth a bit of insurance discount. Make sure that any aftermarket kit actually works, that it looks properly installed, with no stray wires hanging out, and that you get the Thatcham certificate or other paperwork to go with it. If possible, it's worth finding out exactly how it's been wired in - if it goes wrong later, you could be stranded with no chance of disabling the system to get you home.

Model history

Note: *As usual, there's plenty of "special edition" Focus models. Don't pay over the odds for a special edition, unless it's really got some extra kit you actually want.*

October 1998 (S reg) - Focus range introduced. 3- and 5-door Hatch, 4-door Saloon and 5-door Estate models, with CL, Zetec, LX, and Ghia trim levels. 1.4 (75 bhp) and 1.6 (100 bhp) 16-valve Zetec-SE petrol engines, 1.8 (115 bhp) and 2.0 litre (130 bhp) 16-valve Zetec petrol engines, and 1.8 TDi diesel (90 bhp). All models have power steering, twin airbags, central locking (remote, except on CL) and immobiliser. Zetec has alloys, front fogs. 2.0 litre models have rear disc brakes. Various option "packs" available - Style, Reflex and Climate.

October 1999 (V reg) - 2.0 Zetec ESP 3-door introduced. Electronic Stability Program, ABS and traction control. Top of the range sports model at this time.

October 2001 (51 reg) - Facelift models introduced, with new jewel-type headlights incorporating the front indicators. LX models gain heated windscreen, remote CD and alloys, Zetec gains leather steering wheel.

January 2002 (51 reg) - 2.0 litre ST170 introduced, with 171 bhp engine and 6-speed gearbox. 3- and 5-door Hatch, 17-inch alloys, perimeter alarm and half-leather sports seats. 6-disc CD changer, ABS brakes with front and rear discs.

February 2002 (51 reg) - 1.8 TDCi diesel engine introduced, with 115 bhp.

August 2002 (02 reg) - Second 1.8 TDCi diesel engine variant introduced, with 100 bhp.

October 2002 (52 reg) - 2.0 litre RS introduced, with turbocharged 213 bhp engine and 5-speed gearbox. 3-door Hatch, 18-inch OZ alloys, Cat 1 alarm, leather/alcantara interior with Sparco seats and trim parts. Carbon fibre centre console with starter button. ABS brakes with front and rear discs.

Performance figures

	0-60 (sec)	Top speed (mph)
1.4 CL	13.7	108
1.6 LX	11.2	115
1.8 Zetec	10.1	118
2.0 ESP	9.2	126
ST170	8.9	130
RS	6.3	143
1.8 TDi	13.1	114
1.8 TDCi 115	10.8	120

03

Insurance & The Law
A necessary evil

Ah, insurance - loads of money, and all you get's a piece of paper you're not supposed to use! Of course, you must have insurance - you're illegal on the road without it, and you won't be able to get the car taxed, either. If you're ever caught driving without insurance, you'll have great trouble ever getting insurance again - insurance companies regard this offence nearly as seriously as drink-driving, so don't do it!

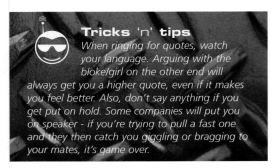

Tricks 'n' tips

When ringing for quotes, watch your language. Arguing with the bloke/girl on the other end will always get you a higher quote, even if it makes you feel better. Also, don't say anything if you get put on hold. Some companies will put you on speaker - if you're trying to pull a fast one and they then catch you giggling or bragging to your mates, it's game over.

The way insurance companies work out premiums and assess risks is a mystery to most of us. In general, the smaller the engine you have in your Focus, the less you'll pay. However, if one company's had a lot of claims on Foci in the past, the RS factor might 'unfairly' influence the premiums of lesser models, too (this is why it's important to shop around). An 'insurance-friendly' 1.4 or 1.6 should be a good bet for a sensible premium, but remember that insurance companies aren't stupid - if you swap in that ST170 / RS engine and turn your LX into a rocket, they may well 'load' the premium to RS level (and that's Group 16). Insurance is a game you can't win, but you must play.

If your annual premium seems like the national debt of a small African country (and whose isn't!), always ring as many brokers and get as many quotes as you possibly can. Yes, there's loads better ways to spend an evening/afternoon than answering the same twenty questions over and over again, but you never know what the next quote will be. A few extra minutes spent on the phone (or on the 'net) once a year may result in an extra few hundred quid in your back pocket. Well, you live in hope don't you!

With modified cars, insurance becomes even more of a problem. By putting on all the alloys, trick body kits, nice interiors, big ICE, you're making the car much more of a target for thieves (yes, ok, we know you know this). The point is, the insurance companies know this too, and they don't want to be paying out for the car, plus all the money you've spent on it, should it go missing. There is a temptation 'not to tell the insurance' about the mods you've

made. Let's deal with this right now. Our experience has been that, while it can be painful, honesty is best. Generally, the insurance company line is: '…thanks for telling us - we won't put the car 'up a group' (ie charge you more), but we also won't cover the extra cost of your alloy wheels/body kit/tasty seats in the event of any claim…'. This is fair enough - in other words, if your car goes missing, you get paid out, based on a standard car, minus all the goodies. If you particularly want all the extras covered, you might have a long hard search - most companies only offer 'modified for standard' policies. There are specialist insurers who are more friendly towards fully-loaded cars, but even they won't actually cover the cost of replacement goodies.

What type of cover, Sir?

For most of us, cost means there's only one option - TPF&T (third party, fire and theft). Fully-comp insurance is an unattainable dream for most people until they reach the 'magic' age of 25, but what's the real story?

Third Party only

The most basic cover you can get. Basically covers you for damage to other people's cars or property, and for personal injury claims. Virtually no cover for your own stuff, beyond what you get if you take the optional 'legal protection' cover.

Third Party, Fire and Theft

As above, with cover for fire and theft, of course! Better, but not much better. This is really only cover in the event of a 'total loss', if your car goes missing or goes up in smoke. Still no cover for your car if you stack it into a tree, or if someone breaks in and pinches your stereo (check your policy small-print).

Fully-comprehensive

In theory at least, covers you for any loss or damage. Will cover the cost of repairing or replacing your car, often with discounted windscreen cover and other benefits. If you lose control of the car on an icy road (arguably, not your fault) you get paid. If someone pinches your wheels and drops the car on the floor, you get paid - at least for the damage done to the underside, and for standard wheels and tyres. Most policies include provision of a hire car after a shunt, which is pretty useful. Some offer cheap breakdown cover packages in with the main policy. With a fully-comp policy, you can 'protect' your no-claims bonus for a small fee so you don't automatically lose all those hard-earned years' worth of discount if you prang it (generally, you can only do this on fully-comp).

All this extra cover costs, obviously, but how much? You might be surprised what the actual difference is. Think about it, anyway - it's got to be worth a couple of hundred quid more to go fully-comp, if your car's worth into four figures, surely?

Valuing your car

When your insurance pays out in the event of a total loss or write-off, they base their offer on the current market value of an identical standard model to yours (less your excess). The only way you'll get more than the average amount is to prove your Focus is in above-average nick (with photos?) or that the mileage was especially low for the year.

With this in mind, don't bother over-valuing your Focus in the hope you'll get more in the event of a claim - you won't! The only way to do this is to seek out an 'agreed-value' deal, which you can usually only get on classic-car policies (with these, the car's value is agreed in advance between you, not worked out later by the company with you having no say in it). By over-valuing your Focus, you could be increasing your premium without gaining any benefit - sound smart to you?

Equally though, don't under-value, in the hope you'll get a reduction in premium. You won't, and if there's a total loss claim, you won't get any more than your under-valued amount, no matter how loudly you complain.

Work on what you paid for the car, backed up with the sort of prices you see for similar cars in the ads (or use a secondhand car price guide). Add no more than 10% for the sake of optimism, and that's it.

Your car? Or your Dad's?

Insurance really costs when you're the wrong side of 25. Ever been tempted to tell your insurance that your full-on sorted Focus belongs to your Dad (old insurance-friendly person), then get him to insure it, with you as a named driver? Oh dear. This idea (known as 'fronting') is so old, it's grown a long white beard. And it sucks, too. First of all, insurance companies aren't stupid. They know your Dad (or your Mum, or old Uncle Bert) isn't likely to be running around in a kid's pocket-rocket, and they treat any 'named driver' application with great suspicion. Even if they do take your money, don't imagine they've been suckered. In the event of a claim, they'll look into everything very carefully, and will ask lots of awkward questions. If you get caught out in the lie, they've taken your money, and you've got no insurance - who's been suckered now?

This dubious practice also does you no favours in future years. All the time you're living the lie, you're not building up any no-claims bonus of your own - you're just delaying the pain 'til later, and without having real cover in the meantime.

value of your car, should it be stolen. Most policies have 'compulsory' excess amounts, which you can do nothing about. By increasing excesses voluntarily, you're limiting the amount you'll get still further. Insurance companies like this, and should reduce your premium in return - but this only goes so far, so ask what the effect of different voluntary excesses will be. Don't increase your excess too far, or you'll get paid nowt if you claim!

Limit your mileage. Most companies offer a small discount if you only cover a small annual mileage. To get any meaningful reduction, the mileage has to be a lot less than 10,000 per year. Few companies, though, ever ask what the car's current mileage is - so how are they gonna know if you've gone over your self-imposed limit?

Make yourself the only driver. Pretty self-explanatory. The more people who drive your car, the greater the risk to the company, and a car's owner will always drive more carefully (it's their money that bought it) than any named driver. If you've built up 2 years' worth of no-claims, but your partner hasn't, putting them on your insurance will bump it up, due to their relative inexperience.

Get a garage - and use it. Where you park can have a big effect on your premium. Parking it on the street is the worst. Park off the road (on a driveway) when you're at home. The best thing is to have a garage of your own (don't pretend you use your Dad's garage) - see if you can rent one locally, even if it means walking a few hundred yards. If you're a student living away from home, tell your company where the car will be parked during term-time - if you're at Uni in London, this is a bigger risk than living at home 'in the country', and vice-versa.

Fit an approved alarm or immobiliser. See if you can get a list from your company of all their approved security devices, and fit whatever you can afford. Not all companies approve the same kit, so it might even be worth contacting more than one company for advice. Any device with a Thatcham or Sold Secure rating should be recognised. In some cases, the discounts offered are not that great any more - but an alarm is still a nice way to get peace of mind.

Build up your no-claims bonus. You'll only do this by owning and insuring a car in your own name, and then not making any claims. Simple really. One rather immoral (but not actually illegal) dodge is to buy an old banger, insure it cheap, then never drive it. You'll need to keep it fully road-legal (with tax, MOT) if you park it on the road. For every year you do this, you'll build up another year of NCB.

Hang onto your no-claims bonus. Obviously, the less you claim, the less your insurance will cost. If something happens to your car, don't be in too big a hurry to make a claim before you've thought it all through. How much will it cost to fix? How much is your excess? How much will your renewal premium be, next year? If you have a big enough accident which you're sure isn't your fault, ring your company, but make it quite clear you're NOT claiming yet - just informing them of the accident. It should be down to the other driver's insurance to pay. You don't always lose all your no-claims, either, even if it was your fault - depends how many years you've built up. Once you've got a few years, ask whether you can 'protect' your no-claims.

Avoid speed cameras and The Law. Yes, okay, easier said than done! But anything less than a clean licence is not good from the insurance perspective. One SP30 won't hurt much, but the second strike will, so take it easy. Don't get caught on traffic-light cameras, either - just one is a major no-no.

'Legit' ways to limit your premium

If you do enough ringing around for quotes, you'll soon learn what the 'right answers' to some of the questions are - even if you can't actually give them (don't tell lies to your insurance company). Mind you, with a little thought, you can start to play their game and win - try these:

Volunteer to increase your excess. The 'excess' is put there to stop people claiming for piddling little amounts - when they pay out, it's always the repair/replacement cost minus whatever the 'excess' is. So, for instance, if you've got a £200 theft excess, it means you'll automatically get £200 less than the agreed

Insurance-friendly mods?

Insurers don't like any changes from standard, but some things you'll do are worse from their viewpoint than others. The guidelines below are just that - for guidance. No two companies will have the same outlook, and your own circumstances will play a big part too.

Golden Rule Number One: If in doubt, declare everything. Insurance companies are legally entitled to dispute any claim if the car is found to be non-standard in any way.

Golden Rule Number Two: Before you spend huge money modifying the car, ring your insurance, and ask them how it will affect things.

Body mods – Even a tiny rear spoiler could be classed as a 'bodykit' (yes, it's daft, but that's how it is). Anything which alters the exterior appearance should be declared. As long as the mods don't include a radical full-on bodykit, the jump in premium should be fairly small. Any genuine Ford add-ons (ST170 bumpers, headlights) might not cost at all - bonus.

Brakes – The companies view brake mods as tampering with safety-related kit, and modifying the brakes implies that you drive fast and hard. You might get away with standard-sized grooved/drilled discs and pads, but fitting bigger discs and replacement calipers will prove expensive.

Engine mods – 'Mild' mods such as induction kits and exhausts don't give much more power, so don't generally hurt. But 'chipping' your Focus will lead to drastic rises in premiums, or a complete refusal of cover. With complete engine transplants, you'll be required to give an engineer's report, and to get your wad out.

Interior mods – Don't assume that tarting up the inside won't interest the insurance company. By making any part of the car more attractive, you're also attracting the crims. Cars get trashed for parts, as often as not - and your racing seats and sexy steering wheel could be worth major money. Still, the effect on premiums shouldn't be too great, especially if you've got an approved alarm.

Lights – Change the car's appearance, and are safety-related. You'll probably get asked for lots of details, but as long as you've kept it sensible (and legal, as far as possible), the effect on your wallet shouldn't be too harsh.

Security – Make sure you mention all security stuff - alarms, immobilisers (including mechanical devices), locking wheel nuts, large Alsatian in the back seat… But - don't over-sell the car. Tell the truth, in other words. If you've got a steering wheel lock, do you always fit it? If you didn't when your car went missing, you're in trouble. Don't say you've got a Cat 1 alarm if it really came from Argos, and don't tell them you garage the car at night if it's stuck out in the road.

Suspension – Changes the car's appearance, and is safety-related. Some enlightened companies once took the view that modded suspension helps the car corner better, so it's safer. Drops of only 30 to 40 mm shouldn't mean bigger premiums.

Wheels – Very appearance-altering, and very nickable. At least show some responsibility by fitting some locking nuts/bolts and an approved alarm. Quite likely to attract a low-to-moderate rise in premium, which still won't cover your wheels properly - you could arrange separate cover for your wheels, then at least you'll get paid. Some companies may ask for a photo of the car with the wheels on.

And finally - a new nightmare

Not telling the insurance the whole truth gets a little tricky when you make a claim. If the insurance assessor comes to check your bent/burnt/stolen-and-recovered 'standard' Focus, and finds he's looking at a vehicle fitted with trick alloys/bodykit/radical interior, he's not going to turn a blind eye. Has the car got an MoT? Oh, and did you declare those points on your licence? No? You're then very much at the mercy of your insurer, especially if they can prove any mods contributed to the claim. At best, you'll have a long-drawn-out battle with your insurer to get a part-payout, and at worst they'll just refuse to get involved at all.

One more thing - *be careful what you hit.* If your insurance is declared void, they won't pay out for the repairs to the other car you smacked into, or for the lamp-post you knock down (several hundred quid, actually). And then there's the personal injury claims - if your insurance company disowns you, it'll be you who has to foot the bill. Even sprains and bruises can warrant claims, and more serious injuries can result in claims running into lots of zeroes! Without insurance cover, **you'll** have to pay. Probably for a long, long time. Think about it, and we won't see you in court.

Insurance & The Law

Big Brother in a Box

Speed cameras have to be one of the most unpopular things ever. We're talking worse than exams, dentists, alcohol-free beer, and the Budget. Does anyone actually like them? Well, the makers do - they should all be living it up on a beach in the Bahamas. The people making speed camera signs are obviously lovin' it. And the Chancellor? Nuff said.

Speed, of course, is fun. The sensation of speed is the main reason we enjoy driving, and it's one of the best ways to show off your motor. There's nothing like giving your ride a good caning, being pushed back in the seat, exhaust snarling, engine singing. Sounds like fun to me - so these things are really fun cameras, then?

Like it or not, we live in a world obsessed with limiting speed. Excess speed, we're told, causes accidents and costs lives. As most of us have realised by now, excess speed really means more money for the Government. What causes accidents is driving like a tw*t. But they don't have cameras for that.

Before we get ourselves in too much trouble, we have to admit the cameras might save lives in built-up areas with lots of peds, kids and old folk about. Driving like a hooligan in those situations probably should get you a slap on the wrist for 'endangering lives'. But at night, on a dead-straight road with no traffic? We think not.

Pay attention

The best you can say about cameras is that they're a necessary evil which we all have to live with. So what's the best way of avoiding the 'bad news' letter in the post?

There is one 100% foolproof method, which is totally legal, and it's dead simple - don't ever speed. That should do the trick. Yeah, right. Back in the real world, everyone speeds some time, even if it's only by a few mph. Add a few more miles-per because you weren't really watching your speed, and then do it somewhere there's a camera (or a sneaky mobile trap you'd never spotted before), and you're nicked. Is it any wonder that clean licences are getting as rare as rocking-horse leftovers?

Even on roads you know well, the do-gooders are forever lowering the limits, so if you don't watch it, you'll be sailing through more than 10 mph over today's new limit. And that's definitely worth a few points! You've gotta concentrate, to stay clean.

Know your enemy

First of all, you've got to know what you're up against. It's the only way (short of the fantasy world of never, ever speeding) that you stand a chance. And the first thing to know is - not all cameras are the same. Some can even be beaten.

Gatso (and PEEK)

The first, the best-known, the most common, and probably the most-hated. Invented by the winner of the 1953 Monte Carlo Rally, Gatsos are the familiar large, square box in stealth grey or high-viz yellow, with a square lens and flash unit (the later, less-common PEEK cameras have two round items, set one above the other). These are radar-operated (type 24) and can only 'get' you from behind, because they use a flash to take the photo, and this would blind you if it went off with you coming towards it. These cameras, therefore, cannot in theory catch you speeding towards them (don't quote us on that). As a result of this limitation, some authorities will turn the cameras round from time to time, to catch you out.

Gatsos have 35 mm film inside, with about 400 shots possible before the film runs out. It's obviously vital that the film is recovered from the camera, or a prosecution can't be made - these cameras get vandalised for all sorts of reasons. Some cameras are rumoured not to contain any film, so they flash without recording any evidence (that bloke down the pub could be wrong, though).

If the radar detects excess speed, the flash is triggered twice as you pass over the measured line markings on the road. From the distance you travel between the set flashes, your speed can be proved. It's anyone's guess where the trigger speed for a camera will be set, but it's almost bound to be quite a few mph over the posted limit - if it wasn't, the camera would quickly catch dozens of speeders, and run out of film. Be more wary of inner-city Gatsos, as they're probably 'emptied' more often, allowing a lower speed tolerance.

tricks 'n' tips
In a thirty limit, you're less likely to speed if you hook a lower gear than normal. Most cars will comfortably cruise through a thirty in 4th gear, but it's too easy to add speed in 4th. Try using 3rd, and the natural engine braking (and extra engine/exhaust noise) will help you keep a lid on your speed. It's not foolproof, but give it a try anyway.

RLCs are also Gatso-based, but they work through sensors in the road, which are active when the lights are on red. If your car passes over them in this condition, it's gotcha. Some RLCs use radar too, so if you speed through on red, you'll also get a speeding fine. Gee, thanks.

Truvelo
Oooh, nasty. The forward-facing 'gatso' is particularly unpleasant, but luckily for us, it's also more expensive than the rear-facing Gatso, so not as common. Yet. The Truvelo camera can be recognised by two round lenses side by side in the centre of its box, and one of these is a pinky-red colour (hence the 'pinkeye' nickname). The unusual pink 'lens' is actually a flash unit, fitted with a red filter to avoid blinding the driver. Because the photo's taken from the front, it's hard for the driver to claim someone else was driving, or that they 'don't know'

who was driving (a common ploy to try and 'get off' Gatso offences). The less-visible flash gives less warning to following motorists, too. Not that we're suggesting they're out to get us. Oh no.

These babies are triggered by the car passing over piezo sensors set into the road, not radar. If you see three stripes across your path, slow the heck down.

Red Light Cameras
Intended to catch people who go through traffic lights on red. Which, you have to say, is pretty dodgy. And have you ever risked it on a single amber? If you remember your Highway Code, this means stop, the same as a red light. 'Amber-gamblers' should also beware the traffic-light cams, 'cos they'll get you one day. Unlike (a few) points for speeding, points for traffic light offences will really hurt your insurance premiums, so watch it.

SPECS
Yikes - this really is Big Bro stuff. This system uses digital cameras (no film needed), mounted high on special gantries - these are a set distance apart, and create a speed monitoring zone. When you 'enter the zone', your number plate is recorded digitally, with a date and time stamp (regardless of whether you're speeding). When you leave the zone, another camera does the same thing. Because you've travelled a known distance between the two cameras, it's possible to calculate your average speed - if you're over the limit for the stretch of road, the computer spits out a fine in your direction.

What's really worrying about this technology is that it can be used to cross-check you and your car for other offences (whether your car's taxed and MoT'd, for instance). Anything dodgy, and the next time you pass by those cameras at that time of day, you could be in for a jam-sandwich surprise. Still, it could also catch the crims making off with your motor...

Mobile or temporary speed traps

These are either Gatso, Mini-Gatso, or laser type.

The potential Gatso sites are easy enough to spot - look for three shiny strips across the road, with a sturdy grey metal post alongside, on the pavement. Mr Plod comes along, sets up his camera (which uses sensors in the road strips not radar to detect your speed), catches his daily quota of speeders, and moves on. Don't give him a short day by being one of his victims.

Mini-Gatsos are just smaller, mobile versions of the UK's least-favourite roadside 'furniture', operated out of cop-cars and anonymous white vans - to get you, you have to be driving away from them.

More sinister (and much on the increase) are the laser cameras, which are aimed at your number plate (usually the front one) and record your speed on video. Often seen mounted on tripods, on bridges overlooking busy roads, or hidden inside those white 'safety camera partnership' vans. Lasers have quite a range (1000 metres, or over half a mile), so by the time you've spotted them, they've spotted you speeding. It's up to the operator to target likely speeding vehicles - so will they pick on your maxed motor? You bet!

Achtung!
Do you live in, or regularly drive through, Northamptonshire or North Wales? We've got two words for you. Oh, dear. Northamptonshire is the area with the most cameras, and where new camera technology is often first tried out, while North Wales has one of the most active safety cam partnerships, with many roaming vans. But don't feel too bad, guys - the way it's going, the rest of us will soon catch you up.

Beating the system

No-one's condoning regular speeding, but these days, it's just too easy to get 'done' for a fairly minor speed infringement. Which hardly seems fair. There must be some way of fighting back, surely?

Cheap and legal

Don't. Ever. Speed. Simple, but not easy in the real world. Next!

Neither cheap nor legal

The James Bond option

One of 007's older cars had self-changing number plates - this may have been the inspiration for a highly-illegal speed camera dodge. Since all the detection systems rely heavily on your number plate, some skankers drive round with false plates - they might even have copied yours. Worth remembering if you ever get accused of speeding in the Outer Hebrides. Getting caught on false plates could be a £1000 fine, so is it worth the risk?

For ages now, companies have been advertising 'photo-reflective' plates (they're not illegal, but the dibble take a dim view). Most are a rip-off, but some do appear to work – on traps which flash. Speed cameras take very high-res pictures, however - even if your plates don't give you away, the coppers might i.d. your motor from its non-standard features. Money wasted, then.

Cloaking device?

The mobile laser speed trap is one of the most common, and most hated, in the UK. It sends out a laser beam which targets your front number plate. Wouldn't it be great if you could buy something to mess up its signal, so it couldn't 'lock on' ? You can - it's called a laser diffuser (sometimes marketed under the guise of a remote garage door-opener). And yes, they do work - but careful fitting is needed, and the lenses need regular cleaning. If you're caught using it for speed trap evasion, you can be done for obstruction, or perverting the course of justice - it pays to have a well-placed 'off' switch.

Gatso-beating radar 'scramblers' are said not to work, while radar jammers are an illegal transmitter - using one could see you inside for much longer than a speeding conviction.

A sound investment?

Radar detectors

These have been around for ages, and started life in the US. They're good for detecting radar-based speed cameras (most Gatsos), and any old police radar guns still in use, but that's all. Don't buy an old one (you'll get lots of false alerts if it's not meant for Euro/UK use), or a cheap one (it might not have enough range to give you a chance). **Stop press: Looks like radar detectors are finally going to be made illegal – only GPS systems will be legal after this.**

GPS systems

Using Global Positioning Satellite technology, these devices are really speed camera site locators, not detectors. Using an onboard database of camera locations, they constantly monitor your car's position, and warn when you're approaching a 'danger area'. Providing you keep your dash-mounted podule updated (by downloading the latest camera/blackspot info from the maker's website), these will warn you of virtually every potential camera in the country, including Truvelo and SPECS. The only limitations are a lack of laser detection, and it won't get all the mobile sites.

You must download new info regularly, and this costs (you buy a subscription to the website). Also, if your system hasn't been in use for a while, it can take quite a few minutes for the pod to pick up the satellites it needs - during this time, you're unprotected. Don't buy secondhand units with no subscription left, as the makers sometimes can't (won't?) re-activate them.

Laser detectors

The makers say this is essential kit to combat the roaming camera van threat, but be careful. We said earlier that laser cams have a range of up to 1000 metres, but most operators don't trigger theirs until you're much, much closer than that. Which means you have far less time to react. As long as you're not the first car along, your laser detector may pick up laser 'scatter' from cars in front, but there isn't much scatter with a laser. It's said that some laser detectors will only go off if your car's already been targeted - and of course, it's too late by then.

A final word

Don't rely too heavily on even the best anti-camera technology - try and drive within the spirit, if not the letter, of the Law, with a detector as backup.

Road **Angel**

The most effective way to 'detect' a camera is to know where it is. Yeah – obviously! But with cameras still being hidden behind road signs and bridges, and increasing numbers of camera-kitted white vans, knowing where the cams are ain't easy.

A GPS locator monitors your car's position relative to known camera sites, and warns you when you're getting close. The latest offerings also warn when you're approaching schools and other areas where extra care is needed. These devices are definitely not illegal. They increase road safety, by telling you where 'accident blackspots' are – not when to brake…

tricks 'n' tips
Don't leave the mounting cradle fitted when you leave the car – it's all the clue a thief needs that there's some serious money's worth hidden in your glovebox. Even if it's not there (because you've sensibly taken it with you) you're still making it too tempting.

This Road Angel offers two main mounting options – a sticky-backed magnetic mount directly on the dash, or this rather neat screen-mounted cradle (also with a mag mount).

01 Either way, make sure the wipers don't obscure the unit's 'view', or the laser detection function won't stand a chance.

02 A GPS unit like this is only as good as the info it's working from – update it regularly by downloading the latest camera locations, or it's worse than useless. If you can use a PC well enough to download stuff from the Internet, you've got no worries.

03 Plug the unit into its lighter socket power supply (assuming it's not already taken by your phone charger or hands-free kit), then fit the unit to its bracket. First, you're greeted by a friendly message, then the unit starts searching for its satellites. While this is going on, remember that you're not protected.

04 Depending which system you've got, when you're getting near a camera site (sorry – accident blackspot), you'll get a warning beep or message, and the display will flash. If you miss all that lot, you probably need to downgrade your ICE install.

Look Mum, no hands!

As of December 2003 (okay, March 2004 really) it became illegal to hold your mobile while driving. Well, brilliant - something new to get done for. Like we were really getting short of that kind of thing. But you have to say, yipping and driving always was a pretty dodgy pastime, with driving coming off worse - if only all the UK's traffic legislation made this much sense.

Of course, the people who really benefit are the ones making hands-free car phone kits - you're looking at upwards of £50 (for a conventional kit) to get anything worth fitting. Which one do I go for? Will I have to make holes in my dash? Good questions. But we're jumping ahead - let's deal first with what the new law means in the real world.

Points of law

First, fitting a hands-free kit is merely a way of getting round part of the new legislation. They're not 'fully-legal', they're just 'not prohibited'. Even using a hands-free set-up is a distraction while you're piloting your machine, and if you start weaving about, carve up a cyclist, or run a red light, you're still likely to face

a 'driving without due care' charge, or worse. The best solution for making a call is to stop where it's safe - have voicemail enabled if you get called while you're driving.

Answering a call, even with hands-free, might not be safe in all circumstances. Let it ring. As for what you're allowed to do with the phone itself - it's just pressing the buttons (and no, this doesn't mean it's ok 2 txt). Holding the phone in any way is not permitted. Even if you're stuck in traffic, completely stationary, the engine would have to be off before you can use your mobile normally - only then could you really say you weren't 'driving'.

At the moment, getting caught using a phone on the move only carries a fixed fine. But it looks like this hasn't worked, because it's soon going to be a bigger fine, and points on the licence. Use your moby sensibly (better still, don't use it, in the car at least), or it could mean re-sitting your driving test. Paying attention now, aren'tcha?

Achtung! *Don't just pull over and screech to a stop when the phone rings. If you do this somewhere stupid, you're just as likely to get fined as you would for using the phone on the move.*

tricks 'n' tips *If you've got a passenger in the car, it's perfectly legal for them to use a mobile, so if yours rings, let them answer it, and relay the message to you - can't be done for that.*

What's available?

Conventional kits

The new law has brought a whole range of new product to the market, so there's no need to settle for the old-style in-car kits, which leave holes all over your dash. Most of the latest kits have adhesive pads, and just plug into your fag lighter. The most essential item, to comply with the rules, is a phone holder or 'cradle' (holding phone bad - cradle good).

As no-one keeps the same phone for very long, it's worth looking for a kit which you can convert from one make of phone to another - by buying a different adapter lead, for instance.

Look for kits offering 'full duplex' operation - this means you can talk and listen at the same time. Just like real life. What it really means is conversations are easier and more natural - to understand fully why you need this feature, try one without it. Non-duplex kits cut out the speaker when they pick up any sound - this could be you talking (as intended), or it could just be noise inside the car. Very irritating, especially in an area where you've already got poor reception to deal with.

Some kits feature 'infra-red technology', which means you can answer/end calls by waving your hand in front of the phone. Proper hands-free operation, and great for impressing your passengers. Maybe not so good if you make lots of hand gestures while driving?

Car stereo kits

One of the newest ideas, and catching on fast. Uses a radio transmitter clipped over the phone speaker to transmit calls over a radio channel on your car stereo. When the phone rings, flick on the radio to the preset channel, speak into the phone's mike as normal, and hear your caller through your car speakers (since it's your stereo, you have easy control over call volume). They're cheap, and they appear to work, though there are potential problems with interference. Remember, this is a developing technology - it pays to buy the latest model you can find.

Bluetooth headsets

Bluetooth offers wireless operation, so get yourself a headset with mike, and you can chat away without having the phone up to your ear. Most modern handsets are Bluetooth-capable, and really new ones also have voice-activated dialling, which offers true hands-free operation in the car. Downsides? Some doubts over sound quality, and do you really want to wear a headset all the time you're driving?

Kit fitting

Fitting details are obviously going to vary, depending on what you've bought – the main trick is to get one which doesn't require you to go drilling holes in your dash. Luckily, this is now so unpopular that most modern kits don't even offer hole-drilling as an option.

Mr Handsfree

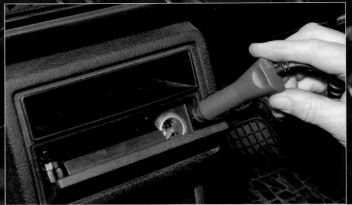

01 All these kits (apart from the Bluetooth headset) need power, usually conveniently taken from the fag lighter socket. Umm, yeah... right... Not easy getting the adapter in the socket, with the ashtray in place, is it? Proof that the Focus comes from a time before mobile phones.

02 If you're not going to drill holes, you'll be sticking stuff on. If you want things to stay stuck (and you usually only get one shot at this) a little cleaning is in order first.

03 Mostly, it's Velcro pads you get for sticking the various kit bits in place (so they can be easily ripped off and stashed when you leave the car). Leave the two 'halves' of Velcro stuck together while fitting. With the mounting area clean, it's peel . . .

04 . . . and press firmly. This is the main unit, which contains the speaker. We thought the centre console was too good a spot to ignore. You only have to ensure the two curly-cords will reach the lighter socket and the phone.

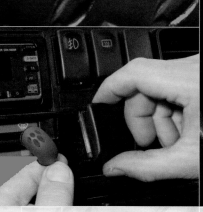

05 Not all fitting is quite this simple, though. With a little clever thinking, you can do a much neater fitting job than one which leaves all the wires hanging out. Take this little mike which comes with the Mr Handsfree kit – by prising out one of the Focus's blank switches, we hid the wire inside the dash and stuck the mike to the switch, right where it's needed. Result.

06 For mounting the phone itself, we have a magnetic bracket, again stuck with sticky pads. It's only an old Nokia, but we'd still better make sure it doesn't hit the deck, by making sure it's firmly attached.

07 And there it is – the phone's nice and handy, the mike's discreetly mounted, and the speaker unit's tucked in the console. And this is the first one of these we've fitted!

Pama Plug n Go

This is one neat unit – no dangling wires, a well-designed mounting bracket with a huge sucker for sticking to the windscreen, and a built-in speaker which faces the glass, so sound is 'reflected' back. The unit is self-contained, with a built-in battery (car charger supplied), so it can be used anywhere, not just in-car. Looks sweet, works a treat.

01

Jabra Bluetooth headset

Only any good to you if your phone's got Bluetooth, but like the Pama unit we fitted earlier, there's no mess. The headset needs charging before use, but after that, you just 'pair' your phone and headset together, and start jabbering. If your phone's trendy enough to have voice-activated dialling, this is about as hands-free as you'll get. You don't even need a cradle for your mobile with this one!

01

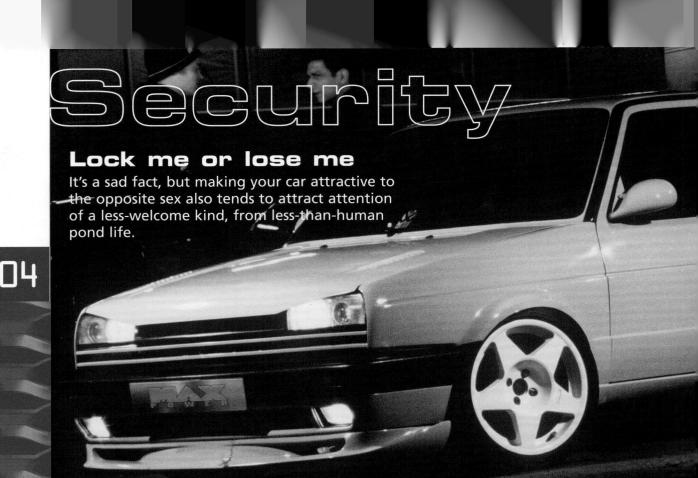

Security

Lock me or lose me

It's a sad fact, but making your car attractive to the opposite sex also tends to attract attention of a less-welcome kind, from less-than-human pond life.

Avoiding trouble

Now come on - you're modifying your car to look cool and to be seen in. Not a problem - but be careful where you choose to show your car off, and who to. Be especially discreet, the nearer you get to home - *turn your system down* before you turn into your road, for instance, or you'll draw unwelcome attention to where that car with the loud stereo's parked at night.

Without being too paranoid, watch for anyone following you home. At night, if the car behind switches its lights off, be worried. If you suspect this is happening, do not drive home - choose well-lit public places until they give up. Believe us - it happens.

If you're going out, think about where you're parking - well-lit and well-populated is good.

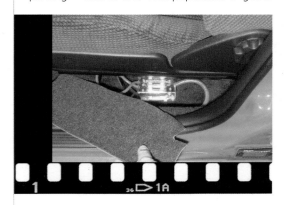

Thieves hate light being on them, so don't make it easy by parking somewhere dark - think about this if you park up in daylight, knowing you won't be back 'til late.

Hands up, who doesn't lock their car when they get petrol? Your insurance company has a term for this, and it's 'contributory negligence'. In English, this means you won't get a penny if your car goes missing when you haven't locked it.

If you're lucky enough to have a garage, use it. On up-and-over garage doors, fit extra security like a padlock and ground anchor.

A clever thief will watch your movements and habits over several days before trying your car. Has it got an alarm, and do you always set it? Do you only fit your steering wheel lock when you feel like it? Do you always park in the same place, and is the car hidden from the house or from the road? Don't make his life easier. Ask yourself how you'd nick your car…

A word about your stereo

From the moment you bolt on those nice alloys, it's taken as read that you've also got stereo gear that's worth nicking - and the thieves know it. All the discreet installation in the world isn't going to deter them from finding out what's inside that nice motor.

Please don't advertise your love of ICE around your car. Your nice stereo gear will fit other cars too, and can be ripped out in nothing flat. You may be very proud of your ICE install, but nothing is more of an 'invite' than a huge ICE sticker or sunstrip. If you've fitted one just to look cool, replace it now with something less provocative - seriously. Your set might not actually be very expensive, but you could still lose a side window for advertising something better.

You'll have got a CD player, obviously, but don't leave discs or empty CD cases lying around inside the car. A nice pair of 6x9s in full view on the back shelf is an invite to having your rear window smashed - stealth shelf, anyone? When you're fitting your system, give some thought to the clues you could accidentally leave in plain view. Oxygen-free speaker cable is great stuff, but it's also a bit bright against dark carpets, and is all the clue necessary that you're serious about your tunes. Hide amps and CD changers under your front seats, or in the boot.

Most modern sets are face-off or MASK, so if they've got security features like this, use them - take your faceplate off when you leave the car, and take it with you rather than leaving it in the door pocket or glovebox (the first places a thief will look).

Things that go beep in the night

Unless your insurance company demands it up front, fitting an alarm is something generally done as an after-thought. We know alarms aren't exactly sexy, but don't skimp - an alarm may never be put to the test, but if it is, you'll be glad you spent wisely…

The simplest first step to car security is to fake it. Tacky *'This car is fitted with an alarm'* stickers won't fool anyone, but if you want cheap, just fit a flashing LED. We know it's not the real thing, but everyone else will think you've got a posh alarm. An LED is cheap to buy and easy to fit, and can be rigged to a discreet switch inside the car.

Don't overlook the value of so-called 'manual' immobilisers, such as steering wheel locking bars and gear-to-handbrake lever locks. These can be a worthwhile deterrent - a thief not specifically after your car may move on to an easier target. Some of the items offered may be 'Sold Secure' or Thatcham Cat 3, accolades well worth checking out, since it means they've withstood a full-on brute force attack for a useful length of time.

The only way to combat the more determined thief is to go for a well-specified and intelligently-installed alarm. Immobilisers alone have their place, but sadly, even a pro-fitted immobiliser on its own won't stop someone pinching your wheels, or having it away with the stereo gear. Neither, incidentally, will a cheap alarm - you have to know how the thieves operate to stand any chance defeating them. Any alarm you fit yourself probably won't gain you any insurance discount, but it will give you peace of mind, and DIY means you can do a real trick installation, to make it very hard work for the gyppos.

Finally, one other scam which you might fall victim to. If you find your alarm is suddenly going off a lot at night, when previously it had been well-behaved, don't ignore the problem. It's an old trick for a thief to deliberately set off your alarm several times, each time hiding round the corner when you come out to investigate, then to wait until the fifth or sixth time when you don't reset it (in disgust), leaving him a clear run. If your alarm does keep false-alarming

without outside assistance, find out the cause quickly, or your neighbours will quickly become 'deaf' to it.

Thatcham categories and meanings:

1. **Cat 1.** For alarms and electronic immobilisers.
2. **Cat 2.** For electronic immobilisers only.
3. **Cat 2-1.** Electronic immobilisers which can be upgraded to Cat 1 alarms later.
4. **Cat 3**. Mechanical immobilisers, eg snap-off steering wheels, locking wheel bolts, window film, steering wheel locks/covers.
5. **Q-class.** Tracking devices.

Other alarm features

Two-stage anti-shock - means that the alarm shouldn't go off, just because the neighbour's cat jumps on your car roof, or because Little Johnny punts his football into your car. Alarm will only sound after a major shock, or after repeated shocks are detected.

Anti-tilt - detects any attempt to lift or jack up the car, preventing any attempt to pinch alloys. Very unpopular with thieves, as it makes the alarm very sensitive (much more so than anti-shock). Alarm may sound if car is parked outside in stormy conditions (but not if your suspension's rock-hard!).

Anti-hijack - immobiliser with built-in delay. If your motor gets hi-jacked, the neanderthals responsible will only get so far down the road before the engine cuts out.

Rolling code - reduces the chance of your alarm remote control signal from being 'grabbed' by special electronic equipment.

Total closure - module which connects to electric windows/sunroof and central locking, which closes all items when alarm is set. Alarms like this often have other nifty features such as remote boot opening.

Pager control - yes, really - your alarm can be set to send a message to your pager (why not your mobile?) if your car gets tampered with.

Current-sensing disable - very useful feature on some cars which have a cooling fan which can cut in after the ignition is switched off. Without this feature, your alarm will be triggered every time you leave it parked after a long run - very annoying.

Volumetric-sensing disable - allows you to manually disable the interior ultrasonics, leaving the rest of the alarm features active. Useful if you want to leave the sunroof open in hot weather - if a fly gets in the car, the alarm would otherwise be going off constantly.

Talking alarms - no, please, please no. Very annoying, and all that'll happen is you'll attract crowds of kids daring each other to set it off again. Unfortunately, these are becoming more popular, with some offering the facility to record your own message!

The knowledge

What people often fail to realise (at least, until it happens to them) is the level of violence and destruction which thieves will employ to get your stuff - this goes way beyond breaking a window.

It comes as a major shock to most people when they discover the serious kinds of tools (weapons) at many professional thieves' disposal, and how brutally your lovingly-polished car will be attacked. Many people think, for instance, that it's their whole car they're after, whereas it's really only the parts they want, and they don't care how they get them (this means that these parts are still attractive, even when fitted to a basic car which has yet to be fully modded). Obviously, taking the whole car then gives the option of hiding it to strip at leisure, but it won't always be the option chosen, and you could wake up one morning to a well-mangled wreck outside.

Attack 1

The first option to any thief is to smash glass - typically, the toughened-glass side windows, which will shatter, unlike the windscreen. Unfortunately for the thief, this makes a loud noise (not good), but is a quick and easy way in. The reason for taking this approach is that a basic car alarm will only go off if the doors are opened (voltage-drop alarm) - provided the doors aren't opened, the alarm won't go off.

Response 1 A more sophisticated alarm will feature shock sensing (which will be set off by the impact on the glass), and better still, ultrasonic sensing, which will be triggered by the brick coming in through the broken window.

Response 2 This kind of attack can also be stopped by applying security film to the inside of the glass, which holds it all together and prevents easy entry.

Attack 2

An alternative to smashing the glass is to pry open the door using a crowbar - this attack involves literally folding open the door's window frame by prising from the top corner. The glass will still shatter, but as long as the door stays shut, a voltage-drop alarm won't be triggered.

Response This method might not be defeated by a shock-sensing alarm, but an ultrasonic unit would pick it up.

Incidentally, another bonus with ultrasonic alarms is that the sensors are visible from outside - and act as a deterrent.

Attack 3

The next line of attack is to disable the alarm. The commonest way to kill the alarm is either to cut the wiring to the alarm itself, or to disconnect the battery, 'safely' hidden away under the bonnet. And just how strong is a bonnet? Not strong enough to resist being crowbarred open, which is exactly what happens.

Response 1 If your alarm has extra pin-switches, be sure to fit one to the bonnet, and fit it in the bonnet channel next to the battery, so that it'll set off the alarm if the bonnet is prised up. Also make sure that the wire to the pin-switch cannot be cut easily though a partly-open bonnet.

Response 2 Make sure that the alarm module is well-hidden, and cannot be got at from underneath the car.

Response 3 Make the alarm power supply connection somewhere less obvious than directly at the battery terminal - any thief who knows his stuff will immediately cut any 'spare' red wires at the battery. Try taking power from the fusebox, or if you must source it under the bonnet, trace the large red battery lead to the starter motor connections, and tap into the power there.

Response 4 Always disguise the new alarm wiring, by using black insulating tape to wrap it to the existing wiring loom. Tidying up in this way also helps to ensure the wires can't get trapped, cut, melted, or accidentally ripped out - any of which could leave you with an alarm siren which won't switch off, or an immobiliser you can't disable.

Response 5 An alarm which has a 'battery back-up' facility is a real kiss of death to the average thief's chances. Even if he's successfully crow-barred your bonnet and snipped the battery connections, the alarm will still go off, powered by a separate battery of its own. A Cat 1 alarm has to have battery back-up.

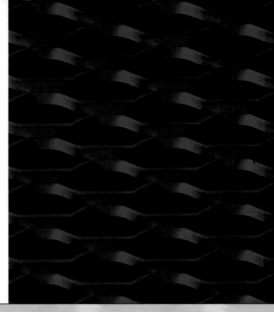

Fitting a basic LED

All you need for this is a permanent live feed, an earth, a switch if you want to be able to turn it on/off, and the flashing LED itself (very cheap, from any car accessory shop).

An LED draws very little current, so you'll be quite safe tapping into almost any live feed you fancy. If you've wired in your ICE, take a live feed from the permanent (radio memory supply) wire at the back of your head unit, or have a delve into the back of the fusebox with your test light. An earth can easily be tapped again from your head unit, or you can make one almost anywhere on the metal body of the car, by drilling a small hole, fitting a self-tapping screw, then wrapping the bared end of wire around and tightening it.

The best and easiest place to mount an LED is into one of the many blank switches the makers seem to love fitting. The blank switch is easily pried out, and a hole can then be drilled to take the LED (which usually comes in a separate little holder). Feed the LED wiring down behind the dashboard to where you've tapped your live and earth, taking care not to trap it anywhere, nor to accidentally wrap it around any moving parts.

Connect your live to the LED red wire, then rig your earth to one side of the switch, and connect the LED black wire to the other switch terminal. You should now have a switchable LED! Tidy up the wiring, and mount the switch somewhere discreet, but where you can still get at it. Switch on when you leave the car, and it looks as if you've got some sort of alarm - better than nothing!

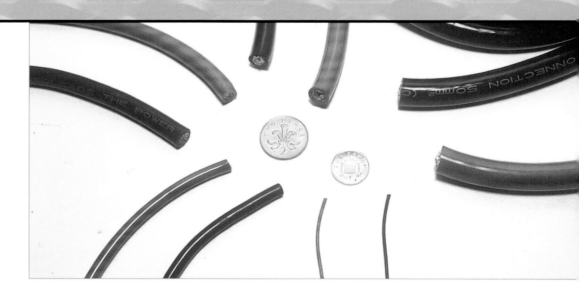

Wiring basics

With your wires identified, how to tap into them? Before we even get that far, is that wire you're planning on playing with live?

Switch off the ignition at least - and ideally disconnect the battery before you do anything else. On cars with airbags, don't go tapping into any of the airbag wiring, which is usually bright yellow. With that cleared up, how were you planning on joining the old and new wires together?

Here's our advice:

Soldering - avoids cutting through your chosen wire - strip away a short section of insulation, wrap your new wire around the bared section, then apply solder to secure it. If you're a bit new to soldering, practice on a few offcuts of wire first - it ain't rocket science! Re-insulate the soldered connection afterwards, with tape or heatshrink tube.

Bullet connectors - cut and strip the end of your chosen wire, wrap your new one to it, push both into one half of the bullet. Connect the other end of your victim wire to the other bullet, and connect together. Always use the 'female' half on any live feed - it'll be safer if you disconnect it than a male bullet, which could touch bare metal and send your motor up in smoke.

Block connectors - so easy to use. Just remember that the wires can come adrift if the screws aren't really tight, and don't get too ambitious about how many wires you can stuff in one hole (block connectors, like bullets, are available in several sizes). Steer clear of connectors like the one below - they're convenient, but they can give rise to problems.

With any of these options, always insulate around your connection - especially when soldering, or you'll be leaving bare metal exposed. Remember that you'll probably be shoving all the wires up into the dark recesses of the under-dash area - by the time the wires are nice and kinked/squashed together, that tiny bit of protruding wire might just touch that bit of metal bodywork, and that'll be a fire...

Fitting an auxiliary fusebox

You'll need plenty of fused live feeds from the battery during the modifying process, for stereo gear, neons, starter buttons - and alarms, and it's always a pain working out where to tap into one. If you make up your own little fusebox, mounted somewhere easy to get at, you'll never have this problem again - and it's easy enough to do.

The first job is to run a main supply cable from the battery positive terminal, to inside the car - but don't connect the wire up to the battery terminal just yet. Make sure that the main cable is man enough for all the loads you're likely to put on it - starting with eight-gauge wire (available from all good ICE suppliers) will mean you're never short of current.

Make a note of which fuse is for which circuit, and carry the paper around in the glovebox (along with some spare fuses). If a fuse ever blows, you won't end up with your head stuck under the dash, trying to remember where you tapped in, and where the fuse is. You'll just pull the cover off, and replace the fuse. Who would've thought electrical safety could be so cool?

01 First job is to find a suitable place to mount the fusebox. This may prove a little more difficult than it sounds, given that there are few flat surfaces within the interior of a Focus! We chose to mount ours on the driver's lower facia panel, so first job is to remove this panel. Simply remove the three retaining screws and lever the plastic grommet away.

02 Next, unclip the wiring plug from the back on the facia panel, and lift the panel from the car.

03 Offer the fusebox into position on the panel and mark the area for cutting. Then using a suitable tool cut out the shape.

04 Pop the box into its new hole and drill the mounting holes.

05 Use the hardware provided and secure the fusebox in place. If you're mounting your box in the same place as us, you'll have to cut off the excess threads from the screws so they don't foul anything that it comes into contact with, when the panel is refitted to the car.

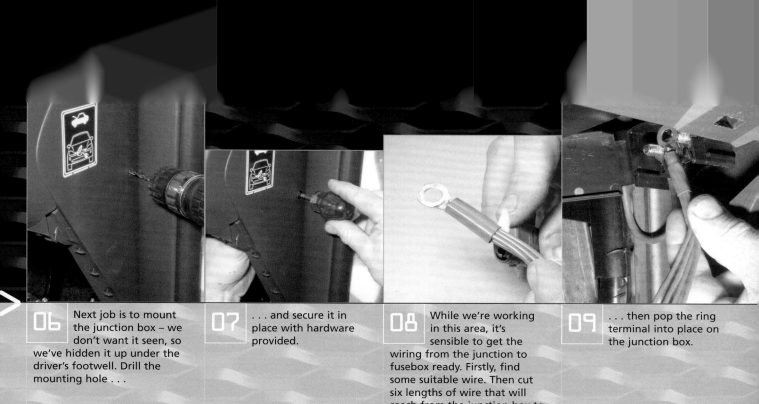

06 Next job is to mount the junction box – we don't want it seen, so we've hidden it up under the driver's footwell. Drill the mounting hole . . .

07 . . . and secure it in place with hardware provided.

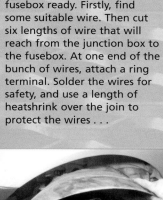

08 While we're working in this area, it's sensible to get the wiring from the junction to fusebox ready. Firstly, find some suitable wire. Then cut six lengths of wire that will reach from the junction box to the fusebox. At one end of the bunch of wires, attach a ring terminal. Solder the wires for safety, and use a length of heatshrink over the join to protect the wires . . .

09 . . . then pop the ring terminal into place on the junction box.

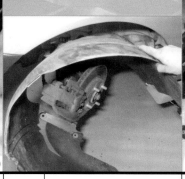

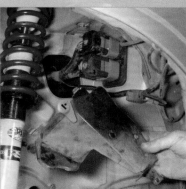

10 At the other end of the wires, crimp the connectors into place, and pop them into the upper pins on the fusebox. Tidy the wires with cable-ties. As and when you need a live feed, all you need to do is take a wire from whatever you're fitting, and connect it to the lower pins on the fusebox – simple!

11 The next part of the process is feeding a cable from the battery to the driver's footwell and to be honest, it's a little time-consuming. The easiest way is to feed the wire from the battery into the wheelarch and through a plug that carries the main wiring loom into the car. Get yourself a length of eight-gauge (thick) wire, attach a ring terminal and pop it onto the battery.

12 Next, feed the wire down towards the passenger wheelarch, using cable-ties to attach it to the loom. Jack up the front corner of the car, and take off the left-hand front wheel (see 'wheels & tyres' for jacking information). Remove the four screws securing the wheelarch liner, and take it off.

13 At the back of the wheelarch, look for a black plastic panel held in place with two pop-rivets. Drill out these rivets, and remove the cover.

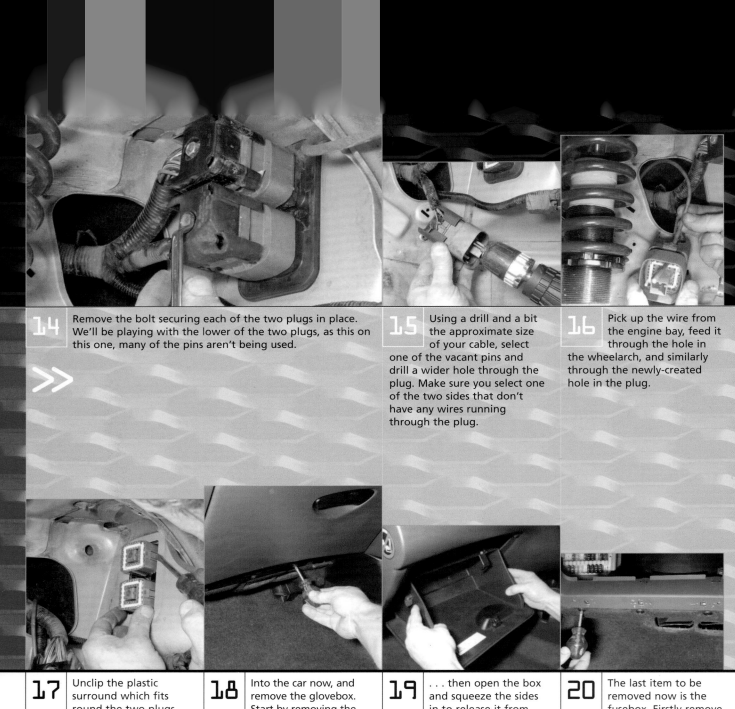

14 Remove the bolt securing each of the two plugs in place. We'll be playing with the lower of the two plugs, as this on this one, many of the pins aren't being used.

15 Using a drill and a bit the approximate size of your cable, select one of the vacant pins and drill a wider hole through the plug. Make sure you select one of the two sides that don't have any wires running through the plug.

16 Pick up the wire from the engine bay, feed it through the hole in the wheelarch, and similarly through the newly-created hole in the plug.

17 Unclip the plastic surround which fits round the two plugs, then detach the back halves of both plugs by depressing the plastic tabs (one either side of each plug).

18 Into the car now, and remove the glovebox. Start by removing the three lower retaining screws . . .

19 . . . then open the box and squeeze the sides in to release it from the plastic retaining tabs, and lift the box from the car.

20 The last item to be removed now is the fusebox. Firstly remove the three screws, which releases the trim panel to allow you to slide the box down and out . . .

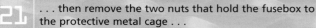

21 ... then remove the two nuts that hold the fusebox to the protective metal cage ...

22 ... and finally, prise the plastic tabs to release the fusebox from the cage. Slide the box downwards into the footwell.

23 Grab a torch and pick up the point where those plugs from the wheelarch come into the car (directly behind the fusebox). Unclip the plastic surround fitted round the two plugs on the inside, then disconnect the two plugs from the body and lower the wiring loom that includes the plugs down into the footwell. Unclip the lower (brown) plug by releasing the two tabs each side.

24 Check which pin in the plug under the wheelarch you drilled through previously. Drill out the corresponding pin in the plug inside the car, large enough to take your new thick wire.

25 Pick up the wire from the plug in the wheelarch, and feed it into the car. Route the wire towards the footwell, and thread it through the newly-created hole in the back half of the plug.

26 We're nearly finished now – it's just a case of passing the wire through the car across to the junction box in the driver's footwell. When it reaches the junction box, attach a ring connector and connect it onto the remaining terminal. Refit everything in the car and wheelarch, and you're finished.

Fitting an alarm

If your Focus already has a decent aftermarket alarm on it, don't mess with it. Otherwise, be prepared for some nasty surprises when you dive behind the dash. How the heck have they wired this in? Will chopping that wire mean the car won't start? If it looks a mess behind there, it's best to leave it - and then hope it never goes wrong, or you'll have to suss it all out anyway.

If your Focus is still a virgin in the aftermarket alarm sense, things are a bit easier. The alarm we've chosen to fit is a MicroScan, which still offers a decent level of protection, and a useful array of features for a sensible price.

As with everything else in this book, remember that we're showing you just how this *particular* alarm is fitted. All the same, whatever alarm you fit, it'll still be useful to pick out the fitting principles and tips. Always refer to the instructions which come with your alarm, and don't go joining the red wire to the yellow wire, just because WE say so...

01 Disconnect the battery negative lead, and move the lead away from the battery, or you'll be blowing fuses and your new alarm will go mental the minute it's rigged up.

02 Decide where you're going to mount the alarm/siren. Choose somewhere not easily reached from underneath, for a start, and if you can, pick a location away from where you'll be topping up washers, oil or coolant - fluids and alarm modules don't mix. The only spot on our Focus was on the passenger's-side inner wing, so we tried the alarm module and its bracket first for fit.

07 As long as the battery stays off, you might as well plug in the loom to the back of the module now.

08 The bonnet pin switch should be close to the battery, but it must hit a 'good' (flat) spot on the bonnet - getting this right can be tricky. The Focus has an ideal spot on the slam panel behind the headlight - there's even a hole there already.

09 All we need now is a smaller hole for the switch self-tapping screw (which also provides the earth connection) . . .

10 . . . then fit a spade terminal to your pin switch wire (brown in our case), and plug it onto the switch.

03 Getting a drill into this part of the engine bay wasn't easy - we cheated with this 'snake' flexible drive attachment, a very handy gizmo which effectively lets you drill round corners.

Testing's a lot easier with a posh multi-meter, set to read continuity (resistance), and with an audible signal. Connect one terminal to the pin switch spade, and the other to a good earth (like the battery '–' terminal). Shut the bonnet, and when the beep stops is the point your alarm would go off. You can duplicate this test with a simple test light, but instead of a good earth, connect one

11 test light wire to the battery positive (+) terminal.

04 With the hole drilled and the bracket mounted, the alarm module was lowered into place.

Trimming the pin switch down will make it 'go off' sooner, but only take off a little plastic at a time, then re-test. If you go too far when trimming down a pin switch, you can sometimes rescue the situation by screwing a little self-tapping screw into the top of the plunger. You can then 'adjust' the length of the plunger at will. The

12 proper answer, though, is to buy a new switch.

05 Well, that was the easy bit - now there's wires to play with. Most of them should go through into the car, but not all - check your alarm's instructions. We've got a bonnet pin switch wire which can stay in the engine bay. The rest? Get out the electrical tape, and wrap that bunch of wires into a neat loom, to go inside.

Once the rest of the alarm wiring's made it inside the car, it's time for some serious wiring-up. Let's do the ultrasonic sensors first (you didn't skimp, and buy an alarm without ultrasonics?). Best place to mount these is on the A-pillar trim panel. If you're careful, you can unclip this

13 without breaking any of the plastic clips inside.

06 We're getting quite good at feeding wires into our Focus. Look in the auxiliary fusebox section for one method, or the 'wiring' section of the ICE chapter for an alternative. We drilled another hole in the wheelarch, above the one we'd done for the ICE live feed. Poke the alarm harness through the hole, which must be fitted with a grommet if you want the alarm to be reliable.

Decide where the sensor should go for maximum interior coverage, then hold it

14 up to the trim panel, and mark it for drilling.

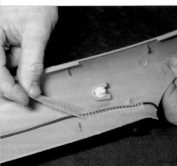

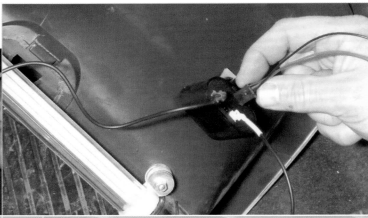

15 With the sensor in place, the wire from it must be fed down inside, to end up at the separate ultrasonic module (on this alarm). Notice we made a small notch at the top of the trim panel, to take the wire? It's called Attention To Detail.

16 We can do without creating any annoying rattles when modding our Focus. Taping the ultrasonic sensor wire to the panel avoids this, and also makes sure the wire doesn't get trapped when the panel goes back on. ATD once again.

17 Like we mentioned earlier, this alarm has a cheeky little ultrasonic module, separate to the main alarm. Which has to go somewhere - we mounted ours behind the driver's lower dash panel, along with our fusebox and one of the neons - getting crowded. Besides plugging in the two sensors, the ultrasonic module has a further plug, for live (red wire), earth (black), and the boot/bonnet switch circuit (blue).

. . . after which, joining the alarm's two grey wires to the blue (left) and blue/red (right) wires is very, very easy indeed.

22

More flashing lights now - the alarm LED needs to be somewhere highly-visible. Like here, in the centre of the dash (while we had the centre panel out, getting in behind here was simple). Okay, so it's pretty scary drilling holes in the middle of your dash, but make sure you've got the right size drill bit, and you can't go wrong.

23

Feed the LED and wiring up from behind, then fit the LED into its holder, pop it in the neat hole you just made, and it's another job to tick off the list. Tidy up the LED wiring behind, so it doesn't get ripped out when you put the stereo back in.

24

The final chapter in this alarm-fitting epic is wiring it in so the central locking works when you zap the alarm remote. This neat feature also gives owners of lowly CL-spec Foci the remote locking they need, once they've de-locked their handles. Under the dash, to the right of the throttle pedal, is the central locking ECU, held in place by a metal bracket with two screws.

25

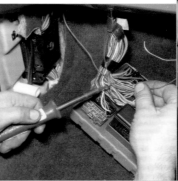

18 The ultrasonic live supply can, in our case at least, easily be taken from our fusebox (bit silly not to use it, really) . . .

19 . . . while the earth can be taken from this point, below the glovebox (along with the main earth for the alarm system).

20 Next, we have to tap into the supplies for the interior light and the boot light, at the back of the car's fusebox (which we removed while fitting our own auxiliary fusebox). The alarm's main feed (a red wire) taps straight into the interior light wire (which is orange/blue) - here, we're soldering one onto the other, which avoids cutting wires. The boot light wire's a blue/black one, but check your Haynes manual wiring diagrams to be sure.

21 Nice to have the indicators flash when the alarm's working, so now we have to tap into them too. You could trace the wires to the fusebox, but we went for the hazard lights switch. With the stereo removed, there's four screws inside the hole to remove, then the dash centre panel unclips, and you can access the hazard light switch plug . . .

With the ECU temporarily removed, it's a bit easier to join on the alarm wires. In this case, a blue one and a green one, which join to the orange/black and green/black wires on the central locking ECU respectively. This is the result of our strip-and-solder operations - two **26** neat, insulated joints.

So come on - does it work? Most alarms require you to 'programme in' the remotes before they'll work. Test all the alarm features in turn, remembering to allow enough time for the alarm to arm itself (usually about 30 seconds). When you test it for the first time, don't forget to either shut the bonnet completely, or do like us, and hold the bonnet pin switch down. Our way, **27** you can pull out the alarm fuses and shut it up, if something goes wrong!

Set the anti-shock sensitivity with a thought to where you live and park - will it be set off every night by the neighbour's cat, or by kids playing football? Finally, and most important of all - next time you park up, **28** remember to set it!

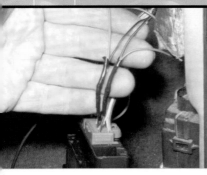

Body styling

If you're planning a major body job, you've probably already got some good ideas about how you want your Focus to look, from *'Max Power'* or *'Revs'*, or maybe from a friend's car. While it can be good to have a target car to aim for, if you're just starting out on the road towards a fully-loaded car, you probably don't want (or can't quite afford) to go 'all the way' all at once.

If you're new to the world of modifying, it's a good idea to start with smaller jobs, and work up to the full body kit gradually, as your skills increase; spending loads on a body kit is a pretty lame idea if you then make a mess of fitting it! There's plenty of small ways to improve the look of your Focus, which don't cost much, and which are simple enough to fit; start with some of these before you go too mad!

One golden rule with any body mods is to plan what you're going to do, and don't rush it. It's better that the car looks a bit stupid for a week (because you couldn't get something finished) than to rush a job and have the car look stupid forever. Do half the job properly instead of messing up all of it. Try and think the jobs through - plan each stage. Have you got all the tools, screws or whatever before you start, or will you have to break off halfway through? If you get stuck, is there someone you can get to help, or have they gone off for the weekend? Above all, if something goes wrong - don't panic - a calm approach will prove to be a huge bonus (that job doesn't have to be done today, does it?).

If a piece of trim won't come off, don't force it. If something feels like it's going to break, it probably will - stop and consider whether to go on and break it, or try another approach. You could even try the Haynes manual… Especially on an older car, things either never come off as easily as you think, or else have already been off so many times that they either break or won't fit back on properly. While we'd all like to do a perfect job every time, working on an older car will, sooner or later, teach you the fine art of 'bodging' (finding valid alternative ways of fixing things!). Don't assume you'll have to bodge something back on, every time - if a trim clip breaks when you take something off, it might be easier and cheaper than you think to simply go to your Ford dealer, and buy a new clip (remember, even Ford mechanics break things from time to time, so they will keep these things in stock!).

Mirror,
mirror

Mirrors are a simple to fit, must-have accessory. The DTM or M3-style door mirrors are well established on the modified car circuit, but there are lots of variations of mirror styles and finishes, so finding some you like won't be hard.

If you want to be just a little different, try some 'California' mirrors. The trouble with being different is it's always more work - California mirrors are 'universal fit', meaning you have to make them fit your car. You bought a Focus 'cause it's a popular car, so why make life difficult? Buy some Focus mirrors (or at least some Focus mirror bases), and your new mirrors could be fitted in minutes.

There's more to mirrors than just looks, though - some have toys attached. Like side repeater lights (in a Merc stylee) or thumb switches for releasing your de-locked, de-handled doors. We want some of that.

DTM cup mirrors

01 Removing the old mirror is easy, and takes just a few minutes. If you've got electric mirrors, disconnect the battery negative (earth) lead. Unclip the mirror bezel.

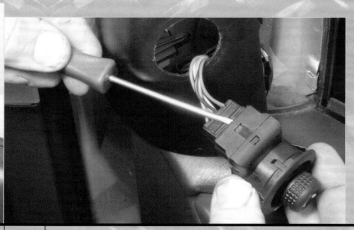

02 Because our new cup mirrors aren't even slightly electrical, we can totally remove the mirror switch by feeding it out through the hole in the bezel, and disconnecting the wiring multi-plug.

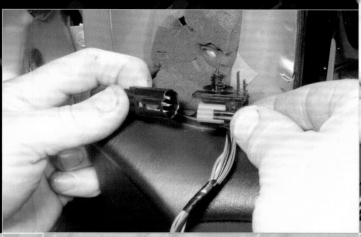

03 Next, locate the second of the wiring plugs that should be found behind the mirror bezel. If the plug is nowhere to be seen, gently pull the remaining wire upwards to free this plug, as it could be caught just under the door card - don't yank it. Disconnect the plug.

04 Pull away the foam membrane to find the mirror mounting bolt and remove the bolt. Support the mirror with one hand or find an assistant to hold it. Once the bolt has been removed, the mirror is free to be lifted from the car. Store the mirrors in a safe place – you may want to re-fit them when selling the car, or keep them handy in case of emergencies.

Onto the new mirrors now – begin by fitting the mirror unit to the base. If you're using universal mirrors, you may struggle to find a base that fits. From past experience, we seriously **05** recommend you buy mirrors designed for a Focus - remember 'Universal' means 'Won't fit anything to start with!'

Offer the mirror to the door to check the fit. Hold the mirror in place with one hand (or track down that assistant again) and refit the mirror mounting bolt. Pop the now-redundant wiring under **06** the door card and refit the trim bezel. You can plug the mirror switch hole with a black rubber grommet, or put the dead switch back in - it's up to you!

Smoothly does it

If you've bought a basic Focus, it's understandable that you might not want to declare this fact loudly from the rear end of your car. Badges also clutter up the otherwise clean lines, and besides, you're trying to make your Focus look different, so why give them obvious clues like a badge? Most Foci also come with admittedly-useful but actually quite ugly side rubbing strips of some sort - lose these, or at least colour-code, if you're at all serious about raising your game.

General bodywork smoothing (including de-seaming) takes time and skill, and is probably best done on a car which is then getting the full bodykit and wicked respray treatment. There's no doubt, however, that it really looks the business to have a fully-flushed tailgate/boot lid, or even to have those ugly roof gutters smoothed. Probably best to put the pros at a bodyshop to work on this. De-badging you can definitely do at home, so get to it.

Body styling

De-stripping

Side rubbing strips. Good - they save your paint if Mr Numpty opens his rusty Metro door into your car. Bad - they look hideous. If looks are important, removal is an option (though colour-coding's easier).

Once the strips are off, you've got a problem - they leave recesses in the door and wings, plus a few holes. So just a filler job, then? Well, yes, but the doors may be a problem. The filler tends to break up and fall out at each end of the door's strip recess, unless you weld on a small plate across the ends. Let's see how the pros at Avon Custom tackle this.

To remove the side rubbing strips, find a flat prising tool – a pallet/putty knife or spatula is an excellent choice. The strips are held on by adhesive tape, and plastic plugs located in holes in the bodywork. Take care not to dent the panels - it's also a good idea to wrap the blade end in masking tape to avoid scratching the paint. That adhesive tape's strong stuff, so expect to use plenty of effort.

01

Using the trusty spatula, carefully scrape off all the evidence of where that nasty sticky stuff was on the car . . .

02

. . . then give the area a good clean using a suitable cleaning/degreaser solution. You may find the paint under the strip's a different shade, as it won't have faded in the sun. But think twice before attacking the paint with ordinary T-Cut, because you're dealing with a lacquered finish, which you'll wreck very fast if you go in too hard with the wrong stuff.

03

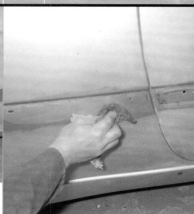

04 Our bodywork expert has elected to weld these holes up, rather than just fill them. Which means the paint round the hole needs to be totally removed, using a grinder and a file.

05 The next stage is tricky. For a start, the rear side trim panel has to come off. Then you need an assistant inside the car holding a piece of metal plate in place, and the hole is welded up from outside.

06 The angle grinder is then used to remove the big blobs of weld in order to achieve a flat surface for a thin layer of filler to smooth the area.

07 After the skim of filler has been left to dry (overnight), it is rubbed down for a smooth finish and is ready for painting.

De-badging

The blue oval Ford badge on the front hides the bonnet lock, but as we'll see in the meshing section, that's no excuse for not removing it. Virtually all the other badges just peel off - try softening the glue up with a heatgun first, which makes it more likely they'll come off in one piece. Clean off the gluey remains with some solvent, and you're a step closer to cleaning up your bodywork.

Fill 'er up!

With most owners trying to smooth and colour-code everything they possibly can, it's a bit odd to take the already-smooth and colour-coded filler cap, and make it stand out! But for those of you who can't leave anything alone…

At least the Focus filler cap is round, so it's easier to re-create the 'racing' look. If you don't want to make too much of the flap, there are stick-on/screw-on fuel cap covers available. Easy to fit, and quite effective.

For those who really want to impress, it's got to be a complete racing conversion, which does away with the flap and the dull black filler cap below, in favour of a fully-functional alloy item to grace the Focus flanks. So let's see - will a pukka working cap need bodyshop assistance to fit successfully?.

Our new collar will be held in place with mastic (such as 3M Panelbond), and a layer of filler. In order for the mastic/filler to stick to the car, the paint needs to be removed and bare metal exposed. An angle grinder is great for these jobs - Avon Custom ace Kevin is trying out his new Bristledisc tool here.

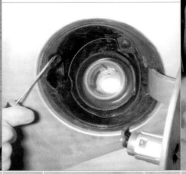

01 Unlock the fuel cap and open. Just inside the cap you will see two retaining screws that need to be removed. Once these screws are removed, prise the rubber washers away.

02 The black rubber collar seated between the filler neck and the car body is now ready to be removed, and it has to be from behind (nice). Our rear bumper had already been removed for painting, so by snaking an arm up behind the wheel arch and pushing, with the other hand pulling at the collar from in front, we could tackle it. Pull the left side of the collar out first, then the right, because . . .

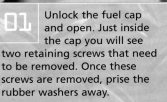

Take your new glassfibre collar, and try it in the wing. If it's a perfect fit first time, you win a prize. Much filing and shaping is usually needed to get a sensible fit (at least this stuff's easy to work to the required shape). This one, apparently, went straight in. Flippin' amazing.

Before bonding the new collar in place, it's a good idea to make holes for two screws, which you can use to keep it in place while the mastic dries. Drill the mounting holes so they align with the metal tabs just inside the filler neck.

03 . . . the flap's hinge is on the right, and makes the flap and collar awkward to remove. But at last we're there.

04

05

06

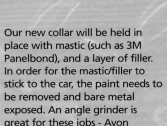

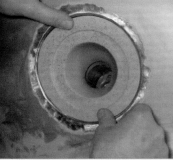

07 Now the collar can be removed, and a nice thick layer of mastic gets applied around the contact area of the filler neck.

08 To get a decent seal between the collar and the top of the filler neck, apply some of that mastic on the collar's inner rim, too. Pays not to overdo it here - any excess mastic might end up in the tank, which probably isn't exactly good news.

09 Screw the collar into place. Some of the mastic will have oozed out from behind the collar – this isn't a problem, just smooth it round the edges and wipe off any excess before it dries. Leave to dry for 24 hours.

10 Once the mastic's fully dry, the bodywork of the car must be rubbed down ready for the filler. All traces of mastic must also be removed from the face of the collar, for the filler to stick to the surface. A clean piece of rag pushed into the filler neck will stop any dust or debris getting into the fuel tank.

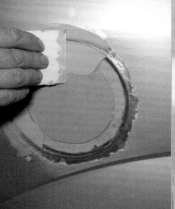

11 The retaining screw holes should really be filled using fibreglass, rather than filler, like this.

12 Final job is to add a layer of filler to blend the collar into place. A piece of cardboard over the hole stops any filler getting in now, and prevents any dust entering when the filler is rubbed down. Once dry, the area is ready to be prepped for painting.

13 Now offer up the sexy new alloy cap, making sure you've got it and the surround straight, and mark the positions of the holes.

14 Drill the holes one at a time . . .

15 . . . and secure with one screw at a time. If you drill all the holes at once, you might get one in just the wrong place, and it could ruin the finished effect.

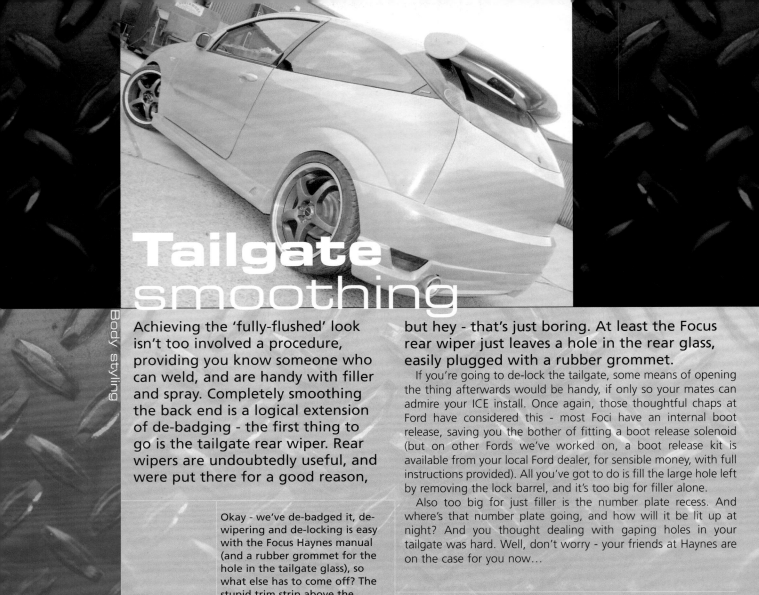

Tailgate
smoothing

Achieving the 'fully-flushed' look isn't too involved a procedure, providing you know someone who can weld, and are handy with filler and spray. Completely smoothing the back end is a logical extension of de-badging - the first thing to go is the tailgate rear wiper. Rear wipers are undoubtedly useful, and were put there for a good reason,

but hey - that's just boring. At least the Focus rear wiper just leaves a hole in the rear glass, easily plugged with a rubber grommet.

If you're going to de-lock the tailgate, some means of opening the thing afterwards would be handy, if only so your mates can admire your ICE install. Once again, those thoughtful chaps at Ford have considered this - most Foci have an internal boot release, saving you the bother of fitting a boot release solenoid (but on other Fords we've worked on, a boot release kit is available from your local Ford dealer, for sensible money, with full instructions provided). All you've got to do is fill the large hole left by removing the lock barrel, and it's too big for filler alone.

Also too big for just filler is the number plate recess. And where's that number plate going, and how will it be lit up at night? And you thought dealing with gaping holes in your tailgate was hard. Well, don't worry - your friends at Haynes are on the case for you now...

Okay - we've de-badged it, de-wipering and de-locking is easy with the Focus Haynes manual (and a rubber grommet for the hole in the tailgate glass), so what else has to come off? The stupid trim strip above the number plate, that's what. Not an especially taxing task - it's

01 held on by four nuts, behind the tailgate trim panel . . .

. . . then can be pulled off from outside. This strip also contains the number plate lights - disconnect the wiring, but keep

02 track of it for re-using when your number plate's been relocated.

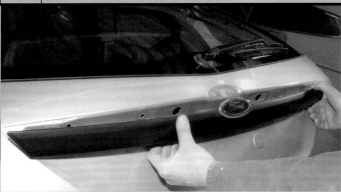

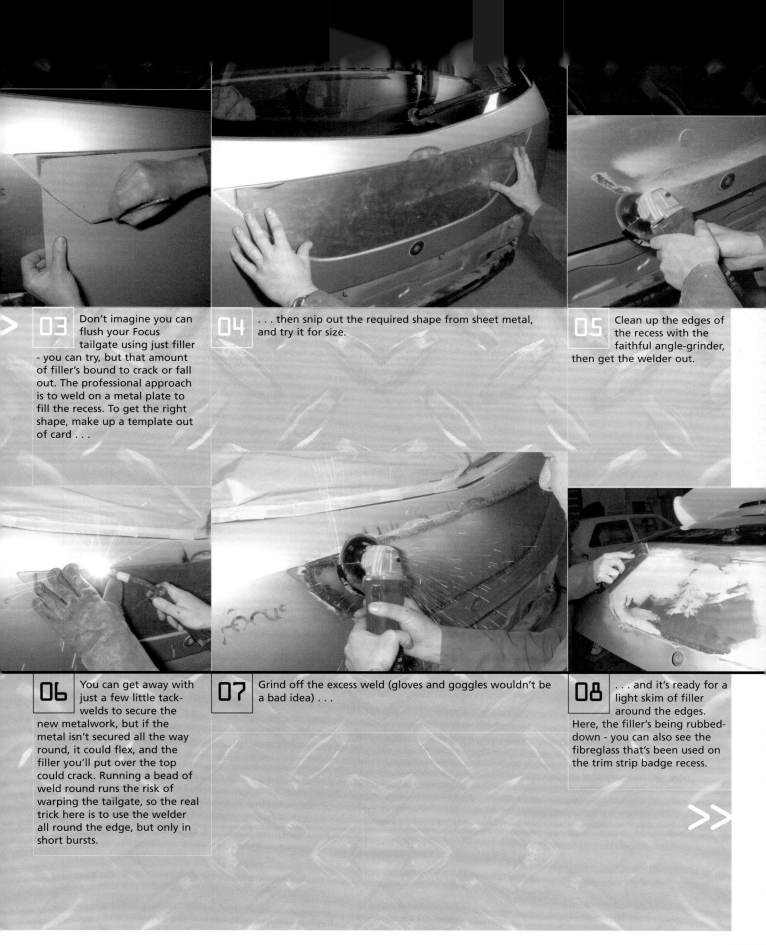

03 Don't imagine you can flush your Focus tailgate using just filler - you can try, but that amount of filler's bound to crack or fall out. The professional approach is to weld on a metal plate to fill the recess. To get the right shape, make up a template out of card . . .

04 . . . then snip out the required shape from sheet metal, and try it for size.

05 Clean up the edges of the recess with the faithful angle-grinder, then get the welder out.

06 You can get away with just a few little tack-welds to secure the new metalwork, but if the metal isn't secured all the way round, it could flex, and the filler you'll put over the top could crack. Running a bead of weld round runs the risk of warping the tailgate, so the real trick here is to use the welder all round the edge, but only in short bursts.

07 Grind off the excess weld (gloves and goggles wouldn't be a bad idea) . . .

08 . . . and it's ready for a light skim of filler around the edges. Here, the filler's being rubbed-down - you can also see the fibreglass that's been used on the trim strip badge recess.

>>

09 The tailgate lock hole gets treated to a circular piece of metal from inside, welded from outside, followed by grinding . . .

10 . . . rubbing-down, and a skim of filler all its own. Looks like this fella's about ready for some paint.

Number plate mounting and lighting

Though you probably wouldn't think it, this is one of the most forgotten-about items - and it causes no end of problems. Try and think ahead when planning a boot-smooth, as an illegal number plate is a bit of a come-and-nick-me to you-know-who.

01 If your rear bumper has no provision for a number plate (and there's plenty out there without this rather essential feature), contact Venom Motorsport, who produce a quality ready-made number plate recess in fibreglass. Bonus. All you do then is offer it up, and mark the bumper for cutting it in.

02 This rear bumper didn't give much scope for plate mounting, so we made two little brackets, and slung it underneath. Fortunately, it still shows up well enough not to attract the flashing-blue-light kind of attention.

03 This lighting solution might not be strictly legal, but at least we tried, and again, this might be enough of a gesture to avoid getting pulled. A row of white LEDs mounted above the plate will hopefully be bright enough to do the job. Wired, in case you wondered, from the existing number plate light circuit.

Travelling incognito

If you is a gangsta wiv da Staines massive, blacking those windows is a must. Window tinting is also one of the best ways to disguise a naff standard interior, or a good way to hide a sorted interior (or ICE install) from the pikeys…

Tints look right with almost any car colour (limo-tint on a black Focus is virtually essential, while mirror film looks trick on a silver car), and with 'reflex film' available in various rainbow colours, there's something for everyone. Only downside is - not all tints are legal to be run on the road, and you'll be chancing it buying any advertised as 'for show cars only'. The boys in blue don't like to see tinted front windows (at cruises, it can be an instant pull), but just doing the rear windows looks a bit stupid. Tints don't suit everybody - if you're doing your car to pose around in (and why not?) it's hard enough to see you in there anyway, without blacking-out the windows!

Because window tinting involves sticking a layer of film to the inside of the glass, fitting tints might help to prevent a break-in, since your side windows won't shatter when hit. Car security firm Toad market an adhesive film specifically designed to prevent break-ins in this way, and even humble window-tinting kits are claimed to offer the same effect.

Generally, window tint comes on a roll, but you can sometimes buy pre-cut kits for popular cars. Buying a kit (if you can) sounds a better deal, but if you muck up fitting one section, you'll be buying another complete kit. With a roll of film, check how many windows you'll be able to do with it - one roll usually isn't enough for the whole car.

At this point, we'd better 'fess up and tell you that tinting will severely try your patience. If you're not a patient sort of person, this is one job which may well wind you up - you have been warned. Saying that, if you're calm and careful, and you follow the instructions to the letter, you could surprise yourself - our mechanic did, when we tried it for the first time and got a near-perfect result!

In brief, the process for tinting is to lay the film on the outside of the glass first, and cut it exactly to size. The protective layer is peeled off to expose the adhesive side, the film is transferred to the inside of the car (tricky) and then squeegeed into place (also tricky). All this must be done with scrupulous cleanliness, as any muck or stray bits of trimmed-off film will ruin the effect (impossible, if you're working outside). The other problem which won't surprise you is that getting rid of air bubbles and creases can take time. A long time. This is another test of patience, because if, as the instructions say, you've used plenty of spray, it will take a while to dry out and stick… just don't panic!

Legal eagle

The law on window tinting currently is that there must be no more than a 25% reduction in light transmission through windscreens, and a limit of 30% reduction on all other glass. How the heck do you measure light reduction? Also, many cars come with tinted glass as standard - so can you fit a tinting kit on top and still be legal? Hard to know what line to take, if you're stopped by Plod - try and choose a tinting kit which is EC-approved (ask before you buy, and if you think it could be a serious issue, get a letter from the company to support the legality of the kit, to use in your defence). Some forces now take this seriously enough to have portable test equipment they can use at the roadside - if your car fails, it's an on-the-spot fine.

Tinting windows

It's worth picking your day, and your working area, pretty carefully - on a windy day, there'll be more dust in the air, and it'll be a nightmare trying to stop the film flapping and folding onto itself while you're working.

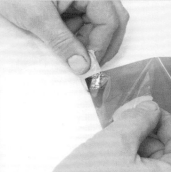

Applying window tint is best done on a warm day (or in a warm garage - if there is such a thing), because the adhesive will begin to dry sooner. For fairly obvious reasons, don't try tinting when it's starting to get dark! It's a good idea to have a mate to help out with this job, but you might get fed up hearing 'you've missed another bubble' or 'you can still see that crease, y'know'.

01 Get the window being tinted clean - really clean - inside and out. Don't use glass cleaners (or any other product) containing ammonia or vinegar, since both will react with the film or its adhesive, and muck it up. Also clean the area around the window - it's too easy for stray dirt to attach itself to the film - and by the time you've noticed it, it could be too late. On door windows, wind them down slightly, to clean all of the top edge, then close them tight to fit the film.

02 Before you even unroll the film, take note - handle it carefully. If you crease it, you won't get the creases out - ever. First work out which way up the film is, by applying a small bit of really sticky tape to the front and back side - use the tape to pull the films apart, just at one corner.

03 Lay the film onto the glass, with the clear side facing you. Unroll the film, and cut it roughly to the size of the window (on a door window, leave plenty at the bottom edge for now). Some kits have a logo on the film, which seems daft - tinting's difficult enough, without having to get a logo straight! The only benefit of a logo is to establish which layer is the tint. Make life easier - lose the logo.

04 Spray the outside of the window with a weak soapy water solution (Folia Tec supply a small bottle of Joy fluid in their kit, but you could use a few drops of ordinary washing-up liquid). Get one of those plant sprayers you can buy cheap in any DIY store, if your kit doesn't contain a sprayer.

05 Lay the roughly-cut sheet of tint back onto the glass, and spray the outside of the film with soapy water . . .

06 . . . then use a squeegee to get out the air bubbles, sticking the film to the outside of the glass.

07 On a door window, trim the bottom edge to leave some excess to tuck down inside the door - this stops the film peeling off on the bottom rubber when you roll the window down!

08 Using a sharp knife (and taking care not to damage your paint or the window rubber), trim round the outside of the window. An unimportant piece of plastic (like an expired video club card) is brilliant for tucking the film into the edges to get the shape right, but don't trim the film right to the absolute edge - leave a small, even gap of just a few mill all round (this helps to get rid of excess water when you squeegee it on the inside - you'll see).

09 Now go inside, and prepare for receiving the tint. On fixed glass, waterproof the side trim panels in anticipation of the soapy water which will be used, by taping on some plastic sheet (otherwise, you'll have some very soggy panels. And seats. And carpets). Spray the inside of the glass with the soapy solution.

10 Back outside, it's time to separate the films. Use two pieces of sticky tape to pull the films slightly apart at one corner. As the films come apart, spray more solution onto the tinted piece underneath, to help it separate cleanly. Try not to lift the tint film too much off the glass when separating, as this increases the risk of creasing.

11 Have your willing helper on standby, to assist with transferring the film to the inside (a prime time for messing it all up). Peel the tint film off the glass, keeping it as flat as you can. Without letting it fold onto itself, move it inside the car and place it fairly accurately on the inside of the glass. The surface which was outside should now be on the inside of the glass (now that you've cut it, it will only fit one way!). Carefully slide the film into the corners, keeping it flat.

12 On a door window, use your unimportant plastic to tuck the film into the door - try to stick it to the glass by wedging-in a wad of paper cloth too.

13 Spray the film with the soapy water . . .

14 . . . then carefully start to squeegee it into place, working from top to bottom. We found that, to get into the corners, it was easier to unscrew the blade from the squeegee, and use that on its own for some of it.

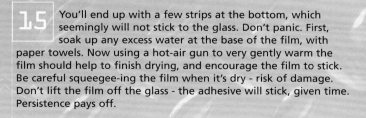

15 You'll end up with a few strips at the bottom, which seemingly will not stick to the glass. Don't panic. First, soak up any excess water at the base of the film, with paper towels. Now using a hot-air gun to very gently warm the film should help to finish drying, and encourage the film to stick. Be careful squeegee-ing the film when it's dry - risk of damage. Don't lift the film off the glass - the adhesive will stick, given time. Persistence pays off.

Fitting a sunstrip

The modern sunstrip, first seen as a lovely green shadeband on Cortinas and Capris back in the 70s, usually bearing imaginative slogans such as 'DAVE AND SHARON'. Just goes to show that some things improve with age.

There are two options to make your car look (and maybe even feel) cooler:

a The sunvisor, a screen tint band inside the screen, which is usually a graduated-tint strip. As this fits inside, there's a problem straight away - the interior mirror. Your Focus mirror may be bonded to the screen, and it seriously gets in the way when trying to fit a wet and sticky (nice!) strip of plastic around it. Go for a sunstrip instead.

b The sunstrip, which is opaque vinyl, colour-matched to the car, fits to the outside of the screen. Much more Sir.

A really wide sunstrip imitates the 'roof chop' look seen on American hot rods, and colour-coded, they can look very effective from the front - plus, of course, you can use the space to advertise your preferred brand of ICE (no, no, NO! Not a good idea!). As it's fitted to the outside of the screen, the sunstrip has a good chance of seriously interfering with your wipers (or wiper, if you've been converted). If this happens to the point where the wipers can't clean the screen, Mr MOT might have a point if he fails your car… The wiper blades may need replacing more often, and the sunstrip itself might start peeling off - still want one? Well, you've got to, really.

Legal eagle

The rule for tinting or otherwise modifying the windscreen is that there must be no more than a 25% light reduction from standard. In theory, this means you can have a sunstrip which covers up to 25% of the screen area, but some MOT testers may see it differently. A sunstrip's got to come down the screen a fair way, to look any sense (otherwise, why bother?). You could argue that accurately measuring and calculating the windscreen area isn't actually that easy, if you get stopped, and anyway, a sunstrip also cuts out harmful glare! If you go so far down the screen that you can't see out, though - well, that's just stupid.

01 This is only stuck to the outside, so only the outside of the screen needs cleaning - excellent! Do a good job of cleaning, though - any dirt stuck under the strip will ruin the effect.

02 With the help of an assistant (if you have one handy), lay the strip onto the car, and decide how far down the screen you're going to go. Legally-speaking, you shouldn't be lower than the wiper swept area - so how much of a 'badboy' are you? If you measure and mark the bottom of the strip with tape, you'll be sure to get it level, even if it's not legal.

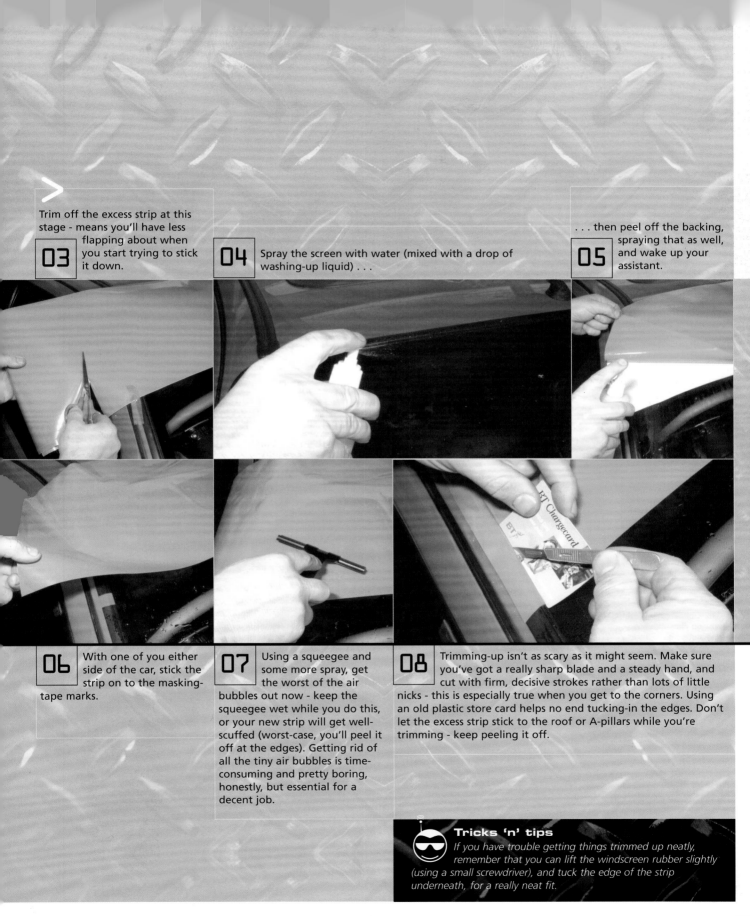

03 Trim off the excess strip at this stage - means you'll have less flapping about when you start trying to stick it down.

04 Spray the screen with water (mixed with a drop of washing-up liquid) . . .

05 . . . then peel off the backing, spraying that as well, and wake up your assistant.

06 With one of you either side of the car, stick the strip on to the masking-tape marks.

07 Using a squeegee and some more spray, get the worst of the air bubbles out now - keep the squeegee wet while you do this, or your new strip will get well-scuffed (worst-case, you'll peel it off at the edges). Getting rid of all the tiny air bubbles is time-consuming and pretty boring, honestly, but essential for a decent job.

08 Trimming-up isn't as scary as it might seem. Make sure you've got a really sharp blade and a steady hand, and cut with firm, decisive strokes rather than lots of little nicks - this is especially true when you get to the corners. Using an old plastic store card helps no end tucking-in the edges. Don't let the excess strip stick to the roof or A-pillars while you're trimming - keep peeling it off.

Tricks 'n' tips
If you have trouble getting things trimmed up neatly, remember that you can lift the windscreen rubber slightly (using a small screwdriver), and tuck the edge of the strip underneath, for a really neat fit.

Glow for it

Ever since 'The Fast and the Furious' first glued us to our screens, every cruise-goer wants a cool neon glow under their car.

Wanting's one thing - make it a reality, and you'll have to explain it to the Law. Under-car neons are totally illegal on the road, and rather an obvious 'come-and-nick-me' to Plod (who will then have a field day with any other semi-legal features on your Focus). So - you have been warned. But we know you still want them, anyway…

Courtesy of our friends at Sargents in Yeovil, prepare to be blown away by a set of the coolest under-car neons ever! With over 2 million different colours from anywhere around the light tubes, you can have patterns of light that are as subtle or shocking as you want, but the best bit – the lights actually respond to music beats via built-in microphones! You can even set your lights to reflect your mood - there's a strobe effect if you're bouncing off the walls, or a cool phasing-colour mode for when you're just chilling out. Sweet. Would you believe there's even a "street-legal" mode, too - yet to be tested in the real world, you understand…

01 First job is to get the car off the ground, and nothing beats a workshop lift. However, if you don't happen to have one in your garage, axle stands are required. With the car off the ground, the next job is to offer the tubes into place to see where they can be mounted, starting with the side tubes first (these are the longest two tubes of the four).

06 As you can see, we drilled another hole in our now-empty spare wheel recess, and fed all the neon tube black wires up through. For maximum safety, you should really use a grommet in any metal hole that has a wire passing through. At least seal the hole up with sealant, to keep the elements where they should be.

07 After deciding exactly where you want to mount the ECU, any excess wire can be trimmed off. Now it's time to wire in the tubes. First attach a green plug to each of the four wires from the tubes, which isn't much different to wiring a household plug (wires, grub screws, etc). Just read the instructions.

08 Take your freshly 'plugged' wires and slot them into the correct terminal on the ECU. Due to the 'chasing' light function, the plugs must be connected in the correct order.

09 Next, the wiring plug for the remote control gets plugged into the ECU, and it has two wires (red and black). As you may have guessed, these are live and earth. Add a ring terminal to the black wire, and screw it to a good earth point on the car's metal bodywork. The red wire should be connected to the battery (or auxiliary fusebox, in our case).

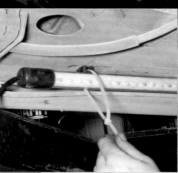

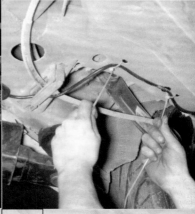

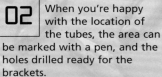

02 When you're happy with the location of the tubes, the area can be marked with a pen, and the holes drilled ready for the brackets.

03 With the brackets in place, it's a simple case of threading a cable-tie through the holes, popping the bracket into place and pulling the cable tight. Repeat the process in the middle and the opposite end of the tube, and you'll have one securely-mounted tube. Do the same for the other side of the car.

04 At the rear, we had some trouble locating the tube, due to the large Peco exhaust and bodykit fitted previously. In the end we mounted the tube so the light shines out through the mesh in the rear bumper, which gives a really good effect. The brackets were mounted under the spare wheel recess, and the screws came through - luckily, we'd removed the tyre! Trim off the excess threads to stop the tyre going down on you.

05 With all the tubes in place, get all the tube wires routed to wherever the ECU will be mounted. You can route the wires under the car as we have done, or run them inside. The wires mustn't come into contact with any hot or moving parts, and they should be well-secured (cable-ties again).

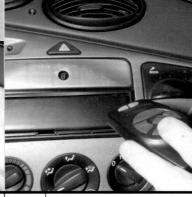

10 Attach the red wire to a live feed (our auxiliary fusebox makes things very easy). This red wire has an in-line fuse, which you need to keep in place if you're attaching the wire straight to the battery.

11 Find the length of black wire with the remote sensor attached. Plug this into the correct hole on the side of the ECU (the holes are labelled).

12 Feed the wire towards the central part of the dash, then unclip the blanking plate fitted above the new stereo. After drilling a hole in the blanking plate, fit the sensor in behind for a very neat result. It's up to you where you mount it - if you don't want any holes in your dash, simply stick the remote in place with double-sided tape.

13 Time for a system test. As you can see, when we work the remote, the neon mode we've selected comes up on the sensor display, visible through the hole we made in the stereo blanking plate. How sweet is that? Well, we're off now to see if we can find all 2 million colours...

Painting by numbers

This is not the section where we tell you how to respray your entire Focus in a weekend, using only spray cans, okay? Mission Impossible, we ain't. This bit's all about how to spray up your various plasticky bits before final fitting - bits such as door mirrors, light brows, spoilers, splitters - hell, even bumpers if you like. As we've no doubt said before, with anything new, fit your unpainted bits first. Make sure everything fits properly (shape and tidy up all parts as necessary), that all holes have been drilled, and all screws etc are doing their job. Then, and only when you're totally, completely happy with the fit - take them off, and get busy with the spray cans.

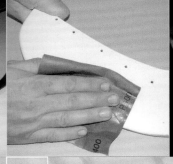

01 The first job is to mask off any areas you don't want painted. Do this right at the start, or you could be sorry; on these door mirrors, we decided to mask off just at the lip before the glass, to leave a black unpainted edge - if we hadn't masked it as the very first job, we would've roughed up all the shiny black plastic next, and wrecked the edge finish.

02 Remove any unwanted 'seams' in the plastic, using fine sandpaper or wet-and-dry. Some of these seams look pretty cool, others don't - you decide. Also worth tidying up any other areas you're not happy with, fit-wise, while you're at it.

Especially with 'shiny' plastic, you must rough-up the surface before spray will 'bite' to it, or - it'll flippin' flake off. Just take off the shine, no more. You can use fine wet-and-dry for this (used dry), but we prefer Scotchbrite. This stuff, which looks much like a scouring pad, is available from motor factors and bodyshops, in several grades - we used ultra-fine, which is grey. One advantage of Scotchbrite is that

03 it's a bit easier to work into awkward corners than paper.

Once the surface has been nicely 'roughened', clean up the surface using a suitable degreaser ('suitable' means a type which won't dissolve plastic!). Generally, it's ok to use methylated spirit or cellulose thinners (just don't inhale!), but test it on a not-so-visible bit first, so you

04 don't have a disaster.

Before you start spraying (if it's something smaller than a bumper) it's a good idea to try a work a screw into one of the mounting holes, to use as a 'handle', so you can

05 turn the item to spray all sides.

Another good trick is to use the screw to hang the item up on a piece of string or wire - then you can spin the item

06 round to get the spray into awkward areas.

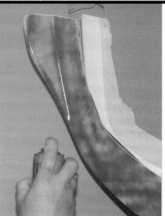

07 If you like a bit of wildlife in your paint, you can't beat the great outdoors. If it's at all windy, you'll end up with a really awful finish and overspray on everything (which can be a real pain to get off). Even indoors, if it's damp weather, you'll have real problems trying to get a shine - some kind of heater is essential if it's cold and wet (but not one with a fan - stirring up the dust is the last thing you want).

08 If you're a bit new at spraying, or if you simply don't want to mess it up, practise your technique first (steady!). Working left-right, then right-left, press the nozzle so you start spraying just before you pass the item, and follow through just past it the other side. Keep the nozzle a constant distance from the item - not in a curved arc. Don't blast the paint on too thick, or you'll have a nasty case of the runs - hold the can about 6 inches away - you're not trying to paint the whole thing in one sweep.

09 Once you've got a patchy 'mist coat' on (which might not even cover the whole thing) - stop, and let it dry (primer dries pretty quickly). Continue building up thin coats until you've got full coverage, then let it dry for half an hour or more.

10 Using 1000- or 1200-grade wet-and-dry paper (used wet), very lightly sand the whole primered surface, to take out any minor imperfections (blobs, where the nozzle was spitting) in the primer. Try not to go through the primer to the plastic, but this doesn't matter too much in small areas.

11 Rinse off thoroughly, then dry the surfaces - let it stand for a while to make sure it's *completely* dry, before starting on the top coat.

12 Make sure once again that the surfaces are clean, with no bits left behind from the drying operations. As with the primer, work up from an initial thin mist coat, allowing time for each pass to dry. As you spray, you'll soon learn how to build a nice shine without runs - any 'dry' (dull) patches are usually due to overspray landing on still-wet shiny paint. Don't worry if you can't eliminate all of these - a light cutting polish will sort it out once the paint's hardened (after several hours).

13 Especially with a colour like red (which is notorious for fading easily), it's a good idea to blow on a coat or two of clear lacquer over the top - this will also give your shine, if you're stuck with a very 'dry' finish. It's best to apply lacquer before the final top coat is fully hardened. The spraying technique is identical, although pro sprayers say that lacquer should be applied pretty thick - just watch those runs! Lacquer also takes a good long while to dry - pick up your item too soon, for that unique fingerprint effect!

Don't mesh with me, boy

A meshed grille or bumper is just one way to demonstrate who's the daddy of the cruise, and it does a great job of dicing any small insects or rodents foolish enough to wander into the path of your motor. So if you're sick of scrubbing off insect entrails from your paint, and fancy getting even, read on...

Which style of mesh to choose? Classic diamond-shape, or round-hole? In our humble opinion, the round-hole mesh works best on modern roundy-shaped cars (like say, a Corsa) - for everything else, we'll settle for the original and best. But wait - the choice doesn't end with what shape you want. Mesh can now be had in various anodised colours too, to match or contrast with the rest of your chosen paint scheme.

01 Anyone can mesh a hole. Ab-so-lutely anyone - it's dead easy. First, measure your hole, then cut out a roughly-sized piece of mesh, leaving some over the sides to bend around the edges of your hole.

There's loads of ways to secure your mesh. One of the most permanent is to use small self-tapping screws, but this won't always be possible. Our hot-glue gun method worked a treat, as the glue flows into place. You can use mastic (quick-setting, exterior-use type) or even builder's 'no-nails' adhesive, but you squirt on a bead of the stuff, and then have to smooth it on by hand, to 'squidge' it over the mesh. Very meshy - sorry, messy.

02 Of course, holes usually have corners - and some of the sides you'll encounter aren't exactly straight. Make small cuts in the edge of the mesh at strategic points . . .

03 . . . and bending over the edges will be much easier. The main mesh panel will also stay flatter, and you'll be less stressed, too.

04

Meshed Ford grille

The Focus grille isn't exactly hideous, but we could do with losing that blue oval, at least. And having a meshed grille's just another essential detail for respect while cruising. Maybe by the time you read this, ready-made meshed grilles will be a reality, but for now, it's all DIY. Be under no illusions - this is not an easy task. It takes time and effort, and several attempts at it to get it right - you have been warned!

01 Refer to the lights and bulbs section, where we show you how to remove the old grille. Find a clean, flat surface to work on, and start by cutting out the big old Ford badge. Don't worry about the bonnet release lock – you can still poke your key through the mesh to open the bonnet. Use a suitable cutting tool for this, and make a neat job of it.

When you're satisfied that the mesh fits the area perfectly, apply a bead of glue all the way around the edge of the grille to hold the mesh in place to the outside of the grille. Once again, the hot-glue gun sorts us out - and the glue is clear, so you don't see it. Keep the screws in place, as this will help the glue to do its stuff.

A final (optional) job is to get rid of the rough edges by applying a bead of silicon around the outside edge of the mesh. Mask around the area to protect the mesh and grille from excess silicon, and to achieve a nicer end result. Best to use clear silicon if you have any – we had to use black, as the mysterious clear-silicon thief had robbed our supply!

Next, take some mesh and cut it to roughly the right size of the grille. Then hold the mesh to the grille with screws, washers and nuts to stop it from moving about whilst you cut. This part is **02** painstakingly slow to get right. It involves precisely cutting and bending the mesh to exactly fit the grille area. Take your time - if you mess up, start again.

03

04

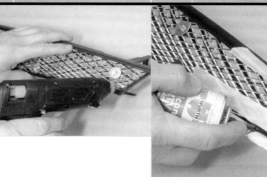

There's no way in

One way to tidy up the Focus lines is to do away with the door locks, and even the door handles - but be careful. Flushing the rear door handles (on 5-door models) is okay, legally/MOT-speaking, but removing the front door handles will land you in trouble, come MOT time.

Construction & Use regs require your car to have an independent mechanical means of door opening from outside (so fire-fighters can get you out, if you stick your all-action Focus on its roof, or in a ditch...) If you must lose the front handles, find some trick mirrors which have door catches built-in, underneath.

At least every Focus (apart from the billy-basic CL) has remote central locking as standard, meaning you're not stuck once you've ditched the lock barrels in your front doors - nice one, Ford.

De-locking

01 First job is to remove the door card, as described in 'interiors'. With the door trim off, locate the grommet at the top section of the door, and remove it.

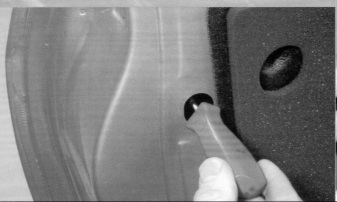

02 Removing the grommet reveals a hole that houses a screw. This little screw is responsible for keeping part of the outer door handle trim in place – in particular, the piece of trim with the hole for the lock barrel, which is the piece we want to get rid of. So, using a Phillips screwdriver, slacken this screw a couple of turns. Don't fully remove this screw – it'll be a nightmare trying to refit it if you do!

03 To the external door handle now and remove the now-loose trim, by unclipping it.

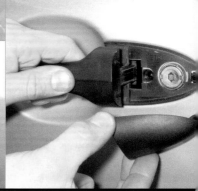

04 Ask your local Ford dealer for a pair of handle trims from the 5-door Focus rear doors, and de-locking couldn't be much easier. Slot the new de-locked trim into place and that's about it. Tighten up the screw inside which you loosened earlier, refit the door trim, and you're done. Course, now you've come this far, colour-coding the handles would be nice...

Remote locking

Only the Focus CL doesn't come with remote locking as standard - if you've got one of these, you'll need to fit an alarm and central locking interface like ours (see 'Security') to remotely trigger the doors.

Tricks 'n' tips
If your battery goes flat, you'll be locked out, thanks to your de-locked handles. But, if it's an emergency, you can always prise off the handle trims you fitted, and use the key. Try not to do too much damage.

Bumpers 'n' bodykits

If you can't find a kit you like for a Focus, you're not trying - and the choice is only going to grow as the Focus gets even bigger on the scene. We went back to our good friends at ESP Design (their website is a good place to start your search), and chose their new "Tornado" front bumper.

One thing you should be concerned about is how well it's all going to fit. Even if you're giving the joy of fitting to a bodyshop, they'll still charge you more if your cheap duff kit takes a week longer to fit than expected. Ask around (or check the Focus chat rooms) before splashing the cash.

Front bumper

Remove the radiator grille and both headlights (as described in "Lights & bulbs"), then dive under the front bumper and disconnect the indicator and front foglight wiring plugs. The bumper has one Torx screw each side at the front of the wheelarches . . .

 01

. . . then three more each side, holding it to the front wings. We're getting in here through the hole where the headlight was - at a push, you could maybe do this from below, without taking out the lights.

 02

Along the front, there are six plastic clips to unhook, with three more in the centre underneath.

 03

>>

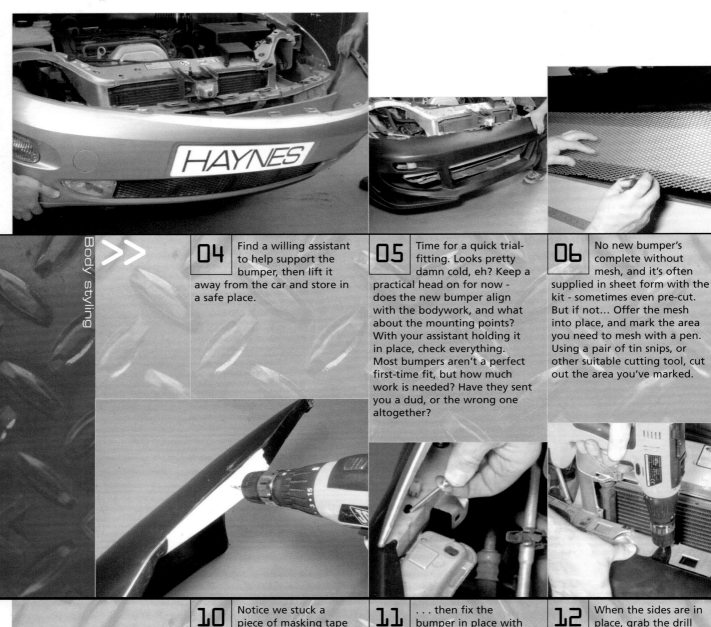

>>

04 Find a willing assistant to help support the bumper, then lift it away from the car and store in a safe place.

05 Time for a quick trial-fitting. Looks pretty damn cold, eh? Keep a practical head on for now - does the new bumper align with the bodywork, and what about the mounting points? With your assistant holding it in place, check everything. Most bumpers aren't a perfect first-time fit, but how much work is needed? Have they sent you a dud, or the wrong one altogether?

06 No new bumper's complete without mesh, and it's often supplied in sheet form with the kit - sometimes even pre-cut. But if not... Offer the mesh into place, and mark the area you need to mesh with a pen. Using a pair of tin snips, or other suitable cutting tool, cut out the area you've marked.

10 Notice we stuck a piece of masking tape to the top of the bumper before marking it - this is easier to show you now. Doing this has two advantages - one, you can see the holes you marked, and two, it stops the drill skating about. Drill the holes . . .

11 . . . then fix the bumper in place with some suitable nuts, bolts and big washers. A trip to the DIY store may be needed at this point (worth reading ahead now, in case there's anything else you need).

12 When the sides are in place, grab the drill again and make some holes to mount the bumper to the front of the car. The original had clips, remember. Your bumper may be different to ours, but the idea's the same - make sure it won't fall off, and be ready to improvise a little.

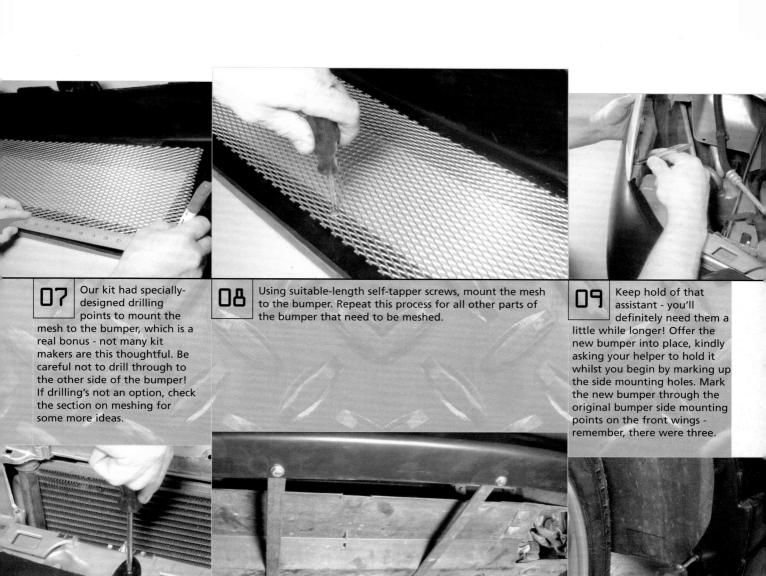

07 Our kit had specially-designed drilling points to mount the mesh to the bumper, which is a real bonus - not many kit makers are this thoughtful. Be careful not to drill through to the other side of the bumper! If drilling's not an option, check the section on meshing for some more ideas.

08 Using suitable-length self-tapper screws, mount the mesh to the bumper. Repeat this process for all other parts of the bumper that need to be meshed.

09 Keep hold of that assistant - you'll definitely need them a little while longer! Offer the new bumper into place, kindly asking your helper to hold it whilst you begin by marking up the side mounting holes. Mark the new bumper through the original bumper side mounting points on the front wings - remember, there were three.

13 With the holes drilled, some self-tappers should do to hold the bumper across the front.

14 After we completed mounting the bumper, we discovered that the bottom of the kit had bowed up. To pull things back into line, our clever mechanic devised a bracket to fit between the bottom edge of the bumper and the radiator support crossmember, which also gives the bumper extra support.

15 A screw in each wheelarch, and the bumper fitment is completed. Now the painful part of getting it re-sprayed and parting with the spons!

Rear bumper

Completely new rear bumper, or bumper extension? An extension's basically a cover which fits over the stock bumper, giving it a different shape (and usually, making it hang lower). Easier to fit than a new bumper? Yes, but only in theory…

You find a bodykit you like, and then what happens? Before you can fit yours, some hooligan up t'road gets the same one. Typical. But why not modify the kit? Adding a personal touch needn't mean messing with large pieces of fibreglass. We livened up our ESP Design rear bumper extension with some mesh, and the end results were stunning. Remember, keep the changes simple - you may end up ruining a good kit and costing yourself a lot of money if it all goes badly wrong!

01 Removed your mudflaps? We know - your Focus never had flaps. Wouldn't know what they look like, even. Good. Pull back the delightful carpet wheel arch liner to reveal the wiring for the foglight and disconnect this plug. Repeat the process for the reversing light on the opposite side.

02 Remove the 'hidden' bumper retaining screw and rubber washer inside the wheelarch at the top, as shown in the picture, and repeat on the opposite side.

03 Next, move to the middle of the rear bumper and armed with your trusty crosshead screwdriver, remove the two lower retaining body clips. These body clips are a two-stage fixing - remove the screw which is the central part of the fixing, and lever out the plastic clip using a flat-headed screwdriver . . .

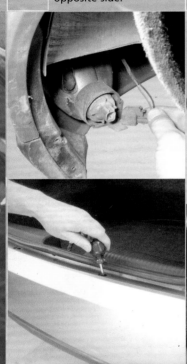

04 . . . attack and remove the four body clips along the top of the bumper in the same way.

05 At this point we tried to lift the bumper away, only to find one more screw on each side of the bumper. Go back to the wheel arch, pull back the liner and find what can only be described as a retaining screw which looks like a rubber bung (see picture). Pull this retaining screw away and the bumper is free to be lifted from the car and stored in a safe place.

06 Modding a new bodykit means you're serious about creating the personal look. Do it right, and it's max respect. We wanted mesh across the back of our new bumper extension, but there isn't even a hole yet. Take your time - no wonky-donkey lines, or the end result will look pants. Use masking tape to mark on, and drill a hole at one corner to start your cut from.

07 Gently sand the area to eliminate rough edges and create a nice finish. Always cut a hole like this slightly smaller than it should be - you can always make it bigger with sandpaper, and tidy up any slips with the saw.

08 Next take some mesh, place it over the area you've cut out, and mark with a pen.

09 Cut out the mesh and secure it to the bumper using a hot glue gun. Snip the mesh at the corners, and fold round the edges of the hole - this makes it much easier to pin in place.

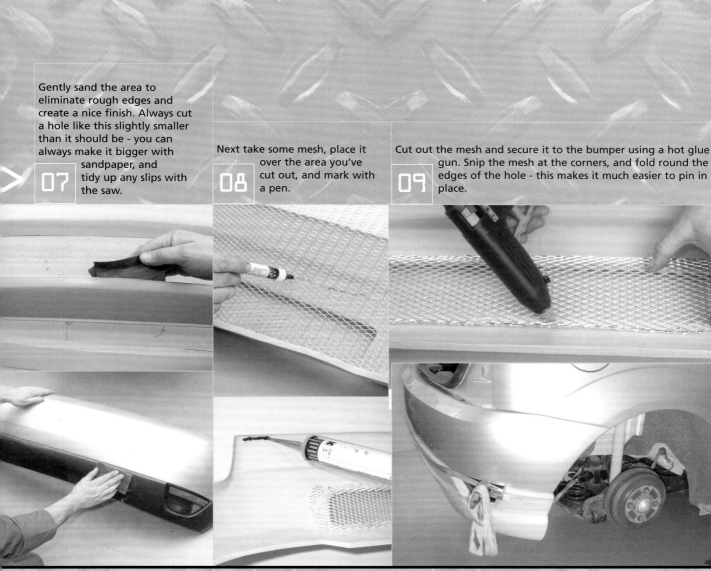

10 Some bumper extensions require the original bumper to be chopped about, but not ours. Our extension slots perfectly onto the bottom of the existing bumper. It will mostly be held in place with strong mastic, possibly with a few screws in the wheelarches. Using a Scotchbrite pad, rub down all areas of the bumper and extension that will come into contact with the adhesive.

11 Before applying any adhesive, offer the extension into place and note the exact points of contact between the bumper and extension. This will save you wasting any valuable adhesive - you don't usually get much (if any) glue supplied with some kits. When you're ready, apply a bead of adhesive to these contact areas.

12 And now we need a volunteer from the audience. Pop the extension into place, and either leave your helper holding it there for 24 hours, or locate some straps/harnesses to hold it on while the glue gets to work. Tie the harnesses round the rear wheels or springs, and don't use the car until the glue's set. Before leaving it to dry, clean off the excess adhesive

Side **skirts**

So what's the deal with side skirts, then? Well, they're an 'artificial' way of visually lowering the car, making it seem lower to the ground than it really is, and they also help to 'tie together' the front and rear sections of a full bodykit. This much we know from our magazines. But where did skirts really come from?

As with so much else in modifying, it's a racing-inspired thing. In the late 70s, the Lotus 'ground-effect' F1 cars ran very, very low (for the time) and had side skirts made of rubber (or bristles), to give a flexible seal against the track. With a clear downforce advantage, Lotus blew the opposition away.

So will fitting skirts to your Focus give you race-car levels of downforce, greatly increasing your overtaking chances at the next roundabout? You already know the answer, I'm afraid…

01 Popping the car on axle stands is not absolutely necessary for this, but it does make the job easier with the car higher off the ground. First, there's the old skirt to remove. Take out the two Torx screws in the rear wheel arch, followed by the five Torx screws located along the length of the skirt under the car.

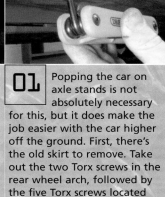

02 Next, there's a bolt underneath at the front. Taking this out allows the wheel arch liner to be pulled back . . .

Tricks 'n' tips
Only attempt to carry out procedures such as this one on a dry day. The car will be out of action for a minimum of 24 hours, so make prior arrangements, and try not to drive the car during this time.

. . . to gain access to a nut holding the skirt to the car body. Didn't want this to just fall off, did they? **03**

Grip the skirt and pull it away from the car. This may be a little difficult, as there are nine plastic clips in total on the inside of the trim that locate into the body of the car - so pull hard to disengage them. **04**

The 'Ultima' side skirts supplied to us by ESP Design require some mesh, so first job is to cut a piece of mesh to size and secure it in place using the trusty hot-glue gun (or mastic). **05**

Some skirts come with pre-drilled mounting holes for fitting to the car. Ours didn't, so with the mesh in place, it's time to drill a suitable-size hole in the three fixing points on the skirt. **06**

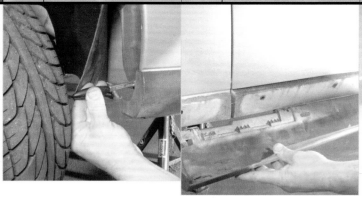

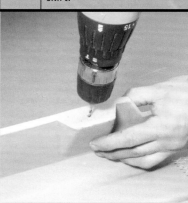

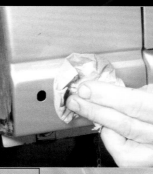

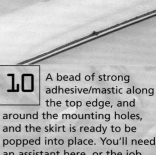

07 After drilling the holes in the skirt, offer it into place on the car, and mark the holes ready for drilling.

08 Once that's done, drill the holes into the body.

09 Wipe the skirt and the car with a good degreaser - the screws only do half the work, and if the mastic's going to stick…

10 A bead of strong adhesive/mastic along the top edge, and around the mounting holes, and the skirt is ready to be popped into place. You'll need an assistant here, or the job could get very messy. Offer the skirt up, and with an assistant holding it in place, secure it with the three screws along the base.

When you're satisfied with the result, support the skirt in place with very strong packing tape. Most adhesives take at least 24 hours to become fully effective, so will need support whilst the glue agents do their thing. After 24 hours, the tape and jacks can be removed and the skirt will be held firmly in place. Now you just gotta get it sprayed - over to you!

With some more help from your assistant, drill a hole in each wheel arch to secure it.

11

Our side skirt had a nasty habit of sagging at the ends and oozing adhesive all over the bodywork, so to hold the skirt in place whilst the adhesive started to work, we installed a jack to save our tired arms!

12

A final bead of adhesive/sealant along the top of the skirt finishes things off nicely. Once this was done, our brave workshop mechanic used his fingers to wipe the excess adhesive away from the skirt, and was still covered in the stuff three days later. So use a cloth to wipe away the excess on the skirt and bodywork.

13

14

This spoiler comes in kit form, in an MFI-stylee. Self-assembly isn't hard, though the endplates needed a little work with the wet-and-dry **01** before they'd fit onto the spoiler ends snugly.

Spoil your
Focus
rotten

A must for any Focus, a rear spoiler makes a very clear statement to the car you just passed - do not mess. Our very fine WRC tailgate spoiler from ESP Design should do the trick. Fitting a spoiler is actually one of the easier jobs in modifying - just take plenty of time making sure you've got it straight, which means lots of eyeing-up, measuring, and getting a second opinion from a mate. Before you drill any holes, make sure you can actually use those holes to fit nuts and bolts - you'll usually also need some sealant, to keep water out of your boot. Some spoilers aren't designed to be bolted on, and you can achieve surprisingly-solid results using good-quality mastic alone (provided you wait for it to go off).

06 . . . then measuring out from there to mark where the spoiler mounting holes need to be. That's one way of getting it right - some spoilers have an even more cunning (and foolproof) method, as we'll see.

07 Often seen on Wings West spoilers, plastic T-strips are a very neat way of getting the mounting holes in the right spot. You fit the strip into the spoiler bolt holes, then when the spoiler's lined up, you tape down the ends of the strips . . .

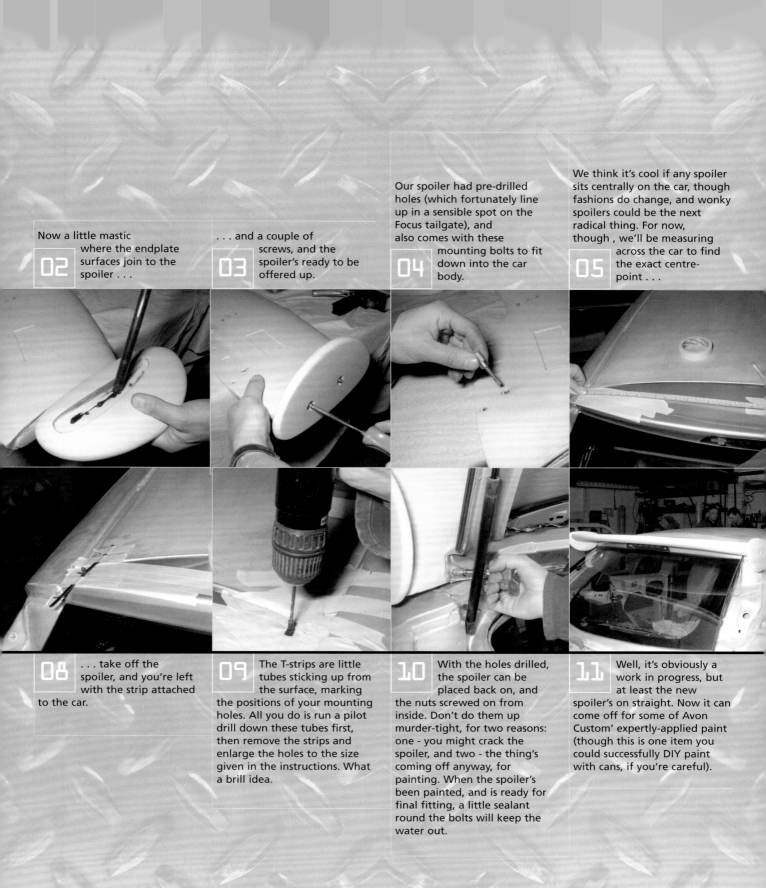

02 Now a little mastic where the endplate surfaces join to the spoiler . . .

03 . . . and a couple of screws, and the spoiler's ready to be offered up.

04 Our spoiler had pre-drilled holes (which fortunately line up in a sensible spot on the Focus tailgate), and also comes with these mounting bolts to fit down into the car body.

05 We think it's cool if any spoiler sits centrally on the car, though fashions do change, and wonky spoilers could be the next radical thing. For now, though , we'll be measuring across the car to find the exact centre-point . . .

08 . . . take off the spoiler, and you're left with the strip attached to the car.

09 The T-strips are little tubes sticking up from the surface, marking the positions of your mounting holes. All you do is run a pilot drill down these tubes first, then remove the strips and enlarge the holes to the size given in the instructions. What a brill idea.

10 With the holes drilled, the spoiler can be placed back on, and the nuts screwed on from inside. Don't do them up murder-tight, for two reasons: one - you might crack the spoiler, and two - the thing's coming off anyway, for painting. When the spoiler's been painted, and is ready for final fitting, a little sealant round the bolts will keep the water out.

11 Well, it's obviously a work in progress, but at least the new spoiler's on straight. Now it can come off for some of Avon Custom' expertly-applied paint (though this is one item you could successfully DIY paint with cans, if you're careful).

Bonnet vents

Once you've got your bodykit on, it's only natural you'll want a bonnet vent, isn't it? Respect.

But this is one scary job to tackle yourself, unless you're really that good, or that brave. Plenty of options - you can get little louvres stamped in as well, to complement your Evo, Impreza, Integrale or F50 main vent. And, like the Focus side repeaters, Focus WRC bonnet vents have now been fitted to everything from Novas upwards (so you may want to scope around for something more original). Speaking of which, there's even been a feature car with a bonnet scoop from a (sensible) Kia Sedona people carrier! Truly, anything goes.

For maximum respect in the bonnet department, you can't beat carbon fibre - on a street-racing Focus, it's pretty much expected these days. Kit yourself out with a ready-made, pre-vented carbon bonnet, and it's not even hard to fit (just hard to pay for??).

Wheelarch mods

The law states that your wide rubber shouldn't be so wide that it sticks out from your arches, and the MOT crew will not be impressed if your new rubber's rubbing, either.

This presents something of a problem, if you're determined to get 19s or 20s on, especially if the car's also having a radical drop job (like our Focus, on coilovers). If you've got rubbing problems on 17s or 18s, something's very wrong. Check that your wheels are the right offset (see 'Wheels & tyres'), or chat to your wheel supplier about spacers. Focus arches are quite roomy, so you should only hit major problems above 18-inch rims.

Sometimes, all you need to stop those nasty grinding noises is a small amount of violence. Any non-vital protrusions into the under-arch area can be trimmed off or flattened with a hammer. Also, try removing those (oh-so-practical) wheelarch liners.

Serious wheelarch mods are best done at a bodyshop. Having the arches professionally rolled, using the proper tool, should only cost

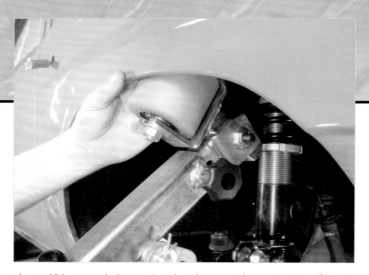

about £50 per arch (assuming they haven't also got rust or filler to deal with as well). Less satisfactory would be having the arch edges cut or ground off - this leaves a bare-metal edge, and encourages rust (as well as weakening the wings).

The best answer to arches which just aren't roomy enough is, of course, a wide-arch bodykit. And bank loans are so cheap these days.

Respraying

Not happy with your Focus's 'pensioner blue' paint? Time to call in the pros. There's no such thing as a simple DIY respray (not one that'll look good afterwards, at any rate). We just thought you'd like to see some of the stages involved.

01 Doing a full respray means getting all those door shuts and other areas of painted metal inside, but not the dash, seats, and carpets (unless you're going to completely gut the entire dash and interior afterwards). You can never do too much masking.

02 Hang on, are you sure that's still our Focus under there? For a full respray, it's often better to remove fixed glass completely, rather than spend time masking it all up. That means windscreen, tailgate, and all the side glass. Still fancy having a go yourself?

03 Mixing the paint is an important, but often overlooked, stage in any spraying process - even ambient temperatures have a bearing on the final paint mix. Topcoats and lacquer especially have complex mixing ratios for the thinners, hardener, activator, and any 'flex' additives for bumpers and such - get it wrong, and even top-notch paint like this won't work.

04 Making sure the paint surface is clean between steps is another often-overlooked essential item. Avon Custom use a water-based wash, as solvent-based products can lift the paint (or react with the next coat). The final stage is cleaning using tack-rags (net-like material, impregnated with resin - very sticky, picks up any bits).

05 What's this? A boring coat of primer? No, despite it being white and looking like primer, this is actually a white base coat. The base coat makes a huge difference to the shade of the final topcoat, especially when you're working with proper custom paint.

06 Now we're ready for some real paint. We're staying silver, but when it's the new ultimate in silver from House of Kolor (Shimrin Platinum), that's a bit of an understatement. Gorgeous. Of course, in proper custom paint like this, there's flakes and pearls as well - the choice is bewildering - ask your bodyshop for some test cards before you decide! Several coats of lacquer later, and we'll have a deep shine.

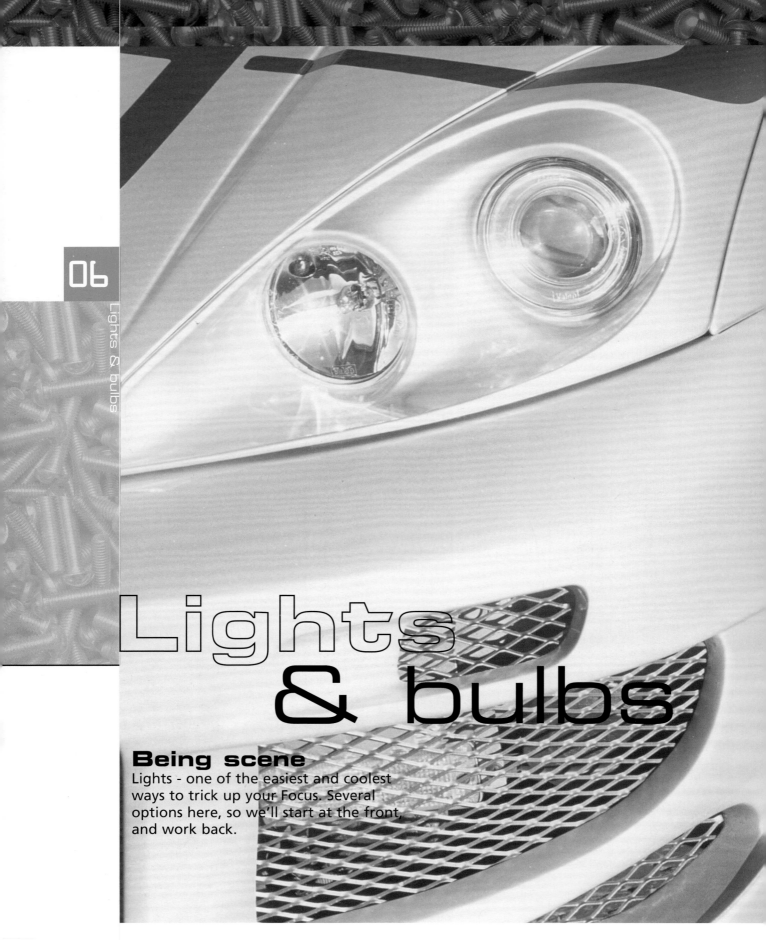

Lights
& bulbs

Being scene

Lights - one of the easiest and coolest
ways to trick up your Focus. Several
options here, so we'll start at the front,
and work back.

Headlights

Almost nothing influences the look of your Focus more than the front end, so the headlights play a crucial role.

What's available?

The popular cheap option is stick-on headlight 'brows', which, depending on which style you choose, either toughen up the front end, or just make it look cute. Hmm - nice. The brows are best sprayed to match the car, before fitting - most are fitted using stick-on Velcro pads. Street-cred on the cheap (as long as you choose wisely).

Another cheap option is again stick-on - this time, it's stick-on covers which give the twin-headlight look. This is basically a sheet of vinyl/plastic (shaped to the headlights, and colour-matched to your car) with two holes cut in it. Dead easy to fit, but dare we say, a bit tacky? Just our opinion. A cheap and simple way to get close to the twin-light look.

If you want tinted headlights, you could try spray-tinting them, but go easy on the spray. Turning your headlights from clear glass to non-see-through is plain daft, even if it's done in the name of style. A light tint is quite effective, and gives you the chance to colour-match to your Focus. With tinted headlights, you'd be wise to tint those front indicators too, of course.

Pub trivia

The popular twin-headlight look was derived from a cunning tweak first employed in the Touring Cars, years ago. Some teams homologated a twin-headlight unit, but for racing, turned one pair of the 'headlights' into air inlets, to direct air from the front of the car to brake ducts or into the engine air intakes, as required. Think about it - why else would the touring cars bother with headlight mods? Until recently, there were no night races!

Assuming your Focus is a pre-facelift model, one headlight upgrade which shouldn't cost too much would be converting to the later (Mk 2) jewel-type headlights - available from Ford dealers and car breakers everywhere. Then there's always the optional xenon lights available for the ST170 - a bargain at £350 each!!

Finally, the most popular choice in headlight upgrades - Morette or Hella twin headlights. Pricey, but so worth it - and you don't even start a Focus project unless you've got cash to splash. Maximum cred, and no-one's gonna accuse you of owning a 'boring' Ford ever again

Headlight
brows

This is the cheap 'n' cheerful approach, and it really doesn't get much simpler than this. This is even a mod you can 'undo' easily, if your MOT geezer objects. So what do you usually get? Two bits of plastic, and two strips of Velcro - but this time, our kit was a little different.

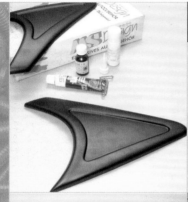

01 First job is to unpack the kit and check to see that everything is present and correct. At this point it is a good idea to check the adhesive hasn't gone off by squeezing the middle of the tube before you open it. We were a little unlucky to discover that our tube of adhesive was rock-hard. If you're one of the unlucky ones, you'll need to track down a suitable adhesive.

02 The brows are supplied unpainted, so before you even think about fitting them, take some time to prep and paint them. The more care you take at this stage, the better the final result. So, take a piece of Scotchbrite and roughen up the surface, then give it a good clean with a suitable degreaser.

03 Next take a can of plastic primer, give it a good shake, point and spray! Spray two or three light layers of primer over the area, allowing a minute or two drying time between each layer. Leave the primer to dry, then give it a light rub over with some fine wet-and-dry.

04 Spray several lighter layers of paint onto the brow, leaving each layer to dry for a minute or two before adding more paint. When you're satisfied with the results, leave the paint to dry. There's no point in rushing now, and ruining all your hard work. With the paint fully dry, add a few glossy coats of lacquer.

05 While the lacquer dries, you can be prepping the headlight. Use a good degreaser (like brake cleaner) and rub the headlight lens. Ensure all the nasty fly guts are gone.

06 With the paint dry and the headlamp ready, it's time to fit the brow to the car. Wipe the back of the brow clean, then apply your Velcro strips or (in our case) a bead of adhesive. If it's Velcro you've got, don't rip it apart - stick both bits on the brows, and peel off the self-adhesive backing, ready to stick to the light. With adhesive, don't put too much on, or you'll spend more time wiping it off everything.

07 Position the brow how you want it, and press it firmly to secure it. If your brows are the adhesive type, use a few strips of masking tape to hold it while the sticky does its stuff. Be careful when removing the tape that it doesn't take the paint off!

Mk 2
headlights

01 To remove the Focus Mk 1 headlights, the grille has to go first. With the bonnet open, unscrew the four plastic body clips from the radiator air deflector, and remove the deflector panel.

02 Unscrew the two radiator grille lower mounting bolts . . .

03 . . . then release the clips at the top ends of the grille.

04 Unclip the centre of the grille from the lock assembly by slackening the clamp screw . . .

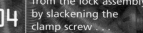

05 . . . then lift the grille out. Nasty plastic fake-mesh effort - do we really want to refit it later?

06 Now remove the three headlight retaining bolts visible on top . . .

07 . . . and the remaining headlight bolt, cunningly hidden underneath. That's why the light won't come out.

08 Lift the headlight partially away from car, then disconnect the wiring plug. Lift the unit away, and store it somewhere safe. Well, you might want to refit it one day - or sell it now after removing the bits you need.

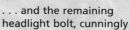

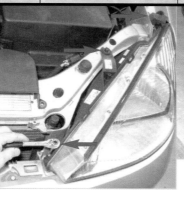

>>

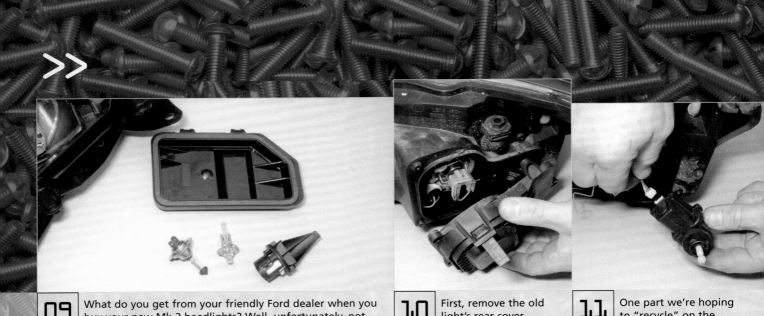

09 What do you get from your friendly Ford dealer when you buy your new Mk 2 headlights? Well, unfortunately, not everything you need to fit them. You also need the rear cover, new (separate) main and dipped beam bulbs each side, and a bulbholder for the in-headlight front indicator. Phew.

10 First, remove the old light's rear cover, which is held on by four Allen screws.

11 One part we're hoping to "recycle" on the new light is the beam adjustment motor, which you twist sideways to release the bayonet fitting, then carefully pull out of its ball-and-socket joint. Unplug the wiring connector . . .

15 Time to put in the new headlight bulbs, which only fit one way, and are pinned in place with a wire clip. Notice we're carefully not touching the bulb glass - it pays to wipe any bulb clean with meths before fitting it, or it may not last long. And they're not cheap.

16 Don't forget to swap over the little sidelight bulb - or you won't have any sidelights.

17 Fit the headlight rear cover, and secure with its wire clip across the back. One fully-assembled headlight. Ready to fit? Well, sort-of.

12 . . . and it's ready to be fitted into the new light.

13 Take the old front indicator bulb out from the bumper light, and fit it to the new bulbholder . . .

14 . . . which then twists into place on the back of the new headlight.

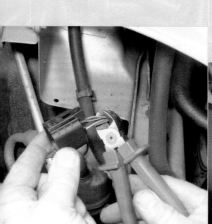

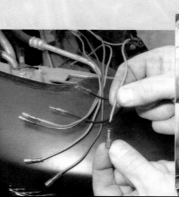

18 Just to make things interesting, Ford have changed the headlight wiring plugs, so old and new don't match. Meaning we're going to chop the old plug, attach some little speaker-type terminals on the ends, and fit our old wires to the plug pins on the new light. Cutting the old plug off's the easy bit . . .

19 . . . while crimping on the new terminals is pretty easy, too.

20 The old front indicator wiring plugs also get the chop. Keep a note of where the wires came from - for instance, this indicator has a blue live wire and a black earth, which shouldn't be confused with any similar-coloured wires from the main headlight plug.

21 With our bunch of headlight and indicator plug wires neatly taped up, all that remains is to plug the wires onto the new headlight plug pins. A bit fiddly, but not a challenge. Of course, what would really help is knowing which wires go where . . .

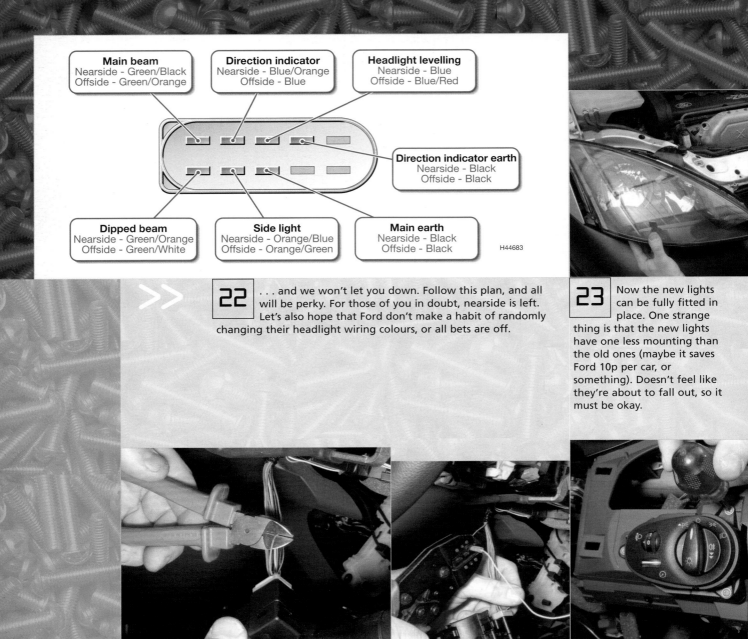

Main beam
Nearside - Green/Black
Offside - Green/Orange

Direction indicator
Nearside - Blue/Orange
Offside - Blue

Headlight levelling
Nearside - Blue
Offside - Blue/Red

Direction indicator earth
Nearside - Black
Offside - Black

Dipped beam
Nearside - Green/Orange
Offside - Green/White

Side light
Nearside - Orange/Blue
Offside - Orange/Green

Main earth
Nearside - Black
Offside - Black

H44683

22 . . . and we won't let you down. Follow this plan, and all will be perky. For those of you in doubt, nearside is left. Let's also hope that Ford don't make a habit of randomly changing their headlight wiring colours, or all bets are off.

23 Now the new lights can be fully fitted in place. One strange thing is that the new lights have one less mounting than the old ones (maybe it saves Ford 10p per car, or something). Doesn't feel like they're about to fall out, so it must be okay.

27 We're looking for a green/blue wire off the column switch, which can be cut close to the plug like this. The short stump of wire you're left with can be left hanging - we want the longer piece, heading off into the loom . . .

28 . . . to which you join on a piece of wire (yellow, in our case), long enough to reach across to the other side of the steering wheel. Feed this wire across to the right-hand side of the car.

29 Remove the panel to the right of the steering wheel (one screw at the base and unclips, as described in the starter button section), then take out three screws and remove the main light switch.

24 Still not quite finished - there's a very necessary wiring mod to do, inside the car. Remove the steering column lower shroud (three screws) . . .

25 . . . and unclip the top shroud, working it carefully out from under the clocks.

26 Unclip the headlight dip/flash column switch (the left-hand one) by releasing the plastic tab at the top of the switch. Lift the switch upwards to get at the wiring on the back.

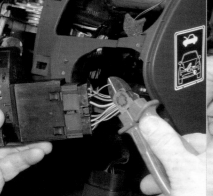

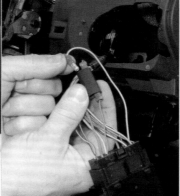

30 At the back of the main light switch, look for a green/red wire. All we need to do is splice our newly-added wire from the column switch onto this green/red joker. Various ways to do this, but our favourite is to strip a little insulation off, wrap the new wire round, and solder. Just to be different, we're going to cut the wire this time . . .

31 . . . and join the new wire in using a bullet-type joiner. Now the headlights should work like they're supposed to.

32 Hopefully, this little wiring diagram will make what we've just done a bit clearer. If not, might we suggest you take the job to someone who isn't scared of car electrics (which rules out about 90% of normal people, unfortunately!).

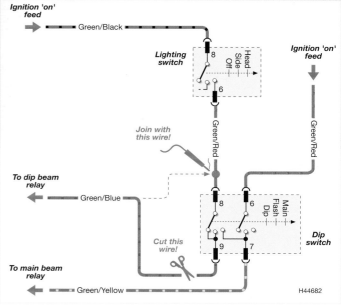

81

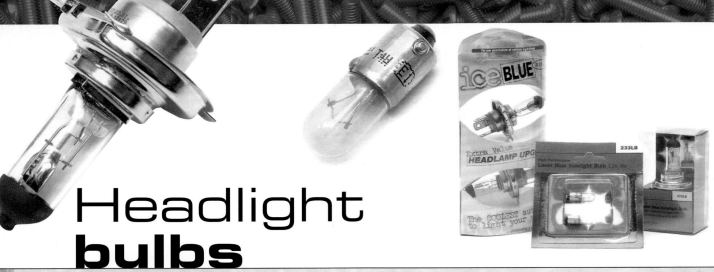

Headlight
bulbs

Make your Focus look like an Audi or a Beemer, the easy way. Bad-weather and 'blue' headlight bulbs are an excellent way to boost headlight performance, and are perfect with other blue LED accessories like washer jets and number plate screws. The blue bulbs you buy in most accessory shops will be legal, 60W/55 bulbs, and are no problem. Don't be tempted to buy the mega-powerful bulbs you can get from rallying suppliers (any over 60W/55 are in fact illegal for use in this country) - as with all other non-standard lights, the boys in blue will love pulling you over for a word about this, so ask before you buy.

Even if you're not bothered about the legality of over-powerful bulbs (and you might well argue that being more powerful is the whole point of fitting), there's other problems with monster bulbs. First, they give off masses of heat, and loads of people have melted their headlights before they found this out. Don't believe us? Try fitting some 100W/90s and put your hand in front of the light, close to the glass. Hot, isn't it? The excess heat these bulbs generate will damage the headlights eventually, either by warping the lens, burning off the reflective coating, or melting the bulbholders. Maybe all three.

The increased current required to work big bulbs has also been known to melt wiring (this could lead to a fire) and will almost certainly burn out your light switch.

Tricks 'n' tips
Put the old bulbs in the glovebox - carrying spare bulbs is a good way to get a let-off from Plod, if they stop you for having a bulb gone. Be smart. Carry spares.

Front fog/spotlights

Extra lights are useful for adding features to the Focus's rather bland front end, even if they are a bit harder to fit than mesh. Most front bumpers have the facility for one or more pairs of lights, so it's gotta be done, really.

If you're fitting fogs, they must be wired in to work on dipped-beam only, so they must go off on main beam. The opposite is true for spotlights. Pop out the main light switch (or pull down the fusebox) and check for a wire which is live ONLY when the dipped beams are on. The Haynes wiring diagrams will help here.

Once you've traced your wire, this is used as the live (+ve) feed for your foglight relay. Did we mention you'll need a relay? You'll need a relay. A four-pin one will do nicely. Splice a new wire onto the feed you've found, and feed it through to the engine (use one of the bulkhead grommets). Decide where you'll mount the relay (next to the battery seems obvious) and connect the new wire onto terminal 86.

For your other relay connections, you'll need an earth to terminal 85 (plenty of good earth spots around the battery). You also need a fused live supply (buy a single fuseholder, and a 15 or 20-amp fuse should be enough) and take a new feed straight off the battery positive connection - this goes to terminal 30 on your relay.

Terminal 87 on your relay is the live output to the fogs - split this into two wires, and feed it out to where the lights will go. Each foglight will also need an earth - either pick a point on the body next to each light, or run a pair of wires back to the earth point you used earlier for your relay. Simple, innit?

With the wiring sorted, now you'd best fit the lights. Over to you. Most decent foglights come with some form of mounting brackets - you must be able to adjust the aim, even if only slightly. To look their best, hopefully your new lights can slot into pre-cut holes in your new front bumper/bodykit.

To connect the wiring to the lights, you'll probably need to splice on your wires from terminal 87 to the new wiring plugs which came with the lights - not too difficult. Plug it all together, and test - you should now have some rather funky fogs!

Front indicators

Got a pre-facelift Focus? Then you're stuck with indicators in the front bumpers. One way to improve this unfortunate situation is to fit later headlights, which have the indicators built in. For those of you who don't fancy this, our friends at ABC Design make crystal replacement indicators, which go straight in, and (especially on a silver Focus) look very trick.

01 Getting the indicators out presents absolutely zero challenge to anyone. Remove one Torx screw in the corner . . .

02 . . . then unhook the light and pull it out. In the opposite corner from where the screw was, the light has a moulded clip which slots into a lug in the bumper (you'll need to know this when you fit the new light).

03 . . . and twist out the bulbholder. Now the light's off, do we mod it or scrap it? Spraying your lights is a top idea if funds are too tight for replacements. Get the light clean, give it a few light coats of light-tinting spray (available from Folia Tec, for instance), and you've instantly got smokes, or any other shade you like.

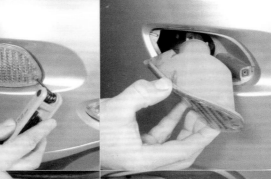

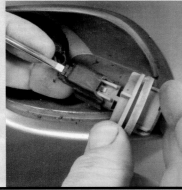

04 Anyway, back to our replacement crystals, which need amber bulbs to keep it all legal. Therefore, the original bulbholder is no good, and must be destroyed (well, removed and kept in safe place!). Remove the holder using a flat-headed screwdriver to depress the plastic lug at the rear of the holder. Retrieve the large rubber washer from the holder - we'll need it later.

05 Now remove the part of the holder that the bulb connects into... You'll understand why in a minute.

06 Our new amber bulb won't fit straight into the old bulbholder - but it does now. With the new holder clipped into place, fit the amber bulb. Remember to refit the rubber sealing washer, which keeps the weather out of the new light unit.

07 Refit the bulbholder to the light, and the light to the car (hook the light retaining lug in at the top outer corner, then secure with the Torx screw), and that's it. Job done. Easy(ish).

There's a range of 'standard' colours that side reps come in, but most people go for clear or smoked, to colour-code with their rear clusters. Clear lenses can be coloured using special paint, but the paint must be applied lightly and evenly to the lens, or this will invite an easily-avoided MOT failure. Bodyshops can colour clear lenses to the exact shade of your car, by mixing a little paint with loads of lacquer - very trick.

Side repeaters must still show an orange light, and must be sufficiently bright (not easy to judge, and no two coppers have the same eyesight!). The stock bulbs are clear, so make sure you get orange bulbs too. You can actually get orange bulbs that look clear, to avoid the 'fried egg' effect. Alternatively, get LED side repeaters, like we did on our Fiesta project car.

Besides the various colour effects, side repeaters are available in many different shapes. But - Focus side reps are so cool, people fit 'em to loadsa cars, so why change the shape? Besides, you'll be making work if you do - the Focus front wings have a triangular recess, which you'd have to smooth before you start.

Or how about ditching the repeaters altogether, and get some tasty Merc-style mirrors, with side reps built-in? You could smooth your front wings, then…

Side
repeaters

01 Grip the side repeater at either end, and slide the assembly downwards. If this proves impossible, use a screwdriver to lever the repeater away, but protect the bodywork when doing this. We don't want any tears.

02 Turn the bulbholder anti-clockwise and disconnect it from the light. Pull the clear bulb from the holder . . .

03 . . . and pop the new amber bulb into its place. You'll need to swap bulbs for virtually every modded side rep out there - remember, it still has to show an orange (or sort-of orange) light afterwards.

04 Pop the bulbholder assembly into the new crystal side repeater unit, and re-fit the unit to the car. Slip it in and slide it upwards. Nice.

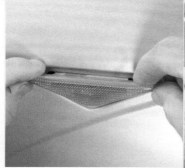

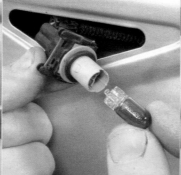
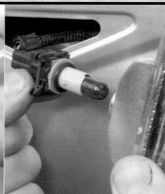

Rear lights

Oh boy - spoilt for choice already, and more to come as the Focus grows in popularity. There's obviously Lexus-style (tired of it yet?), and Morette do some tidy afterburner-style rears. Because the rear lights are quite a styling feature on the Focus, it pays to choose carefully. As they join together the side glass and rear window, we decided not to break up the smoked glass with any other colour, and went for the 'Black Magic' clusters from ABC Design. Your car, your look, you decide.

Light legality

Lots of Focus rear clusters there may be, but - often, they're not UK-legal (even lights which are E-marked sometimes have no rear fogs or reflectors). Mr. Plod is well-informed on this point, and those sexy rear lights are way too big a come-on for him to ignore.

The rear foglight/reflector problem isn't such a huge one on Foci, as they have discreet little reflectors and a fog under the standard rear bumper. Get crystal replacements, or spray-tint the originals, and you're sorted. Course, if the stock bumper goes when the bodykit arrives, you could've created yourself a problem. And discreet they may be, but those standard lower rear lights are right in the way of a twin-exit exhaust.

You can buy stick-on reflectors, but these are about as sexy as NHS specs, so there's no easy answer on this. You'd have to be pretty unlucky to get pulled just for having no rear reflectors, but don't say we didn't warn you. And what happens if your car gets crunched, parked at night with no reflectors fitted? Will your insurance try and refuse to pay out? You betcha.

If you've got a rad rear bumper planned, with no chance of refitting the standard fog, why not cut a hole in your new rear bumper/mesh, and find a cool-looking rear fog to mount inside (the Peugeot 206 unit's pretty sweet). If you don't mind a bit extra work, source an exhaust tailpipe trim roughly the same size as your existing single pipe, mount it on the opposite side of the car, and fit a round foglight inside the end.

Any questions on light legality? Why not check out the ABC Design website tech tips page - if you've any questions after that, you can e-mail them. We're so good to you.

Rear foglights/reversing lights

We're not fitting a complete new rear bumper, so the standard reversing and fog lights need to be sexed-up a little, as they're still on show. We decided to tint the lights using a special Folia Tec taillight tinting kit, so they'll match our sexy smoked clusters. Tinting is easy and takes very little time to do.

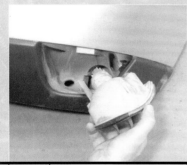

01 With the rear bumper removed as described in the bodywork section, we can simply pop out the two light units (one positioned at either end of the rear bumper).

02 Give the light lens a good clean with a suitable degreaser - we use brake cleaner for these types of jobs, which (surprisingly) doesn't melt or discolour the plastic lens. You might not be so lucky with all solvents, so watch it. Petrol might be ok, but meths would be safer. Then, using a Scotchbrite pad (bodyshop 'scouring pad'), gently roughen the surface. You don't want to deeply scratch the plastic lens, just take a bit of the shine off.

03 Mask the back of the light unit, to protect from over-spray.

04 As with most spray-painting, the trick is to get the stuff on evenly, which means applying light coats. Blasting it on too thick will give you the runs, which is never pleasant. How thick is too thick? See what it looks like after a few light coats - somewhere between standard and completely black is the target. Don't go too mad if you want to avoid attention from the Law.

Rear lights

Open the tailgate and you will see the rear light cluster retaining screw. Grab your trusty Philips screwdriver, and remove said screw.

01

05 Temporarily remove the rubber sealing washer from the indicator bulbholder, and keep it in a safe place as we'll be re-using it later.

06 Prise off the part of the holder that the bulb locates into - the new amber bulbs have different pins, and won't fit the standard holders.

07 Fit the new section of bulbholder supplied with the kit, then refit the rubber washer and add the amber bulb.

02 Into the boot now, and look round the corner until you can see the light cluster's flat plastic wingnut (the left-hand one's just back from the boot light) - unscrew and remove it.

03 Lift the cluster away from the car and support with one hand, while disconnecting the bulbholders with the other hand to free the unit from the car. You may find the wiring has been cable-tied in several places on the back of the light – cut these ties off to free the unit from the car. When the cluster's been stored safely, clean the bodywork behind the light cluster.

04 Remove the clear indicator bulb. Our new lights require us to fit an amber bulb for the clear indicator lens, and this gives us some extra work.

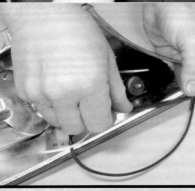

08 Now the lights need waterproofing. In our kit, we find four adhesive rubber strips, which fit at the top and outer edges of the new light, to keep the rain out. Peel off the backing, and slide the rubber into the grooved channel along the side and top of the light cluster. Take care to ensure the rubber strips lie perfectly in the grooved channels, with no air bubbles left that might let in water. If your lights aren't as posh as this, you might use a little silicone sealant instead.

09 Fit the bulbs into the new light, and tidy the wire as best you can behind the unit, so that it won't be damaged when refitting the unit to the car.

10 Offer the cluster into place, ensuring that it locates properly. Refit the outer and inner retaining light cluster screws, and that's it! Check it all works before venturing out into Plod-land. The original clusters had a reflector section at the top - our new ones don't. By law, you must have a minimum of two rear reflectors, fitted symmetrically, one on each side. If you keep the standard lights below the bumper, you're ok - otherwise, reflectors are cheap to buy. It's up to you.

Wheels & tyres

Your most important decision ever?

This is where it's at - alloy wheels are the most important styling decision you'll ever make. No matter how good the rest of your car is, choose the wrong rims and your car will never look right. Choose a good set and you're already well on the way to creating a sorted motor. Take your time and pick wisely - wheel fashions change like the weather, and you don't want to spend shedloads on a set of uncool alloys.

For a change, some standard Focus alloys are quite tidy (ST / RS), but Zetec 15s are a bit too common, and should really be ditched when funds allow it. Advice on which particular wheels to buy would be a waste of space, since the choice is so huge, and everyone will have their own favourites. For what it's worth, though, something in a multi-spoker usually looks sweet on a Focus (multi-spoke ST170 wheels get nicked on a regular basis - there must be a reason), so maybe some OZ's? For something close to an RS wheel, check Compomotive's offerings (or OZ again, who make the real thing). Turning all-American, this year's look is chrome, and the US-based sites have plenty to see (MSI Online, for starters, and DM Tech America). Even Wolfrace have recently jumped on the chrome bandwagon - or try Cam chromes for a value choice.

One point not to overlook when choosing wheels is the wheel offset. Most normal cars fall somewhere in the mid-30s to early 40s, but the Focus is an oddball, at 52. Make sure you mention they're for a Focus at an early stage in negotiations. Going lower than a 52 offset makes the wheel 'stick out' more - for really big rims, your arches won't just have to be 'trimmed' - they'll be butchered! Fitting wheels with the wrong offset may also do unpleasant things to the handling.

Lead us not into temptation

Before we go any further into which wheels are right for you, a word about insurance and security. Fitting tasty alloys to your Focus is one of the first and best ways to make it look cool. It follows, therefore, that someone with dubious morals might very well want to unbolt them from your car while you're not around, and make their own car look cool instead (or simply sell them, to buy spot cream and drugs).

Since fitting a set of top alloys is one of the easiest bolt-on ways to trick up any car, it's no surprise that the market in stolen alloys is as alive and kicking as it currently is - your wheels will also look very nice on any number of other cars, and the owners of those cars would love to own them at a fraction of the price you paid... It's not unknown for a set of wheels to go missing just for the tyres - if you've just splashed out on a set of fat Yokohamas, your wheels look even more tempting, especially if you've got a common-size tyre.

Tell your insurance company what you're fitting. What will probably happen is that they'll ask for the exact details, and possibly a photo of the car with the wheels on. Provided you're happy to then accept that they won't cover the extra cost of the wheels if they get nicked (or if the whole car goes), you may find you're not charged a penny more, especially if you've responsibly fitted some locking wheel nuts. Not all companies are the same, though - some charge an admin fee, and yes, some will start loading your premium. If you want the rims covered, it's best to talk to a company specialising in modified cars, or you could be asked to pay out the wheel cost again in premiums. The daftest thing you can do is say nothing, and hope they don't find out - we don't want to go on about this, but there are plenty of documented cases where insurance companies have refused to pay out altogether, purely on the basis of undeclared alloy wheels.

How **cheap** are you?

Hopefully, you'll be deciding which wheels to go for based on how they look, not how much they cost, but inevitably (for most ordinary people at least), price does become a factor. Surely buying a cheaper wheel must have its pitfalls? Well, yes - and some of them may not be so obvious.

Inevitably, cheaper wheels = lower quality, but how does this manifest itself? Cheap wheels are often made from alloys which are more 'porous' (a bit like a sponge, they contain microscopic holes and pockets of air). Being porous has two main disadvantages for a wheel, the main one being that it won't be able to retain air in the tyres. The days of tyres with inner tubes are long gone (and it's illegal to fit tubes to low-profile tyres), so the only thing keeping the air in are the three 'walls' of the tyre, with the fourth 'wall' being the inside of the wheel itself. If you like keeping fit by pumping up your tyres every morning, go ahead - the rest of us will rightly regard this as a pain, and potentially dangerous (running tyres at low pressure will also scrub them out very effectively - what was that about saving money?).

Porous wheels also have difficulty in retaining their paint, lacquer, or chrome finish, with flaking a known problem, sometimes after only a few months. This problem is made worse by the fact that porous wheels are much harder to clean (brake dust seems to get ingrained into the wheels more easily) - and the more you scrub, the more the lacquer comes off.

The final nail in the coffin for cheap wheels is that they tend to corrode (or 'fizz') more. This not only ruins the looks if visible from outside, but if you get corrosion between the wheel and the hub, you won't even be able to take the damn things off! Yes seriously, grown men with all the specialist tools in the world at their disposal will be scratching their heads when faced with wheels which simply **will not** come off.

Buying an established, popular make of wheel has another hidden benefit, too. Choosing a popular wheel will mean more suppliers will stock it, and the manufacturers themselves will make plenty of them. And if you're unlucky enough to have an accident (maybe a slide on a frosty road) which results in non-repairable damage to one wheel, you're going to need a replacement. If you've chosen the rarest wheels on the planet, you could be faced with having to replace a complete set of four, to get them all matching… A popular wheel, even if it's a few years old, might be easier to source, even second-hand.

The Sunday morning ritual

It's a small point maybe, but you'll obviously want your wheels to look as smart as possible, as often as possible - so how easy are they going to be to clean?

The real multi-spokers and BBS-style 'wires' are hell to clean - a fiddly toothbrush job - do you really want that much aggro every week? The simpler the design, the easier time you'll have. For those who like nothing better than counting their spokes, though, there are several really good products out there to make your life less of a cleaning nightmare.

Bound to drive you nuts

Don't forget about locking wheel nuts (see *'Hold on to your wheels'* further on) - bargain these into a wheel/tyre package if you're buying new.

A word of warning about re-using your existing wheel nuts, should you be upgrading from steel wheels. Steel-wheel nuts may not be suitable for use with alloy wheels (and vice-versa, incidentally). Make sure you ask about this when buying new wheels, and if necessary, bargain a set of nuts into the price. Most nuts for use with alloys will have a washer fitted, for two very good reasons - 1) the nut will pull through the wheel hole without it, and 2) it protects the wheel finish.

Other options

If you're on a really tight budget, and perhaps own a real 'basic' model Focus, don't overlook the possibility of fitting a discarded set of standard alloys (a set of Zetec rims would do).

Remember the strange 52 offset problem if you get offered a set of rims from another Ford entirely. Escort Cosworth wheels are just about the sexiest thing to grace any Ford, but try fitting them to a Focus, and there'll be trouble - the Cossie has a 25 offset, so unless your Focus has a wide-arch kit, they won't go on. Mondeo wheels are a possibility (the offsets aren't that different), but it's definitely try before you buy.

If the Ford range of wheels is too limiting, don't be too quick buying (for instance) alloys from other car makes altogether. For instance, some Peugeot/Citroen alloys have the same stud pattern (4x108), so they'll go on alright, but the offset's even lower than those Cosworth items we mentioned earlier. In the case of some alloys (BMW, for example), the stud pattern may be only fractionally different (4x100), but if you put these on, the strain on the wheel studs is too great, and they can fracture…

Size **matters**

For us Brits, biggest is best - there are Foci out there with 19s and up. And yes, the mags all say you can't be seen with anything less than 17-inchers. In Europe, meanwhile, they're mad for the small-wheel look, still with seriously dropped suspension of course.

While the Focus will take 8x19-inch rims without sorting the arches, remember that anything bigger than 17s won't do wonders for the ride or handling. If you're bothered about how your Focus takes the bends, stick to 17s instead. Providing the rest of the car's up together, get the car low (35 to 40 mm drop) and you'll still get respect. A comment we saw on one chat room was "get 19s for the look, 17s if you still wanna drive it".

Tricks 'n' tips

When you have your new wheels balanced, make sure the fast-fit centre knows to use stick-on weights, inside the wheel (not on the rim edge) - old-type knock-on lead weights look terrible on the outer wheel edges, and on the inner edges may foul the suspension. Stick-on weights are, however, notorious for falling off easily, even when applied to pristine new alloys.

We like a challenge

To be honest, successfully fitting big wheels in combination with lowered suspension is one of life's major challenges.

As much as anything, tyre width is what ultimately leads to problems, not so much the increased wheel diameter.

If the tyres are simply too wide (or with wheels the wrong offset), they will first of all rub on the suspension strut (ie on the inside edge of the tyre). Also, the inside edges may rub on the arches on full steering lock - check left and right. Rubbing on the inside edges can be cured by fitting offsets or spacers between the wheel and hub, which effectively pull the wheel outwards, 'spacing' it away from its normal position (this also has the effect of widening the car's track, which may improve the on-limit handling - or not). Fitting large offsets must be done using special longer wheel studs, as the standard ones may only engage the nuts by a few threads, which is highly dangerous.

Rubbing on the outside edges is a simple case of wheelarch lip fouling, which must be cured by rolling up (or trimming off) the wheelarch return edge, and other mods. If you've gone for REALLY wide tyres, or have already had to fit offsets, the outer edge of the tyre will probably be visible outside the wheelarch, and this is a no-no (it's illegal, and you must cover it up!).

Foci also have unusual wheel arch liners - they seem to be made of carpet, not plastic, and they can sag down after a while, meaning they rub. Fortunately, removal isn't difficult.

The other trick with fitting big alloys is of course to avoid the 'Focus 4x4 off-road' look, which you will achieve remarkably easily just by popping on a set of 17s with standard suspension. The massive increase in ground clearance is fine for Farmer Palmer, but your 'fistable' arches won't win much admiration at cruises. Overcoming this problem by lowering can be a matter almost of inspired guesswork, as much as anything (see 'Suspension').

Speedo error? Or not?

One side-effect of fitting large wheels is that your car will go slower.

Yes, really - or at least - it will appear to go slower, due to the effect on the speedometer. As the wheel diameter increases, so does its circumference (distance around the outside) - this means that, to travel say one mile, a large wheel will turn less than a smaller wheel. Because the speedometer is driven from the gearbox final drive, the apparent vehicle speed is actually based on the number of complete revolutions of the wheel. Therefore, for a given *actual* speed, since a larger-diameter wheel will be turning at a slower rate than a smaller wheel, and the method for measuring speed is the rate of wheel rotation, a car with larger wheels will produce a lower *speedo reading* than one with smaller wheels - but it's NOT actually going any slower in reality. So don't worry if you think you've reduced your Focus's performance somehow with the monster rims, 'cos you 'aven't.

With the ever-increasing number of those lovely grey/yellow roadside boxes with a nasty surprise inside, spare a thought to what this speedo error could mean in the real world. If (like most people) you tend to drive a wee bit over the posted 30s and 40s, your real speed on 17s could be a bit more than the bit more you thought you were doing already, and you could get an unexpected flash to ruin your day. What we're saying is, don't drive any faster, to compensate for the lower speedo reading. Actually, the speedo error effect on 17s really is tiny at around-town speeds, and only becomes a factor over 70. But then, Officer, you couldn't possibly have been going over 70, could you? Officer?

Jargon explained

Rolling Radius - You may have come across the term 'rolling radius', which is the distance from the wheel centre to the outer edge of the tyre, or effectively, half the overall diameter. The rolling radius obviously increases with wheel size, but up to a point, the effects are masked by fitting low-profile tyres, with 'shorter' sidewalls. Above 16-inch rims, however, even low-profiles can't compensate, and the rolling radius keeps going up.

PCD - this isn't a banned substance, it's your Pitch Circle Diameter, which relates to the spacing of your wheel holes, or 'stud pattern'. It is expressed by the diameter of a notional circle which passes through the centre of your wheel studs, and the number of studs/nuts. Unlike the offset, the PCD often isn't stamped onto the wheels, so assessing it is really a matter of eyeing-up and trying them on the studs - the wheel should go on easily, without binding, if the stud pattern is correct. On a Focus, the PCD is 108 mm with four studs, which is given as 108/4, or 4 x 108.

Offset - this is determined by the distance from the wheel mounting face in relation to its centre-line. The offset figure is denoted by ET (no, I mustn't), which stands for einpress tiefe in German, or pressed-in depth (now I KNOW you're asleep). The lower the offset, the more the wheels will stick out. Fitting wheels with the wrong offset might bring the wheel into too-close contact with the brake and suspension bits, or with the arches. Very specialised area - seek advice from the wheel manufacturers if you're going for a very radical size (or even if you're not). The correct offset for Foci of all sizes is ET 52.

Hold on to your wheels

The minute you bang on your wicked alloys, your car becomes a target. People see the big wheels, and automatically assume you've also got a major stereo, seats and other goodies - all very tempting, but that involves breaking in, and you could have an alarm. Pinching the wheels themselves, now that's a doddle - a few tools, some bricks or a couple of well-built mates to lift the car, and it's easy money.

The trouble with fitting big wheels is that they're only screwed on, and are just as easily screwed off, if you don't make life difficult for 'em. If you're unlucky enough to have to park outside at night (ie no garage), you could wake up one morning to a car that's *literally* been slammed on the deck! Add to this the fact that your car isn't going anywhere without wheels, plus the damage which will be done to exhaust, fuel and brake pipes from dropping on its belly, and it's suddenly a lot worse than losing a grand's worth of wheels and tyres...

The market and demand for stolen alloys is huge, but since most people don't bother having them security-marked in any way, once a set of wheels disappears, they're almost impossible to trace. Thieves avoid security-marked (or 'tattooed') wheels (or at least it's a pretty good

deterrent) - and it needn't look hideous!

When choosing that car alarm, try and get one with an 'anti-jacking' feature, because thieves hate it. This is sometimes now called 'anti-tilt', to avoid confusion with anti-hijacking. Imagine a metal saucer, with a metal ball sitting on a small magnet in the centre. If the saucer tilts in any direction, the ball rolls off the magnet, and sets off the alarm. Highly sensitive, and death to anyone trying to lift your car up for the purpose of removing the wheels - as we said, the crims are not fond of this feature at all. Simply having an alarm with anti-shock is probably not good enough, because a careful villain will probably be able to work so as not to create a strong enough vibration to trigger it - mind you, it's a whole lot better than nothing, especially if set to maximum sensitivity.

Locking nuts/bolts

Locking wheel nuts will be effective as a deterrent to the inexpert thief (kids, in other words), but will probably only slow down the pro.

Thieves want to work quickly, and will use large amounts of cunning and violence to deprive you of your stuff. If you fit a cheap set of locking nuts, they'll use a hammer and thin chisel to crack off the locking heads. Some nuts can easily be defeated by hammering a socket onto them, and undoing the locking nut as normal, while some of the key-operated nuts are so pathetic they can be beaten using a small screwdriver. So - choose the best nuts you can, but don't assume they'll prevent your wheels from disappearing. Insurance companies seem to like 'em - perhaps it shows a responsible attitude, or something...

There's some debate as to whether it's okay to fit more than one set of locking nuts to a car - some people we know value their wheels so highly they've fitted four sets of nuts - in other words, they've completely replaced all the standard nuts! The feeling against doing this is that the replacement locking nuts may not be made to the same standard as factory originals, and while it's okay to fit one set on security grounds, fitting more than that is dangerous on safety grounds (nut could fail, wheel falls off, car in ditch, owner in hospital...).

Obviously, you must carry the special key or tool which came with your nuts with you at all times, in case of a puncture, or if you're having any other work done, such as new brakes or tyres. The best thing to do is rig this onto your keyring, so that it's with you, but not left in the car. The number of people who fit locking nuts and then leave the key to them cunningly 'hidden' in the glovebox or the boot... You don't leave a spare set of car keys in your glovebox as well, do you?

How to change a set of wheels

You might think you know all about this, but do you really?

Okay, so you know you need a jack and wheelbrace (or socket and ratchet), but where are the jacking points? If you want to take more than one wheel off at a time, have you got any axle stands, and where do they go? If you've only ever had wheels and tyres fitted by a garage, chances are you're actually a beginner at this. It's surprising just how much damage you can do to your car, and to yourself, if you don't know what you're doing - and the worst thing here is to think you know, when you don't...

What to use

If you don't already have one, invest in a decent hydraulic (trolley) jack. This is way more use than the standard car jack, which is really only for emergencies, and which isn't really stable enough to rely on. Lifting and lowering the car is so much easier with a trolley jack, and you'll even look professional. Trolley jacks have a valve, usually at the rear, which must be fully tightened (using the end of the jack handle) before raising the jack, and which is carefully loosened to lower the car down - if it's opened fully, the car will not so much sink as plummet!

Axle stands are placed under the car, once it's been lifted using the jack. Stands are an important accessory to a trolley jack, because once they're in place, there's no way the car can come down on you - remember that even a brand new trolley jack could creep down (if you haven't tightened the valve), or could even fail completely under load (if it's a cheap one, or knackered, or both).

Under NO circumstances use bricks, wooden blocks or anything else which you have to pile up, to support the car - this is just plain

stupid. A Focus is not a small car, and weighs quite enough to damage you convincingly if it lands on top of you - if you don't believe us, try crawling under it when it's resting on a few poxy bricks.

Where to do it

Only ever jack the car up on a solid, level surface (ideally, a concrete or tarmac driveway, or quiet car park). If there's even a slight slope, the car's likely to move (maybe even roll away) as the wheels are lifted off the ground. Jacking up on a rough or gravelled surface is not recommended, as the jack could slip at an awkward moment - such as when you've just got underneath…

How to do it - jacking up the front

Before jacking up the front of the car, pull the handbrake on firmly (you can also chock the rear wheels, if you don't trust your handbrake).

If you're taking the wheels off, loosen the wheel nuts BEFORE you start jacking up the car. It's easily forgotten, but you'll look pretty silly trying to undo the wheel nuts with the front wheels spinning in mid-air.

We'll assume you've got a trolley jack. The next question is -

where to stick it? Up front, there's a chunky-looking subframe behind the engine, with the front suspension wishbones attached - as long as you don't jack under the wishbones, this should be fine, but put a flat offcut of wood on your jack head first, to spread the load. There's also a chunky box-section on the floorpan, running back from the subframe, which can be used for jacking, again with some wood on the jack head. You can jack on the sill jacking points, which are marked by an indent in the sill bottom edges (there may be a plastic cover to remove first), but it's better to leave those for your axle stands.

Once you've got the car up, pop an axle stand or two under the front sill jacking points - this is the only part of the sill it's safe to jack under or rest the car on. With the stands in place, you can lower the jack so the car's weight rests on the stands. For maximum safety, spread the car's weight between the stands and the jack - don't lower the jack completely unless it's needed elsewhere.

I'm sure we don't need to tell you this, but don't jack up the car, or stick stands under the car, anywhere other than kosher jacking and support points. This means - not the floorpan or the sump (you'll cave it in), not the moveable suspension bits (not stable), and not under the brake/fuel pipes (ohmigawd).

How to do it - jacking up the rear

When jacking up the rear of the car, place wooden chocks in front of the front wheels to stop it rolling forwards, and engage first gear.

If you're taking the wheels off, you don't have to loosen the wheel nuts before lifting the car, but you'll be relying on your handbrake to hold the wheels while you wrestle with the nuts. Much cooler (and safer) to loosen the rear wheel nuts on the ground too.

Jacking and supporting the Focus back-end is a little trickier. Have a good look under there before making your choice. There's a hefty crossmember between the rear wheels which may be used, but watch that no suspension bits are being compressed, and that no pipes or cables get crushed. Otherwise, it's a bit of a minefield - there's the fuel tank and filler neck, exhaust, anti-roll bar and spare wheel pan to avoid. Not easy.

Although Ford certainly wouldn't recommend it, you can jack under the rear spring plates (the large round plates near the wheels) or the shock absorber lower mounting - just go slowly, as the arm will move and compress the suspension as the jack rises. Jacking under the suspension arm is obviously no use if you're working on the rear suspension itself. There is a strengthened section of floorpan just inside the rear jacking point which you could use while working on the suspension, but watch the fuel lines and handbrake cables - the block of wood on the jack head's essential equipment here.

For axle stands, it's the rear sill jacking point, again marked with an indent on the sill edge. Not so much need for a block of wood here, but still not a bad idea to use one if you can - saves your paint, spreads the load into the car.

Remember not to put your axle stands under any pipes, the spare wheel well, or the fuel tank, and you should live to see another Christmas.

Finally…

As far as possible, don't leave the car unattended once it has been lifted, particularly if kids are playing nearby - football goes under your car, they go under to get it, knock the jack, car falls... it would almost certainly be your fault.

Changing
wheels

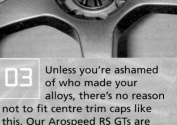

01 Have you got a nice ally/plastic ring inside the wheel hub? Make sure it's there, as it acts to centre the wheel properly, and may help to stop the wheel rusting on. Ever had a rusted-on wheel? Your local fast-fit centre will have, and they'll tell you it ain't funny.

02 Even with the plastic ring of confidence, the metal bits can still corrode on. Equip yourself with some copper brake grease, and smear some on the hub. The pros 'paint' it on with a brush - the rest of us get messy. It's not a bad idea if some of that grease finds its way onto the wheel studs/nuts, too. Keep it off the brake disc, though.

03 Unless you're ashamed of who made your alloys, there's no reason not to fit centre trim caps like this. Our Arospeed RS GTs are no cause for embarrassment, so on it goes.

With the wheel on the ground, tighten the wheel nuts securely (ideally, to the correct torque - 85 Nm). Don't over-tighten, or you'll never get them off if you have a flat! If you've really blown some serious cash on your new rims, why not treat them to a special protected socket for tightening the nuts? Companies like Draper do a set of special sockets with plastic protector sleeves fitted, to stop the metal scratching your fine alloys. Makes sense to us.

04 Pop the wheel onto the hub, then on with the nicely-greased nuts, and tighten up as far as possible by hand.

05 You have got some locking nuts, haven't you? Keep your locking tool (in this case, a fairly mahoosive bolt) somewhere safe, but not obvious. The glovebox is convenient, but way too obvious!

06

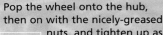

Always nice to see a good brand of tyre on a decent alloy. How cool do cheap tyres look?

Tyres

To some people, tyres are just round and black - oh, and they're nearly all expensive, and don't last long enough. When you're buying a new set of wheels, most centres will quote prices with different tyres - buying a tyred-up set of rims is convenient, and usually good value, too.

Some people try and save money by fitting 'remould' or 're-manufactured' tyres. These aren't always the bargain they appear to be - experience says there's no such thing as a good cheap tyre, with wheel balancing problems a well-known downside, for starters.

Choosing a known brand of tyre will prove to be one of your better decisions. Tyres are the only thing keeping you on the road, as in steering, braking and helping you round corners - what's the point of trying to improve the handling by sorting the suspension if you're going to throw the gains away by fitting naff tyres? Why beef up the brakes if the tyres won't bite? The combination of stiff suspension and cheap tyres is inherently dangerous - because the front end dives less with reduced suspension travel, the front tyres are far more likely to lock and skid under heavy braking.

Cheap tyres also equals more wheelspin - might be fun to disappear in a cloud of tyre smoke, but wouldn't you rather be disappearing up the road? Another problem with really wide tyres is aquaplaning - hit a big puddle at speed, and the tyre skates over the water without gripping - it's seriously scary when your car starts

Tricks 'n' tips

When buying tyres, look out for ones which feature a rubbing strip on the sidewall - these extend over the edge of the wheel rims, and the idea is that they protect the rim edges from damage by 'kerbing'. Any decent tyre has them - discreet and very practical, and much better than a chewed-up rim.

The size markings are obviously the most important, but take note of the directional marks too, if swapping wheels round. Most of the other markings are for anoraks only.

steering for you. Fitting good tyres won't prevent it, but it might increase your chances of staying in control. The sexiest modern low-profile tyres have a V-tread pattern, designed specifically to aid water dispersal, which is exactly what you need to prevent aquaplaning - try some, and feel the difference!

Finally, cheap tyres ruin the look - a no-name brand in big letters on your tyre sidewalls says you're a pikey loud and clear. If you're spending big dosh on wheels, you've gotta kit 'em out with some tasty V-tread tyres, or lose major points for style. Listen to friends and fellow modifiers - real-world opinions count for a lot when choosing tyres (how well do they grip, wet or dry? How many miles can you get out of them?) Just make sure, before you splash your cash on decent tyres, that you've cured any rubbing and scrubbing issues, as nothing will rip your new tyres out faster.

Marks on your sidewalls

Tyre sizes are expressed in a strange mixture of metric and imperial specs - we'll take a typical tyre size as an example:

205/40 R 17 V
for a 7-inch wide 17-inch rim
205 width of tyre in millimetres
40 this is the "aspect ratio" (or "profile") of the tyre, or the sidewall height in relation to tyre width, expressed as a percentage, in this case 40%. So - 40% of 205 mm = 82 mm, or the height of the tyre sidewall from the edge of the locating bead to the top of the tread.
R Radial.
17 Wheel diameter in inches.
V Speed rating (in this case, suitable for use up to 150 mph).

Pressure situation

Don't forget, when you're having your new tyres fitted, to ask what the recommended pressures should be, front and rear - it's unlikely that the Ford specs for this will be relevant to your new low-low profiles, but it's somewhere to start from. If the grease-monkey fitting your tyres is no help on this point, contact the tyre manufacturer - the big ones might even have a half-useful website. Running the tyres at the wrong pressures is particularly stupid (you'll wear them out much faster) and can be very dangerous (too soft - tyre rolls off the rim; too hard - tyre slides, no grip).

Speed ratings

Besides the tyre size, tyres are marked with a maximum speed rating, expressed as a letter code:

T up to 190 km/h (118 mph)

U up to 200 km/h (124 mph)

H up to 210 km/h (130 mph)

V inside tyre size markings (225/50 VR 16) over 210 km/h (130 mph)

V outside tyre size markings (185/55 R 15 V) up to 240 km/h (150 mph)

Z inside tyre size markings (255/40 ZR 17) over 240 km/h (150 mph)

If you've got marks on your sidewalls like this, you're in trouble - this has almost certainly been caused by "kerbing".

08 Suspension

If your Focus is still sitting on standard suspension, it's safe to say it doesn't cut it - yet. If you've decided you couldn't wait to fit your big rims, the chances are your Focus is now doing a passable impression of a tractor. An essential fitment, then - so how low do you go, and what nasty side-effects will a lowering kit have?

The main reason for lowering is of course, to make your car look cool. Standard suspension nearly always seems to be set too soft and too high - a nicely lowered motor really stands out instantly. Lowering your car should also improve the handling. Dropping the car on its suspension brings the car's centre of gravity closer to its roll and pitch centres, which helps to pin it to the road in corners and under braking - combined with stiffer springs and shocks, this reduces body roll and increases the tyre contact patch on the road. BUT - if improving the handling is really important to you, choose your new suspension carefully. If you go the cheap route, or want extreme lowering, then you could end up with a car that doesn't handle at all... And with a fine-handling car like the Focus, that's a real shame.

As for what to buy, there are basically three main options when it comes to lowering, arranged in order of ascending cost below:

1 Set of lowering springs.

2 Matched set of lowering springs and shock absorbers (suspension kit).

3 Set of 'coilovers'.

Lowering springs

The cheapest option by far, but with the most pitfalls and some unpleasant side-effects. Lowering springs are, effectively, shorter versions of the standard items fitted to your Focus at the factory. However, not only are they shorter (lower), they are also uprated (stiffer) - if lowering springs were simply shorter than standard and the same stiffness (the same 'rate'), you'd be hitting the bump-stops over every set of catseyes. With lowering springs, you just fit the new springs and keep the original shock absorbers ('dampers'), so even if the originals aren't completely knackered, you're creating a problem caused by mis-matched components. The original dampers were carefully chosen to work with the original-rate springs - by increasing the spring rate without changing the dampers, you end up with dampers that can't control the springs properly. What this usually does before long is wreck the dampers, so you don't even save money in the end.

The mis-matched springs and dampers will have other entertaining side-effects, too. How would you like a Focus which rides like a brick, and which falls over itself at the first sign of a corner taken above walking pace? A very choppy ride and strange-feeling steering (much lighter, or much heavier, depending on your luck) are well-documented problems associated with taking the cheap option, and it doesn't even take much less time to fit, compared to a proper solution. Even if you're a hard man, who doesn't object to a hard ride if his car looks cool, think on this - how many corners do you know that are completely flat (ie without any bumps)? On dodgy lowering springs, you hit a mid-corner bump at speed, and it's anyone's guess where you'll end up.

If cost is a major consideration, and lowering springs the only option for now, at least try to buy branded items of decent quality - some cheap sets of springs will eat their way through several sets of dampers before you realise the springs themselves have lost the plot. Needless to say, if riding around on mis-matched springs and shocks is a bit iffy anyway, it's downright dangerous when they've worn out (some inside 18 months!).

Assuming you want to slam your suspension so your arches just clear the tops of your wicked new rims, there's another small problem with lowered springs - it takes some inspired guesswork (or hours of careful measuring and head-scratching) to assess the required drop accurately, and avoid that nasty rubbing sound and the smell of burning rubber. Springs are generally only available in a very few sizes, expressed by the amount of drop they'll produce. On a Focus, on 17s, you need to go at least 30 mm to notice the drop, and 35 mm is a popular choice for retaining good handling. Much more of a drop is just for the look - one problem reported with going to 50 mm is that the driveshaft joints wear out prematurely, owing to the extreme angle they're working at when dropped. Take as many measurements as possible, and ask around your mates / 'net forums - suppliers and manufacturers may be your best source of help in special cases.

Suspension **kit**

A far better choice, Sir - a matched set of springs and dampers is a genuine 'upgrade', and respect is due. There are several branded kits available, and some Ford specialists do their own. With a properly-sorted conversion, your Focus will handle even better, and you'll still be able to negotiate a set of roadworks without needing dental work afterwards. Actually, you may be amazed how well the Focus will still ride, even though the springs are clearly lower and stiffer - the secret is in the damping.

Some of the kits are billed as 'adjustable', but this only applies to the damper rates (don't mistake them as being cheap coilovers), which can often be set to your own taste by a few minutes' work. This Playstation feature can be a good fun thing to play around with, even if it is slightly less relevant to road use than for hillclimbs and sprints - but don't get carried away and set it too stiff, or you'll end up with an evil-handling car and a CD player that skips over every white line on the road!

Unfortunately, although you should end up with a fine-handling car, there are problems with suspension kits, too. If you don't have your steering geometry (camber and tracking) reset, you'll eat tyres, and once again, you're into guesswork territory when it comes to assessing your required drop for big wheels. Generally, most suspension kits are only available with a fairly modest drop (typically, 35 to 40 mm).

Coilovers

If you've chosen coilovers, well done again. This is the most expensive option, and it offers one vital feature that the other two can't - true adjustability of ride height, meaning that you can make the finest of tweaks to hunker down on your new rims, or wind it back up when all your mates are on board. Coilovers are a variation on the suspension kit theme - a set of matched variable-rate springs (some have separate 'helper' springs too) and shocks, but their adjustability might not guarantee as good a ride/handling mix as a normal kit.

A coilover set replaces each spring and shock with a combined unit where the coil spring fits over the shocker (hence 'coil' 'over') - nothing too unusual in this, because so far, it's similar to a normal front strut. The difference lies in the adjustable spring lower seat, which can lower the spring (and car) to any desired height, within limits.

Unfortunately, making a car go super-low is not good for the ride or the handling. Coilover systems have very short, stiff springs, and this can lead to similar problems to those found with cheap lowering springs alone. If you go too far with coilovers, you can end up with a choppy ride, heavy steering and generally unpleasant handling. Combine a coilover-slammed car with big alloys, and while the visual effect may be stunning, the driving experience might well be very disappointing. At least a proper coilover kit will come with shock absorbers (dampers) which are matched to the springs, unlike a 'conversion' kit.

Coilover conversion

A better-value option is the 'coilover conversion'. If you really must have the lowest, baddest machine out there, and don't care what the ride will be like, these could be the answer. Offering as much potential for lowering as genuine coilovers (and at far less cost), these items could be described as a cross between coilovers and lowering springs, because the standard dampers are retained (this is one reason why the ride suffers). What you get is a new spring assembly, with adjustable top and bottom mounts - the whole thing slips over your standard damper. Two problems with this solution (how important these are is up to you):

1 Your standard dampers will not be able to cope with the uprated springs, so the car will almost certainly ride (and possibly handle) like a pig if you go for a really serious drop - and okay, why else would you be doing it?

2 The standard dampers are effectively being compressed, the lower you go. There is a limit to how far they will compress before being completely solid (and this could be the limit for your lowering activities). Needless to say, even a partly-compressed damper won't be able to do much actual damping - the results of this could be... interesting...

Front Suspension

Tricks 'n' tips

A few days before attacking your suspension, spray some WD-40 on the various mounting nuts and bolts. Shearing off one of the suspension mountings is a great way to ruin your weekend. If any of the nuts/bolts proves really tough to loosen (or goes a little way, then sticks), try tightening it a small amount before getting out the cracker bars - a little movement, even if it's the wrong way, might prevent a fastener from shearing.

01 Loosen the wheel nuts, jack up the corner of the car you are working on (see 'Wheels & tyres' for more info on jacking and supporting), and remove the wheel. First job is to unclip the brake hose from its bracket and pull the hose to one side, so that it won't get damaged whilst you work. Tie it back if necessary.

02 Next, remove the anti-roll bar drop link nut; this will require the use of a spanner and Allen key.

Tricks 'n' tips

Don't start this job without coil spring compressors, or you'll be sorry! A torque wrench is also pretty important.

03 The strut-to-hub clamp bolt comes out using a socket and wrench - notice the bolt fits from the front.

04 Now persuade that hub to detach itself from the strut. Don't be shy - you (probably) won't damage it. All we're looking to do is break any rust that may have set in, so the hub moves down.

05 Now you need to prise the lower arm down to release the strut completely from the hub mounting. You may be able to just press down by hand, and pop the strut out. This part looks quite hardcore, but don't panic. Our "special tool", consisting of a mother of a bar, some chain and a block of wood, just made things easier for us.

06 Into the engine bay, and remove the three top mounting nuts on the strut housing. Don't touch the nut in the centre of the strut at this stage, or things may start flying apart.

Respect

For the next bit, you MUST use coil spring compressors ('spring clamps'). Medical attention will be required if you don't. Do we have to draw you a diagram? The spring's under tension on the strut, even off the car - what do you think's gonna happen if you just undo it? The spring-embedded-in-the-forehead look is really OVER, too.

07 With everything loosened and removed, drop the strut out from the wheelarch – if it hasn't already fallen out… Best pop a jack under the hub now – that way, you won't be replacing any driveshafts (doesn't do the CV joints any good to be hanging down).

08 Fit the spring compressors to 'grab' as many of the spring coils as you can, and fit them directly opposite each other. Tighten the bolt that runs up the centre of each clamp. Remember to tighten each clamp evenly, or the unclamped side may fly off and cause injury.

09 Compress the spring until the tension is off the strut upper mounting plate. Next job is to remove the upper mounting plate. Use a spanner on the inner nut, and an Allen key to stop the piston from turning. Depending on your choice of suspension, you may need to re-use the top mount plate – so keep it handy for later.

10 It's now time to strip the strut. Start by removing the top mounting plate and upper spring seat.

11 Take care when removing the spring, as it's still under major tension. When removing the spring clamps from the coils, which is the next job, loosen them slowly and evenly, or you'll end up having a very bad day!

12 Take the correct strut for the side of the car you're working on, and prep the piston by pulling it fully out. Then slip the washer (Spax call it a bumpstop protector – check to see if your kit has one) onto the piston and fit the bump stop. You'll either have a new bump stop in your kit, or you'll re-use the original one.

13 Now it's time the shiny new spring goes on. Use the correct spring, the right way up (if it's not obvious which spring to use, check the markings on the spring and refer to the kit manufacturer's notes). Even if the springs look the same, they may have different rates (stiffness) so check first.

14 The upper spring seat is the next part to be added to the strut. Due to the fact that our new springs are a lot smaller in width than the originals, we need to fit the spring seat adapter (supplied with kit) into the original Focus top mount plate. Push this into place - it will click when it has located properly.

>>

15 With the top mount in place on the strut, fit the new Nyloc nut . . .

16 . . . which you either tighten the same way you took the old one off, using the Allen key and spanner routine, or in this case, two different-size spanners.

17 If you're fitting coilovers, set the ride height of the springs evenly on both sides (measure with a ruler). You can adjust the height later when the car is back on the ground, keeping it level by simply turning the height adjuster and locking rings the same number of turns each side.

18 The newly-assembled strut can now go back into position in the arch. Hold it in place by loosely refitting the three upper mounting nuts.

19 Grease the base of the strut, to make refitting it to the hub less hassle.

20 The new strut should go back into the hub easier than the old one came out. There's a raised rib on the back of the strut, which must align with the slot in the hub. Ensure the brake hose is kept out of the way to prevent it from being damaged. Jack up the hub this time, to make sure the strut goes all the way in.

21 If you have some, use a drop of thread-locking fluid on the clamp bolt, and refit it from the front.

22 Torque the clamp bolt up to 90 Nm. If you don't have a torque wrench, do it up very tightly – as if your life depended on it (which it does).

23 Refit the brake hose into its new bracket. If your kit doesn't have a bracket to attach the hose to, you'll be in trouble with the MoT tester – it's a failure to have flapping brake hoses! If this is the case – you will have to engineer yourself a suitable bracket.

24 Using a crowbar, lever for all you're worth under the anti-roll bar to re-attach the drop link to the new strut. Some cheap kits don't have holes for the anti-roll bar drop link, and if this is the case – you're stuffed!

25 The drop link nut should be tightened to 50 Nm - but you try getting a torque wrench on this style fitting... Instead, use a spanner and Allen key, and do it up as tight as you can.

26 Refit the wheel and lower the car now, then torque those strut upper mounting nuts to 25 Nm.

27 You can now set the ride height by winding the top ring up or down (height adjustment ring) using the C spanners supplied, then counter-lock the adjustment ring in position with the lower (locking) ring. A bit of lube on the threads will aid future height adjustment.

28 The final job is to adjust the dampers as you see fit. Don't set the shocks too stiff, as the ride will be very harsh - and with coilovers, the ride is quite harsh to begin with. It's also important that both sides are set to the same rate.

Rear Suspension

From a modifying viewpoint, the Focus rear suspension's a tad comical - it's clever, yes, but not the easiest to work on. Unusually, the rear anti-roll bar has to be removed, to make room for removing the old spring. Even the oldest Focus isn't very old, but a little WD-40 lube spray on the nuts 'n' bolts makes life easier.

01

The back end of the car must be raised and supported safely - but you already knew that. You will need a sturdy trolley jack to remove the spring, though. Now to undo the anti-roll bar - if this doesn't come off, you can't lower the bottom arm, to get the spring out. Anyway, removing isn't hard - there's an outer link bolt with a rubber bush either side . . .

02

07 You'll find that the jack will want to move backwards as the spring is lowered, which might mean the lower arm jams up at the last minute. A little careful levering with the 'universal tool' (large screwdriver) should sort you out.

08 Now the bottom arm drops away, and the spring can come out. In case you were wondering why we didn't just use spring clamps to compress the old spring, and take it out that way - you can't. There's no room.

09 The new springs are way easier to fit than the old ones were to come out - bonus. So the lower arm can now go back up, and the outer bolt back in (well, you wouldn't want to forget it, later on). Torque this bolt to 115 Nm. Now that's tight. Refit the anti-roll bar, too - the clamp bolts are 48 Nm, and the outer link bolts (with two bushes) are 15 Nm.

10 On our luvverly Spax coilovers, the next job is removing this very large bolt from the top of the subframe (spring upper seat). We expected it to be rusted-in, but we were lucky - you might not be, so hit it with some spray-lube first.

03 . . . and a clamp bracket with another bush, Take these off both sides, and the anti-roll bar's outta da way. It will, of course, have to go back on afterwards. And if any of those bushes look shot, you know what to do…

04 Just in case anything slips while you're lowering the spring (and it'll go with a bang if you're unlucky), make up a 'special tool'. Get yourself a sturdy metal strip, drill a hole in for a long bolt and nut, and fit it to the rear suspension as shown. The jack will do the lowering work, but this should stop it all flying apart. Safety is what we're talking here.

05 With a decent trolley jack supporting the bottom arm (compress the spring a little), unscrew the bolt at the outer end of the arm. Once that bolt is tapped out, the jack is the only thing stopping the spring flying out, so take care. Trolley jacks have wheels, and wheels turn - sometimes when you don't expect them to.

06 Undo the nut on the special tool, then lower the jack slightly. Repeat this process until the spring pressure has been safely released.

11 This'll be why the bolt had to come out - you can't beat a bit of purple in the undercarriage, and this is the adjustable top mount for the coilovers. We treated the old bolt to a lick of grease before putting it back, and tightened it to 115 Nm. This bolt holds the rear suspension to the car, so it's pretty important it's tight.

12 Screw the locking ring onto the threaded top mount, then add the new spring upper seat . . .

13 . . . while at the bottom end, the new spring lower seat gets a little love, in the form of loadsa copper grease.

14 More purple-ness with our new spring, which is so much shorter than the original, it's actually a very baggy fit. This is good, because it makes fitting easy . . .

>>

15 . . . but it's also bad, because the spring falls out just as easy. While the car was up in the air, we used a trolley jack to lift the bottom arm, and hold the spring in place. It's obviously pretty important to check the spring's located properly, top and bottom, when the car gets lowered back to the ground.

16 So we've got us a height-adjustable spring, but where's the shocker? Well, they're separate units on the Focus, so there's still some work to do. Undo the shock's bottom mounting bolt . . .

17 . . . then go into the boot, and undo the top mounting nut, holding the shock piston rod still with a smaller spanner . . .

18 . . . then take off the rubber mount - we'll be re-using that later.

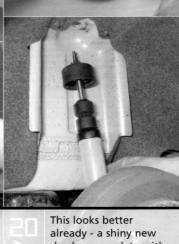

19 The shock absorber may have fallen off by this point, but if it hasn't, take it off. Slide off the other top mount, which we'll also be recycling.

20 This looks better already - a shiny new shocker, complete with the top mount we just took off the old shock. Slide it into place, and tighten the bottom mounting bolt (to, yes, you guessed - 115 Nm). Back in the boot, refit the top rubber mount, then tighten the top nut, using the same two-spanner technique used before.

21 If you've bought adjustable suspension, get adjusting. When you've set one side (a best-guess job, first time), measure the height you set it to, so you can set the other side the same. Lock the spring seat in place with the locking ring - tighten them together with the two spanners provided. Treat the coilover threads to a little lube, to keep the rust at bay.

22 You don't get a suspension kit with adjustable damping, and then not fiddle with it, do you? But - your new suspension's going to be way-stiff anyhow, so making it much stiffer's possibly not advisable unless you're planning to shave a few tenths off the Silverstone lap record. Set both sides the same, to avoid getting strange handling quirks you can live without.

Nasty
side-effects

Camber angle and tracking

With any lowering 'solution', it's likely that your suspension and steering geometry will be severely affected - this will be more of a problem the lower you go. This will manifest itself in steering which either becomes lighter or (more usually) heavier, and in tyres which scrub out their inner or outer edges in very short order - not funny, if you're running expensive low-profiles! Sometimes, even the rear tyres can be affected in this way, but that's usually only after some serious slammage. Whenever you've fitted a set of springs (and this applies to ALL types), have the geometry checked ASAP afterwards.

If you've dropped the car by 60 mm or more, chances are your camber angle will need adjusting. This is one reason why you might find the edges of your fat low-profiles wearing faster than you'd like (the other is your tracking being out). The camber angle is the angle the tyre makes with the road, seen from directly in front. You'll no doubt have seen race cars with the front wheels tilted in at the top, out at the bottom - this is extreme negative camber, and it helps to give more grip and stability in extreme cornering (but if your car was set this extreme, you'd kill the front tyres VERY quickly!). Virtually all road cars have a touch of negative camber on the front, and it's important when lowering to keep as near to the factory setting as possible, to preserve the proper tyre contact patch on the road. Trouble is, there's not usually much scope for camber adjustment on standard suspension, which is why (for some cars) you can buy camber-adjustable top plates which fit to the strut tops. Setting the camber accurately is a job for a garage with experience of modified cars - so probably not your local fast-fit centre, then.

Brace yourself

Another item which is inspired by saloon racing, the strut brace is another underbonnet accessory which you shouldn't be without. Some of them might even work...

The idea of the strut brace is that, once you've stiffened up your front suspension to the max, the car's 'flimsy' body shell (to which the front suspension struts are bolted) may not be able to cope with the 'immense' cornering forces being put through it, and will flex, messing up the handling. The strut brace (in theory) does exactly what it says on the tin, by providing support between the strut tops, taking the load off the bodyshell.

Where this falls down slightly (for road use) is that 1) no-one's going to have the car set that stiff, 2) no-one's going to drive that hard, and 3) the Focus shell isn't exactly made out of tin foil. The strut brace might have a slight effect, but the real reason to fit one is for SHOW - and why not? They look great in a detailed engine bay, and are available in lots of designs and finishes. You're looking at parting with up to a hundred of your finest English pounds, but your mates will be impressed and the girls will love it - and you can't put a price on that!

09 Brakes

Remember the middle pedal?

It's the one next to the throttle - some people don't use it much. Uprating the brakes is actually a very easy bolt-on upgrade, but there are some points to consider.

One of the strangest, given that improving the brakes should in theory also improve your chances of avoiding an accident, is that insurance companies do not like performance brakes. You should still tell them, but be prepared for bad news. To them, it seems that fitting sporty brakes must automatically make you drive like Colin McRae - the clear implication is that if you need better brakes, you've either also uprated the engine (and not told them?), or you simply drive on the limit everywhere. Shame. We just like to know our cars will stop quickly. That, actually, might be another reason why they don't like better brakes - you stop better, but does the old dodderer behind you? Crunch.

Uprating the brakes will be a complete waste of time if you're a cheapskate on tyres. Cheap, no-name tyres (or ones with no tread left) won't always be able to translate extra braking power into actual vehicle-stopping power - they'll give up their grip on the tarmac and skid everywhere. Something like 90% of braking is done by the front wheels - ie the ones you steer with. If you consider that locked-up wheels also don't tend to steer very well, you'll begin to see why top brakes and lame tyres are a well-dodgy mixture.

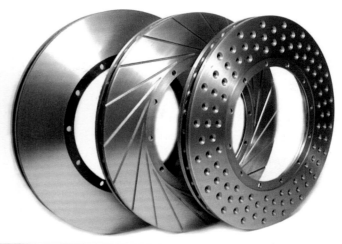

Groovy discs

Besides the various brands of performance brake pads that go with them, the main brake upgrade is to fit performance front brake discs and pads. Discs are available in two main types - grooved and cross-drilled (and combinations of both).

Grooved discs (which can be had with varying numbers of grooves) serve a dual purpose - the grooves provide a 'channel' to help the heat escape, and they also help to de-glaze the pad surface, cleaning up the pads every time they're used. Some of the discs are made from higher-friction metal than normal discs, too, and the fact that they seriously improve braking performance is well-documented.

Cross-drilled discs offer another route to heat dissipation, but one which can present some problems. Owners report that cross-drilled discs really eat brake pads, more so than the grooved types, but more serious is the fact that some of these discs can crack around the drilled holes after hard use. The trouble is that the heat 'migrates' to the drilled holes (as was intended), but the heat build-up can be extreme, and the constant heating/cooling cycle can stress the metal to the point where it will crack. Discs which have been damaged in this way are extremely dangerous to drive on, as they could break up completely at any time. Only fit discs of this type from established manufacturers offering a useful guarantee of quality, and check the discs regularly.

Performance discs also have a reputation for warping (nasty vibrations felt through the pedal). Justified, or not? Well, the harder you use your brakes (and we could be talking serious abuse), the greater the heat you'll generate. Okay, so these wicked discs are meant to be able to cope with this heat, but you can't expect miracles. Cheap discs, or ones which have had a hard time over mega-thousands of miles, will warp. So buy quality, and don't get over-heroic on the brakes.

Performance pads can be fitted to any brake discs, including the standard ones, but are of course designed to work best with heat-dissipating discs. Unless your Focus has something seriously meaty under the bonnet, don't be tempted to go much further than 'fast road' pads - anything more competition-orientated may take too long to come up to temperature on the road. Remember what pushbike brakes were like in the wet? Cold competition pads feel the same, and old dears always step off the pavement when your brakes are cold!

Lastly, fitting all the performance brake bits in the world is no use if your calipers have seized up. If, when you strip out your old pads, you find that one pad's worn more than the other, or that both pads have worn more on the left wheel than the right, your caliper pistons are sticking. Sometimes you can free them off by pushing them back into the caliper, but this could be a garage job to fix. See your Haynes manual for details. If you drive around with sticking calipers, you'll eat pads and discs. You choose.

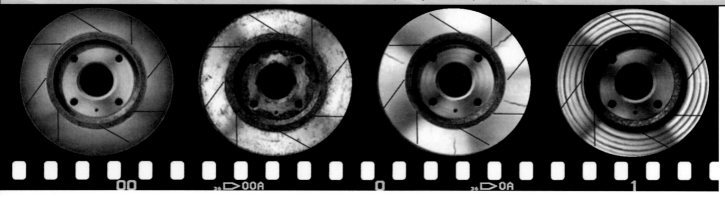

Big disc conversion

Fitting huge multi-spoke wheels makes your factory-fit discs look pretty puny, so many people's idea of impressive brakes is to go large. We can understand that. But it costs, and you might have quite a search to find a company doing the bits, to start with. Then it's got to be decent quality, and fitted properly - play around with brakes, and the only mag feature you'll get is Crash of the Month.

Brake
discs and pads

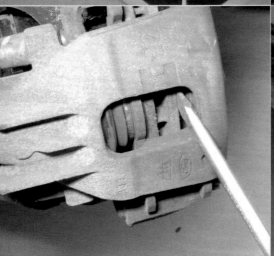

01 Loosen the wheel nuts, jack up the corner of the car you're working on, and take off the wheel. Put an axle stand under a solid part of the car, just in case the jack gives out (see "wheels & tyres" for more info on jacking up). To make room for the new, thicker, pads we'll be fitting, try levering between the old disc and pads as shown. This does risk damaging the old disc and pads, but we're fitting new, so who cares?

02 Remove the rubber caps from the two (top and bottom) caliper guide bolts . . .

03 . . . then remove the guide bolts using a 7 mm Allen key and socket.

04 Using a flat-bladed screwdriver, prise the outer brake pad retaining clip from the caliper. Note how it fits for putting it all back together.

05 Withdraw the caliper from the disc. While the caliper's off, take care you don't strain the rubber hose still attached to it - and don't be tempted to leave the caliper hanging by that hose, either. Pull the inner pad from the piston in the caliper (it's held in there by spring legs).

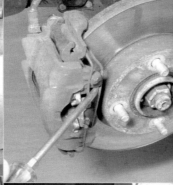

06 Remove the outer pad from the caliper by sliding the pad out, with its securing clip.

07 Now we're finished with the caliper for a bit, so protect the hydraulic hose by hanging the caliper up on the front spring, using wire, string, or even an old bungee-cord. If that hose gets damaged, you'll lose your brakes very quickly - you're supposed to be upgrading them here, remember!

08 The caliper mounting bracket doesn't need to be removed in order to remove the disc. However, you may wish to remove it, to clean it up for painting - it's only held on by two bolts. Removing the disc, meanwhile, is laughably easy - just prise off the disc retaining clip . . .

>>

09 . . . and, possibly with a little persuasion from a hammer, the disc should come away. If it's rusted-on, quite a lot of persuasion with that hammer will be required (swearing optional).

10 Time to clean the rust and muck from the hub face using a wire brush or emery cloth. This is actually more vital than you might think - any muck in there will stop the new disc from sitting on square, and if that happens, your brakes won't work too well, and you'll eat through brake pads. So do a good job.

11 Spread some copper grease on the hub face, to prevent the pain and misery of rusted-on discs in the future.

12 Now's a good time to paint the calipers, as the brakes are apart. Unfortunately, we weren't that organised, but see the caliper-painting section for more info. The new discs must be cleaned using brake cleaner before fitting to the car, as they're covered in sticky stuff to prevent the discs from rusting.

13 Pop your new discs onto the hub, firstly checking you've got the right disc (any grooves must be positioned in a certain way – check your paperwork). Our custom discs supplied to us by Red Dot Racing make it easy to see the fitting direction – why not give them a call, and get your own custom discs?

Remember!
It's a good idea to have your brake mods MOT-tested once you've fitted new discs and pads, and you might even be able to 'blag' a free brake check at your local fast-fit centre if you're crafty! Brakes are a serious safety issue, and unless you're 100% confident that all is well, demo-ing your car's awesome new-found stopping ability could find you in the ditch…

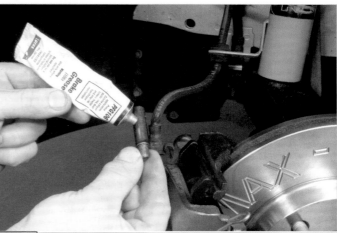

14 Refit the disc retaining clip – but beware that sometimes this clip can score the inside edge of alloy wheels. If you've fitted nice big wheels, check to make sure the clip won't make contact with the alloy - if it does, don't refit the clip (the disc will be firmly held in place once the wheel's back on).

15 Smear a bit of copper grease to the backplates of the pads, to prevent the brakes from squealing. Don't get the grease on the discs (or on the pad friction surface) - if you do, clean them with brake cleaner. Slip the new pads back into position in the caliper, and slip the caliper on over the disc.

16 Our dedication to the happiness of guide pin bolts is so great that we've cleaned them and greased them using brake grease. The bolts don't have to removed, but how much do you love your car?

17 Pop the guide bolts back into place, and tighten them to 28 Nm. Remember to re-fit the rubber covers . . .

18 . . . and finally, clip the brake pad retaining clip back into place.

19 A little copper grease applied where the top of pads make contact with the caliper mounting bracket will prevent the pads seizing. Don't get any grease on the disc or contact surface of the brake pad. When the discs and pads have been done both sides, give the brake pedal several good shoves to bring the pads up to the discs. And remember - run them in gently!

Remember!
New pads of any sort need careful bedding-in (over 100 miles of normal use) before they'll work properly - when first fitted, the pad surface won't have worn exactly to the contours of the disc, so it won't actually be touching it, over its full area. This will possibly result in very under-whelming brakes for the first few trips, so watch it - misplaced over-confidence in new brakes is a fast track to hospital…

Cool coloured **stoppers**

One 'downside' to fitted massive multi-spoked alloys is that - gasp - people can see your brakes! So don't be shy about it - paint some of the brake bits so they look the biz, to match (or clash completely) with your chosen colour scheme. Red is the colour inspired by the racing/touring-car boys, but isn't the only choice.

Many Foci don't have rear discs, but painting the brake drums is acceptable under the circumstances - but then, do you paint 'em black, to de-emphasise them, or in your chosen colour for the fronts? It's all tough decisions, in modifying. If you're really sad, you can always buy fake rear discs… For the less-sad among you, Ford performance specialists may be able to sell you a rear disc brake conversion kit - pricey, but maybe necessary if there's an RS engine going in soon. A rear disc conversion's going a bit far, just to have red calipers front and rear - and remember, the rear brakes don't do much actual stopping…

Painting the calipers requires that they're clean - really clean. Accessory stores sell aerosol brake cleaner, which (apart from having a distinctive high-octane perfume) is just great for removing brake dust, and lots more besides! Some kits come complete with cleaner spray. Many of the kits advertise themselves on the strength of no dismantling being required, but we don't agree. Also, having always successfully brush-painted our calipers, we wouldn't advise using any kind of spray paint.

We know you won't want to hear this, but the best way to paint the calipers is to do some dismantling first. The kits say you don't have to, but trust me - you'll get a much better result from a few minutes' extra work. The best time to paint would be while you're fitting new discs, but nobody thinks that far ahead.

01 Jack car up the front and/or rear of the car (depending on which you choose to do) and support on axle stands, then take a wire brush to your calipers and drums to clean off all that rust and muck. It makes most sense to paint all four corners at once, because the paint won't keep once the tin has been opened.

02 After a good scrub with the brush, further clean the area you are going to paint using a suitable brake cleaning solution – this is sometimes supplied with caliper painting kits (nice one, MHW).

Tricks 'n' tips
If you have trouble reassembling your brakes after painting, you probably got carried away and put on too much paint. We found that, once it was fully dry, the excess paint could be trimmed off with a knife..

Painting brakes

Finally, prise the lid off the paint and find yourself a paintbrush. Some kits require you to mix hardener into the paint, so read the instructions on your kit to be sure, before you start applying paint. Stir the paint before you begin and then slap it on – but don't paint it on too thick, or it'll run, and stone chips will flake the thick paint away faster. We don't really need to tell you not to get it on the brake discs or pads, do we??

Remember to paint the drums too! These need cleaning - and don't get the paint on the wheel mating surface (where the studs are). While the paint's drying, turn the drum every so often, or you might get the runs. Leave the paint to dry for the paint manufacturer's suggested time, to ensure it's totally dry. If the paint is still a bit wet and you drive the car, you'll get all sorts of muck in the paint and it will look awful, so take your time.

03

04

Interiors

What do we think of the standard Focus dash? For once, it's actually nothing to be ashamed of - it's pretty radical, and doesn't feel like it's about to fall apart (something you can't say about certain French cars, for instance). Given the Zetec treatment, it's something we could live with. For a while. But the rest of the interior? Er, no. We're talking dull-as. But nothing was ever built that can't be improved, and the interior really is one area where the goodies are easy to fit. Choose one 'theme' and stick to it, and the end result won't look like anything from a production line.

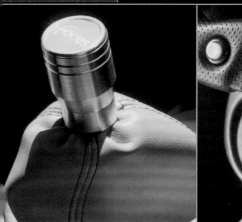

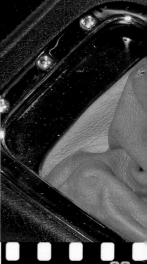

As with exterior styling, fashions can change very quickly - so don't be afraid to experiment with a look you really like, because chances are, it'll be the next big thing anyway. Just don't do wood, ok? We've a feeling it's never coming in, never mind coming back...

Removing stuff
Take it easy and break less

Many of the procedures we're going to show involve removing interior trim panels (either for colouring or to fit other stuff), and this can be tricky. It's far too easy to break plastic trim, especially once it's had a chance to go a bit brittle with age. Another 'problem' with the Focus is that the interior trim is pretty well-attached (and the designers have been very clever at hiding several vital screws), meaning that it can be a pig to get off. We'll try and avoid the immortal words 'simply unclip the panel', and instead show you how properly, but inevitably at some stage, a piece of trim won't 'simply' anything.

The important lesson here is not to lose your temper, as this has a highly-destructive effect on plastic components, and may result in a panel which no amount of carbon film or colour spray can put right, or make fit again. Superglue may help, but not every time. So - take it steady, prise carefully, and think logically about how and where a plastic panel would have to be attached, to stay on. You'll encounter all sorts of trim clips (some more fragile than others) in your travels - when these break, as they usually do, many of them can be bought in packs from accessory shops, and rarer ones will be available from a Ford dealer, probably off the shelf. Even fully-trained Ford mechanics aren't immune to breaking a few trim clips!

Door trim panels

You'll find plenty of excuses for removing door trim panels - fitting speakers, re-trimming the panel, de-locking, even window tinting, so we'd better tell you how ...

01 Removing the door card is really easy, and takes just a few minutes. First, prise out this little plastic screw cover from inside the interior door lock handle . . .

02 . . . and (you guessed it) remove the screw underneath, which then lets you remove the handle surround and window switch panel. Pull the handle like we're doing to work the panel off, and remember the window switches have wiring on the back . . .

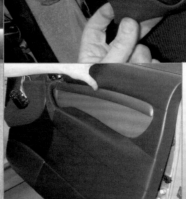

06 All that's holding the door card on now are the little crosshead screws fitted round the edge of the panel. There's a few of these babies (some underneath), and you gotta get 'em all.

07 Lift the panel up to release it from the window channel at the top, and it's free.

08 To remove the rear side panel, this top section of the B-pillar trim has to come off . . .

Tricks 'n' tips
Find something like an old ice-cream or margarine tub to keep all the little screws and bits in, as you take them off. This approach is far superior to the chuck-them-all-on-the-floor method most people use, until they lose something vital.

Ford Focus

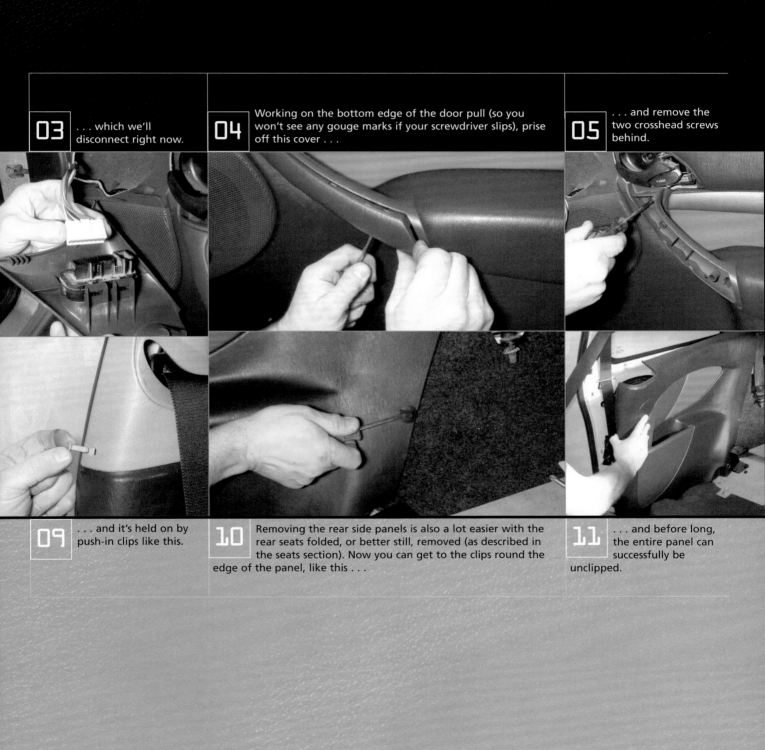

03 . . . which we'll disconnect right now.

04 Working on the bottom edge of the door pull (so you won't see any gouge marks if your screwdriver slips), prise off this cover . . .

05 . . . and remove the two crosshead screws behind.

09 . . . and it's held on by push-in clips like this.

10 Removing the rear side panels is also a lot easier with the rear seats folded, or better still, removed (as described in the seats section). Now you can get to the clips round the edge of the panel, like this . . .

11 . . . and before long, the entire panel can successfully be unclipped.

123

01 Lift out the cupholders from the front of the console, and remove the retaining screws (one in each side).

02 Unclip the ashtray from the rear of the console.

03 When the ashtray has been removed, you can see a small trim cover that hides a retaining screw, prise away this cover and remove screw.

Centre **console**

Unclip the gear lever gaiter from the centre console. Is this the first car we've done that doesn't have a hideous standard gear knob and gaiter? **04**

05 Unclip the handbrake gaiter from the base of the handle, and slide it upwards. When the console is removed, the gaiter will slide off the handbrake lever.

Now the console is ready to be lifted out. Feed the gear gaiter down through the hole as the console comes out, and slide the handbrake gaiter off its lever. **06**

Anything but black?

The interior trim on the Focus at least hides its age well, and doesn't rattle much. And that's about it - for a lover of elephant-hide grey, it's heaven. For normal people, it's something else. Fortunately, there's plenty you can do to personalise it, and there are three main routes to take:

1) Spray paint - available in any colour you like, as long as it's... not black. This Folia Tec stuff actually dyes softer plastics and leather, and comes in a multi-stage treatment, to suit all plastic types. Don't try to save money just buying the top coat, because it won't work! Special harder-wearing spray is required for use on steering wheels. Ordinary spray paint for bodywork might damage some plastics, and won't be elastic - good primer is essential. Make sure you also buy lots of masking tape.

2) Adhesive or shrink-fit film - available in various wild colours, carbon, ally, and, er... walnut (would YOU?). Probably best used on flatter surfaces, or at least those without complex curves, or you'll have to cut and join - spray is arguably better here. Some companies will sell you sheets of genuine carbon-fibre, with peel-off backing - looks and feels the part (nice if you have touchy-feely passengers).

3) Replacement panels - the easiest option, as the panels are supplied pre-cut, ready to fit. Of course, you're limited then to styling just the panels supplied.

If you fancy something more posh, how about trimming your interior bits in leather? Very saucy. Available in various colours, and hardly any dearer than film, you also get that slight 'ruffled' effect on tighter curves.

Get the cans out

Any painting process is a *multi-stage* application. With the Folia Tec system (thanks to Eurostyling for supplying ours), many of you apparently think you can get away just buying the top coat, which then looks like a cheap option compared to film - WRONG! Even the proper interior spray top coat won't stay on for long without the matching primer, and the finish won't be wear-resistant without the finishing sealer spray. You don't need the special foaming cleaner - you could get by with a general-purpose degreaser, such as meths. Just watch the grey/black plastic doesn't suddenly turn white - if it does, you're damaging the finish! This might not be too important to you, as it's being sprayed over anyway, but if you take out the grey too far on a part that's not being sprayed all over, you'll have to live with a cacky-looking white-grey finish to any non-painted surface...

Providing you're a dab hand with the masking tape, paint gives you the flexibility to be more creative. For instance, you could try colour-matching the exterior of the car - but will ordinary car body paint work on interior plastics? Course it will, as long as you prep the panels properly.

Choice of paint's one thing, but what to paint? Well, not everything - for instance, you might want to avoid high-wear areas like door handles. Just makes for an easier life. The glovebox lid and instrument panel surround are obvious first choices, as are the ashtray and fusebox lid. The centre console's not lighting anyone's fire in standard Ford grey, so hit it with some spray too. Any panels which just pop out are targets, in fact (lots less masking needed) - just make sure whatever you're dismantling was meant to come apart, or it'll be out with the superglue instead of the cans.

Don't be afraid to experiment with a combination of styles - as long as you're confident you can blend it all together, anything goes! Mix the painted bits with some tasteful carbon-fibre sheet or brushed-aluminium film, if you like - neutral colours like this, or chrome, can be used to give a lift to dash bits which are too tricky to spray.

01 Place your chosen item of interior trim on a clean, flat surface, and attack with sandpaper. Our aim is to remove the nasty injection-moulded design that looks like elephant hide. Nice. In order to save total disintegration of your hands, wear gloves!

02 When you're satisfied that enough of the grain pattern has been removed by sandpaper (remember that you carry on the smoothing process by priming the area, rubbing the primer back and repeating the process), clean the area with a suitable degreaser. Try 'panel-wipe' from a bodyshop.

03 Plaster the surrounding area with newspaper (to avoid parental unrest), then add your first layer of plastic primer and leave to dry as per instructions on the can.

Painting **trim**

04 Rub the primer back with fine-grain sandpaper. Do not rub the primer off; we're aiming partly to fill any gaps left from the elephant hide by building up layers of primer.

05 Repeat this process of building up the primer until the surface is totally smooth. Ours took three layers until we were happy that all elephant hide had been eliminated. It's time to paint. You could choose to paint things the same colour as your car, but the possibilities are endless. One coat of paint should be enough – but use two coats if you feel it needs it. End by adding a nice layer of lacquer to make it really shiny!

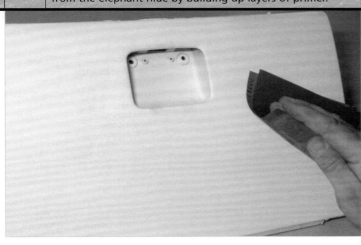

Dash
dynamics

A far easier route to the brushed-ally or carbon look, pre-finished ('here's some we did earlier') panels are available from suppliers.

   Dash kits are available for the Focus from companies like Dash Dynamics, and offer a simpler way of livening-up the dull Focus dash. Did we say simple? It's sometimes not too obvious where the various kit bits are supposed to go! A trial fitting isn't a bad idea, before peeling off the backing. Make sure your chosen trim piece is lined up nice and square, and keep it square as you press it on - the adhesive's usefully-sticky, meaning it will stay stuck whether you get it right or wrong. Still, it's easier by far than trying to mask up and spray the edges of the vents, which is what you'd have to do otherwise.

01 First job is to clean the area to which the kit will be fitted, using the cleaning solution supplied. Give it a good clean to remove any traces of silicone, grease or polish, so that when fitting the kit, the glue will stick properly and hold the kit in place.

02 After all that cleaning, it would be a shame if you touched the area and had to clean it all over again – so don't touch it. Instead, raise the temperature of the surface area of the dash using a hot-air gun or hairdryer, set to a low heat, and not too close!

With a cloth, press each part of the kit firmly into place, paying particular attention to the corner and the edges. It will take 24 hours for the kit to be fully bonded in place. If after a while the edges begin to lift, simply apply some strong adhesive and stick the kit back into place. Continue to heat each panel for a couple more minutes on a low heat to kick-start the glue into doing its stuff

A slight bit of overlap between the panels in places resulted in the need for some very minor trimming – use a sharp craft knife/blade and a ruler, and watch those digits!

One piece at a time, apply the same low heat to each section, then peel off the backing paper. Don't touch the adhesive on the back. **03**

Place the piece into position on the dash – each section of the kit is labelled to show you where to fit it. If it is fitted incorrectly, it is still possible at this stage to remove and reposition each piece to your satisfaction. **04**

Filming your Focus

If you fancy creating a look that's a bit more special than plain paint colours, film is the answer - but be warned - it's not the easiest stuff in the world to use, and so isn't everyone's favourite. If you must have the brushed-aluminium look, or fancy giving your Focus the carbon-fibre treatment, there really is no alternative (apart from the lazy-man option of new panels, of course).

01 Cut the film roughly to size, remembering to leave plenty of excess for trimming - it's also a good idea to have plenty to fold around the edges, because thin film has a nasty habit of peeling off, otherwise.

02 Next, we gently warmed up both the panel, and the film itself. Just following the instructions provided, and who are we to argue?

03 Peel off the backing, being careful that the film stays as flat as possible. Also take care, when you pick the film up, that it doesn't stick to itself (our stuff seemed very keen to do this!).

Stick the film on straight - very important with any patterned finish. Start at one edge or corner, and work across, to keep the air bubbles and creases to a minimum. If you get a really bad crease, it's best to unpeel a bit and try again - the adhesive's very tacky, and there's no slide-age available.

04

Work out the worst of the air bubbles with a soft cloth - get the stuff to stick as best you can before trimming, or it'll all go horribly wrong. To be sure it's stuck (especially important on a grained surface), go over it firmly with the edge of your least-important piece of 'plastic' - ie not a credit card.

05

Once the film's laid on, it's time for trimming - which (you guessed it) is the tricky bit. We found it's much easier to trim the tricky bits once the film's been warmed up using a hairdryer or heat gun, but don't overdo it! Make sure you've also got a VERY sharp knife - a blunt one will ripple the film, and may tear it (one good thing about film is that blood wipes off it easily!).

06

To get the film to wrap neatly round a curved edge, make several slits almost up to the edge, then wrap each sliver of film around, and stick on firmly. If the film's heated as you do this, it wraps round and keeps its shape - meaning it shouldn't try and spring back, ruining all your hard work.

07

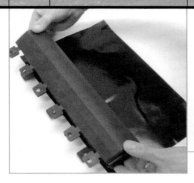

Bum notes

There are limitations to using film, and the quality of the film itself has a lot to do with that. We had major problems doing any kind of job with one particular make of brushed-aluminium-look film - it was a nightmare to work with, and the edges had peeled the next day. Buying quality film will give you a long-lasting result to be proud of, with much less skill requirement and LOTS less swearing. But it still pays not to be too ambitious with it.

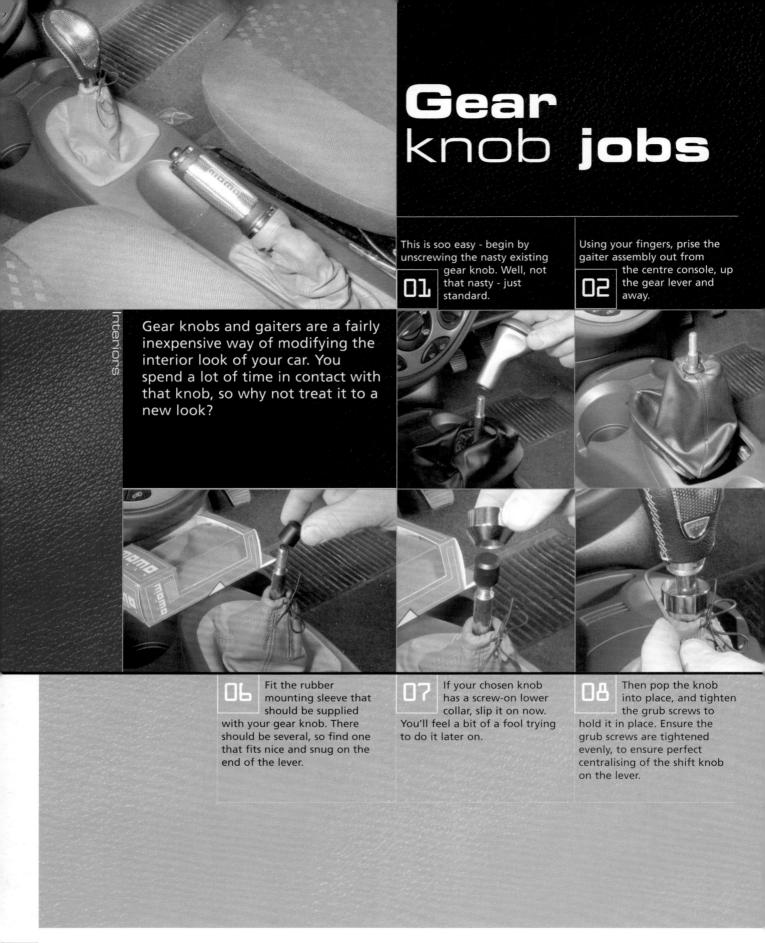

Gear knob jobs

Gear knobs and gaiters are a fairly inexpensive way of modifying the interior look of your car. You spend a lot of time in contact with that knob, so why not treat it to a new look?

01 This is soo easy - begin by unscrewing the nasty existing gear knob. Well, not that nasty - just standard.

02 Using your fingers, prise the gaiter assembly out from the centre console, up the gear lever and away.

06 Fit the rubber mounting sleeve that should be supplied with your gear knob. There should be several, so find one that fits nice and snug on the end of the lever.

07 If your chosen knob has a screw-on lower collar, slip it on now. You'll feel a bit of a fool trying to do it later on.

08 Then pop the knob into place, and tighten the grub screws to hold it in place. Ensure the grub screws are tightened evenly, to ensure perfect centralising of the shift knob on the lever.

03 Find a clean, flat surface to work on, and start by removing the staples that hold the original gaiter to the surround.

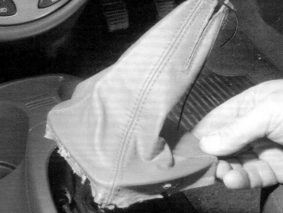

04 Pop the new gaiter onto the surround and pop-rivet into place, exactly the same as the handbrake gaiter. If riveting isn't an option, get hold of a heavy-duty stapler (the absolute daddy for this is an electric stapler). With the gaiter secured to the surround, and any excess material trimmed away, pop it back over the gear lever and into place.

05 Tie the gaiter's laces (preferably at the front, where it's less visible) to hold it in place, and you're ready to start playing with the knob!

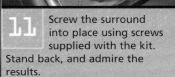

09 Final job is to screw the lower collar to the knob, and that's a wrap - well, actually, that's one sweet-looking knob! Momo Air Metal - you love it.

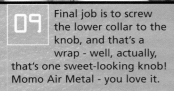

11 Screw the surround into place using screws supplied with the kit. Stand back, and admire the results.

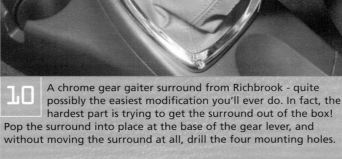

10 A chrome gear gaiter surround from Richbrook - quite possibly the easiest modification you'll ever do. In fact, the hardest part is trying to get the surround out of the box! Pop the surround into place at the base of the gear lever, and without moving the surround at all, drill the four mounting holes.

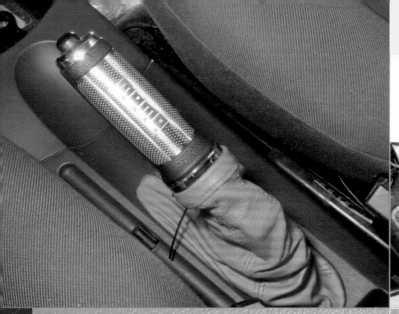

Handbrake
knobs &
gaiters

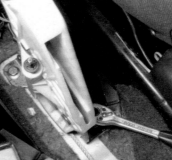

01 Now you've done it - fitting a sexy new gear knob and gaiter's only made the sad black handbrake stick look even worse. Get it sorted. If you haven't already, remove the centre console (see 'removing stuff'). We found the easiest way to fit our gorgeous new Momo handbrake handle, was to remove the handbrake lever. Yes, really. So begin by removing the two (brass-coloured) handbrake lever mounting bolts at the base.

02 Unscrew the plastic locking washer from the handbrake adjustment nut.

03 Before you go any further, measure and note the amount of thread showing on the handbrake adjuster. This is the handbrake setting dimension, so you can re-adjust it perfectly when refitting. Unscrew the adjuster nut completely, and remove the washer underneath.

04 Unplug the handbrake warning light switch in front of the lever, at the base.

05 Lift the assembly away from the car, note that the cable has a square end that must be aligned perfectly in the channel when refitting the handbrake lever.

> **06** Find a clean, flat workspace, and remove the existing handbrake handle. Unless you're super strong, the only way to do this is by hacking it off with a suitable tool. Watch those digits!

07 Take the handbrake centralising guide supplied with the kit, and insert it into the handle.

08 Slide the new handbrake handle into place, and tighten the grub screws to hold it. Now refit the greatly-enhanced handbrake assembly to the car. Use the setting dimension you wrote down earlier to reset the handbrake adjuster as it was.

09 Now for a new gaiter. Unclip the handbrake gaiter from the centre console you removed earlier, and prise away the staples that retain the old handbrake gaiter to the surround. Place your new gaiter over the surround, and check the fit.

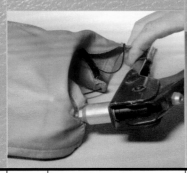

10 We decided the best way to hold our spanking new Simoni Racing gaiter in place was to use pop-rivets. A washer on the inside of the surround will protect the rivets from chewing through the plastic. Drill some mounting holes, and rivet away. If you don't have this tool, you'll need a heavy-duty stapler to do the job instead.

11 Make a slit in the gaiter to allow for the metal lug that locates into the centre console and holds the surround in place.

12 Trim away any excess gaiter to stop it getting caught in the handbrake lever assembly.

13 Pop the gaiter assembly back into the console, fit the console back over the handbrake, and we're talking game, set and matching gaiters.

01 No surprises what the first task is here. We'll be sticking these babies on, so it would be nice if the sills are clean. Use meths, if you can stand the tramp-deterring aroma.

02 A trial fitting is a very good idea. This way, you find out whether there's any potential problems before you're struggling to peel off the high-strength adhesive. At this point, you can also make pencil alignment marks, to ensure you get the things on straight, etc.

Door sill trim plates

You can get these in any colour you like, as long as it's chrome, but a new trick is getting trims which light up, preferably with the interior lights.

We're keeping our Momo "air metal" theme going here, though, with these too-cool-for-school chrome plates. One piece of advice, if you're planning major interior mods - fit the sill trims last. That way, there's less chance of scratching and scuffing 'em up during fitting the rest of the interior.

03 This is where it starts to get serious - that sticky strip's the real deal, and wants to 'love' everything it touches. Once the backing strip's off, watch out!

04 After all that, it all went very smoothly (it's all in the preparation). Press your new plates on firmly and evenly, and await those admiring glances.

All white, dials?

White or coloured dial kits aren't that difficult to fit, but you will need some skill and patience not to damage the delicate bits inside your instrument panel - the risk is definitely worth it, to liven up that dreary grey Focus dash, anyway.

Just make sure you get the right kit for your car, and don't start stripping anything until you're SURE it's the right one - look carefully. Most dial kit makers, for instance, want to know exactly what markings you have on your speedo and rev counter. If they don't ask, be worried - the kit they send could well be wrong for your car, and might not even fit. If you're ordering a kit from the US, remember they get slightly different-spec Foci to us - don't order without checking your clock layout with their website pics.

For safety and electrics to go arm in arm, start by disconnecting the battery. Next you need to get at those clocks, so arm yourself with a screwdriver and remove the two retaining screws that hold the instrument panel surround in place. **01**

Gently pull this panel forward to gain access to the boot release switch that needs to be disconnected, then unclip the panel from the facia and lift the panel from the car. **02**

Unscrew the four mounting screws from the instrument cluster. **03**

Carefully pull the cluster out from its slot in the dash, to reveal a multi-plug that needs to be disconnected. This is a little fiddly - there's a little black plastic arm that needs to be levered downwards to release the plug, and this isn't easy in a tight space. Take your time doing this - you don't want to damage this plug. **04**

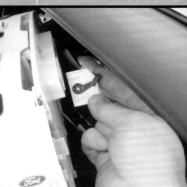

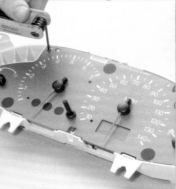

05 Lift the clocks out of the car, and find a clean, flat workspace to dismantle it. Find yourself a little cup or container of some kind, to keep all the little screws, etc in. Remove the clear instrument 'lens' by carefully levering up the tabs at the base and top.

06 Remove the needle stop-pegs where fitted - typically, there'll be three (one at each 'end' of the rev counter, and one on the speedo). Once the pegs have been removed, don't play with the needles. No, stop it. Let them come to their natural resting place, and leave them alone.

07 The trip reset button needs to be removed next. To do this, firstly remove the three Allen screws that secure the dials to the instrument housing . . .

08 . . . then lift the dials out of the housing.

Position the washer centrally, making sure that the movement of the needle is not hindered in any way. When you're satisfied with the position, press it down firmly and cut off the 'handle' of the washer, leaving just the circle around the hub. **13** Repeat this process for all four hub washers.

14 Next, take the new dial face and peel off the backing paper to reveal the adhesive.

Gently move the rev counter and speedo needles to the 12 o'clock position, and enter the tip of the needles through their correct holes in the dials. Bend the dial face inwards to help achieve this. Do not press the dial onto the backplate just yet, or the adhesive will grab, **15** making it difficult to position the other two needles properly.

Again, nice and gently move the temperature needle to the 12 o'clock position, and move that end of the dial face upwards so that the needle enters its hole. Then move the dial downward, over the needle hub – don't press the dial into place until you've **16** repeated this process for the fuel gauge needle.

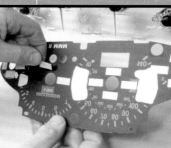

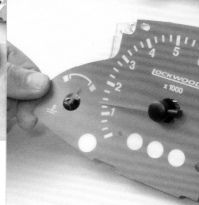

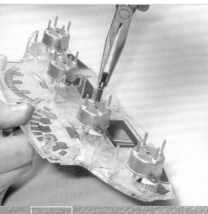

09 Turn the dial plate over, and use pliers to pinch the fat end of the button together, before pulling it out through the front of the dial plate.

10 Now comes the fun bit. Use a sharp knife to cut each dial face in two or more places to remove each section without disturbing the needles. Cut from the centre of the dial out to the edge of the plate. The dials will more than likely have adhesive on the back of them, so carefully peel the pieces of dial away from the mounting plate.

11 Time to clean that mounting plate off using something that will remove glue. Methylated spirit is a good choice - if you can bear the smell. Say, don't those clocks look kinda naked? Steady, now.

12 On a separate sheet supplied with the kit, you'll see some banjo-shaped washers. These are to be fitted around the needles to eliminate any light that may shine through the needle hubs. The two large washers fit around the rev counter and speedo, the smaller two are for the fuel and temperature gauges. Peel off the backing paper to reveal the adhesive, and open the slit in the washer to slide it around the spindle of the needle.

With all the dials in their correct positions, press the dial face to the mounting plate so that the adhesive can do its **17** stuff.

Slip the trip reset button into place, turning the dials over to make sure it's located properly at the **18** back.

Gently lift the rev counter and speedo needles up whilst slotting the stop-pegs back into place. Let each needle drop back down onto the rest position in its own **19** time.

Wipe off any finger-marks from the dials, and re-assemble the instrument pack the same way you took it apart. Give the transparent lens a clean too. Finally, refit the clocks to the car. And feel **20** suitably chuffed.

Racing
starts

The hardest part of fitting this kit is deciding where to mount the Richbrook Pro-start button - yep, that's about as hard as it gets. We decided to mount ours on the dash to the right of the steering wheel, so the first job is to take this bit of the dash off. **01** Remove the single retaining screw at the base, and lift the right-hand vent panel away.

Like to have a racing-style starter button on your Focus? Read on! A very cool piece of kit, and a great way to impress your passengers.

The idea of the racing starter button is the ignition key's made redundant, beyond switching on the ignition lights (it'd be a bit stupid, security-wise, if you could start the engine without the key at all).

 Achtung!
Disconnect the battery before starting this job. You may have ignored this advice in the past – don't ignore it now.

The new starter button needs a flippin' big hole drilled – according to the instructions, 19.2 mm (3/4in in old money). Somehow we doubt you've got either size in your toolbox. Two options: drill a slightly smaller hole and enlarge it **02** with a round file, or get a hole saw.

Pop the button into place to ensure it fits in the hole, and secure it in place using the nut provided with the kit. Try refitting the facia panel now - we had to trim away part of the dash behind our new button, to make room. Don't **03** actually fit the panel right back in just yet, though.

It really is easy from this stage onwards - we found the ultimately easy way to install this kit. All will be revealed, but to start with, remove the **04** steering column lower cowl, held in place by three screws.

To the left-hand side of the steering wheel, you'll see a large grey plastic wiring plug – this is the ignition switch. Disconnect the plug by prising the plastic retaining tabs up with a flat-headed **05** screwdriver - be careful not to snap these tabs off.

On the plug locate pin number 7, which houses a grey and orange wire. When you've found this wire, cut it near the top of the plug.

06

Next, unpick this wire as far as possible down the wiring loom.

07

We want this grey and orange wire to connect up to the back of the starter button, so feed it up to the back of the button. Then connect the wire to one of the terminals on the back of the starter button. At the other end of the grey and orange wire, simply crimp a wire joiner to act as an insulator and make it easy to link the wires together again, should you ever need to.

08

This next stage requires you to find a suitable piece of wire. Begin by stripping the wire and attaching one end of the wire to the other terminal on the back of the starter button. Then refit the facia panel.

09

Feed the new wire towards the ignition switch, routing it tidily using cable-ties.

10

When the new piece of wire reaches the ignition plug, locate the wire found in pin number 1, which should be green and yellow in colour. Don't cut this wire – we're going to splice our new wire onto it, so carefully strip away a section of insulation, to reveal the wire underneath.

11

Strip the end of your new wire, wrap it round the bare section of the existing wire, and join the two together using a soldering iron. Remember to tape it up after the solder has cooled.

12

Reconnect the ignition plug and battery to test that the switch works - if not, go back and check your connections. When you're happy that everything works, refit the steering lower cowl and you're done!

13

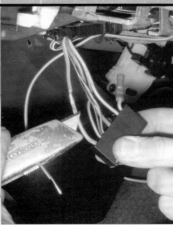

Under neon light

So how much of a poser are you? How'd you like to show off all this shiny chequer floor and sexy pedals to full effect, in the midnight hour? You need some neons, baby! Yeah!

01 First job is to mount the switch in a suitable position within the car. We've chosen to mount ours on the driver's side lower facia panel, next to the auxiliary fusebox we fitted previously (useful for picking up the live feed for the switch too – nice!). Use the switch surround as a template to mark and cut out the slot.

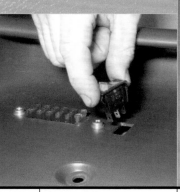

02 Drill a hole into the section you want to cut out, to make it easier to start cutting with a knife.

03 When the slot is ready, pop the switch into place.

04 As we've fitted an auxiliary fusebox, we're able to take a live feed from here to power our switch. The battery is the obvious choice otherwise - check in 'security' to see how we took a live feed into the car. But with a fusebox, it's just a simple job of connecting one end to the live feed (fusebox) and the other end to a pin on the switch.

Bum notes

Interior neons have recently been declared ILLEGAL, and some places don't even sell them any more. Exterior neons have been illegal from day one. If you fit interior neons, make sure they're at least easily switched off, should you get pulled. Remember that driving at night with a brightly-lit interior makes it even harder to see out. Neons are best used at shows, cruises, or when you're parked up.

05 Now it's time to mount the neon tubes. This bit's really up to you, but one favourite spot is under the dash so the neons light up the footwells. Funnily enough, this is where ours are going. For the tubes to be hidden, some chopping of the facia panel in the driver's footwell will be needed. Remove this panel by undoing the screws, levering out the plastic grommet and disconnecting the diagnostic plug.

06 With the panel out of the car, it's much easier to work on. You'll notice that the only way of discreetly mounting the tube is by chopping off the plastic plug surround that the diagnostic plug connects into. To keep it pretty, cut off the bulk of the plastic surround, but make sure you can still pop the blanking plate into place. The diagnostic plug can be cable-tied up under the dash.

07 This is the end result. The tube can now be mounted on the flattest part of the facia, and the blanking plug can still be used without fouling the tube in any way - bargain.

08 To mount the tube to the facia, use the plastic securing clips provided with the kit. Good old Folia Tec - they think of everything. Mark the holes for drilling, and then you guessed it – drill the mounting holes!

09 As pretty much every surface in the Focus is rounded, we're faced with a wee problem when it comes to fastening the tube to the panel. In order to mount the tube squarely, you will have to use some spacers to pad out the space between the tube and facia panel - washers or nuts will do the job just fine.

10 At this point, fit the second tube to the passenger's footwell. The underside of the glovebox is a good place to use. When you've done this, separate the black and red wires from the end of each tube, and route the two red wires towards the switch. Join the two red wires together, crimp a female connector on, and attach that to the middle pin on the switch.

11 The two black wires can then be joined in a ring connector, and routed to a suitable earth point. Here's one we made earlier, while fitting our X-Box screen. Before you re-fit the panel, make sure the lights work by turning on the ignition and flicking the switch. If nothing happens, try swapping the connectors around on the pins on the back of the switch.

Boring flooring?

Alright, so carpets have always been a dull colour because they have to not show the dirt - when was the last time you heard of a car with white carpets? What goes on the floor needn't be entirely dull, though, and can still be easy to clean, if you're worried.

Ripping out the old carpets is actually quite a major undertaking - first, the seats have to come out (you might be fitting new ones anyway), but the carpets and underfelt fit right up under the dashboard, and under all the sill trims and centre console, etc. Carpet acts as sound-deadening, and is a useful thing to hide wiring under, too, so don't be in too great a hurry to ditch it completely. Unless, of course, your Focus is having a full-on race/rally style treatment, in which case - dump that rug!

Chequerplate flooring has an enduring appeal - it's tough but flexible, fairly easy to cut and shape to fit, has a cool mirror finish, and it matches perfectly with the racing theme so often seen in the modified world. Looks trick with interior neons, too.

Tips 'n' tricks

If you're completely replacing the carpet and felt with, say, chequerplate throughout, do this at a late stage, after the ICE install and any other electrical work's been done - that way, all the wiring can be neatly hidden underneath it.

Chequer mats

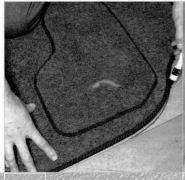

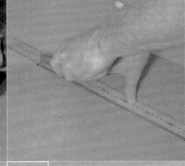

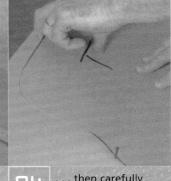

01 The halfway-house to a fully-plated interior is to make up your own tailored mats (hell, you can buy ready-mades if you're not allowed to play with sharp knives). Unless you buy real ally chequer, what you'll get is actually plastic, and must be supported by mounting it on hardboard. Take one of the lovely 'Granny' mats your car might have come with, and use it as a template to mark the shape onto the hardboard (you could always make a template from some thin card).

02 With the shape marked out, it's time for the jigsaw - next to a cordless drill, this has to be one of the most useful tools ever invented for the modder.

03 To make the hardboard fit better into the footwells, score it at the bend where it goes up under the pedals . . .

04 . . . then carefully 'fold' the hardboard back to the required shape - trust us, this will make your new chequer mats fit superbly.

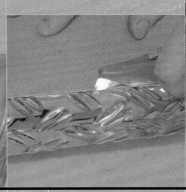

05 Not unlike this in fact. Try your hardboard mat in place, and trim the corners and edges as necessary to get it fitting as flat as poss.

06 Now you can use your hardboard as a template, for cutting out the chequer. Try to make the chequer fractionally bigger overall than the hardboard, so you don't see the wood edge (you shouldn't anyway, if your board is a tidy fit). Stick the chequer to the board, using some decent glue - spray glue's convenient, but usually not quite up to the job. You can't beat good old brush-on Evo-Stik (and no, we're not being paid to say that).

07 Do it right, and you too can have a floor like this - looks sweet, and the mats don't slip. Sorted.

Wheely cool

A new steering wheel is an essential purchase in personalising your Focus. It's one of the main points of contact between you and the car, it's sat right in front of you, and the standard ones are dull and massive!

One bit of good news is that, once you've shelled out for your wheel, it may be possible to fit it to your next car, too. When you buy a new wheel, you usually have to buy a boss (or mount) to go with it - the mounts are less pricey, so one wheel could be fitted to another completely different car, for minimum cost.

A trick feature worth investigating is the detachable wheel/boss. This feature comes in handy when you park up and would rather the car was still there when you come back (something most people find a bonus). It's all very well having a steering wheel immobiliser or steering lock, but not many thieves will be driving off in your car if the steering wheel's completely missing! Also, removing the wheel may remove the temptation to break in and pinch… your wheel!

A word about **airbags**

All Foci (even the RS) have at least a driver's airbag, built into the steering wheel centre pad. So far, the market for replacement wheels with airbags hasn't materialised, so fitting your tasty new wheel means losing what some (old) people think is a valuable safety feature.

So just disconnect the damn thing, right? Wrong. Then your airbag warning light will be on permanently - not only is this irritating, your newly-modded motor will fail the MOT (having the airbag itself isn't compulsory, but if the warning light's on, it's a fail - at least at the time this was written). Two ways round this - either take out the clocks (see the section on fitting white dials) and remove the offending warning light bulb, OR bridge the airbag connector plug pins with two lengths of wire attached to either side of a 5A fuse. Bridging the pins this way 'fools' the test circuit (which fires up every time you switch on the ignition) into thinking the airbag's still there, and the warning light will go out as it should.

Disabling the airbag is yet another issue which will interest your insurance company, so don't do it without consulting them first. We're just telling you, that's all.

Warning: Airbags are expensive to replace (several £100s), and are classed as an explosive!!! Funny, that - for a safety item, there's any number of ways they can CAUSE injuries or damage if you're not careful - check this lot out:

a Before removing the airbag, the battery MUST be disconnected (don't whinge about it wiping out your stereo pre-sets). When the battery's off, don't start taking out the airbag for another 10 minutes or so. The airbag system stores an electrical charge - if you whip it out too quick, you might set it off, even with the battery disconnected. True.

b When the airbag's out, it must be stored the correct way up.

c The airbag is sensitive to impact - dropping it from sufficient height might set it off. Even if dropping it doesn't actually set it off, it probably won't work again, anyway. By the way, once an airbag's gone off, it's scrap. You can't stuff it back inside.

d If you intend to keep the airbag with a view to refitting it at some stage (like when you sell the car), store it in a cool place - but bear in mind that the storage area must be suitable, so that if the airbag went off by accident, it would not cause damage to anything or anyone. Sticking it under your bed might not be such a good idea.

e If you're not keeping the airbag, it must be disposed of correctly (don't just put it out for the bin men!). Contact your local authority for advice.

f Airbags must not be subjected to temperatures in excess of 90°C (194°F) - just remember that bit about airbags being an explosive - you don't store dynamite in a furnace, now do you? Realistically in this country, the only time you'll get THAT hot is in a paint-drying oven.

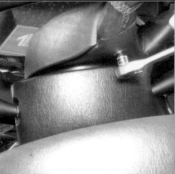

01 Disconnect the battery negative (earth) lead and wait for 10 minutes before proceeding to remove the steering wheel. If you don't disconnect the battery, or don't wait, the airbag will go off in your face. The airbag bolts are in the back of the wheel - turn the wheel a quarter-turn to reach the first one, and remove it. Turn the wheel half a turn from here, and remove the second bolt.

02 Now centralise the steering wheel, and make sure that the wheels are in the straight-ahead position. Using your fingers, unclip the horn pad and airbag by pulling it carefully towards you - remember the airbag wiring is still connected, so don't pull too hard.

03 Disconnect the horn and airbag wiring plug, and lift the pad away from the car. We will be returning to this part later on.

04 Grip the steering wheel with one hand, and using a 19mm socket, remove the steering wheel bolt. Our wheel came off easily - if yours doesn't, put the bolt back on by a few threads, and give it some pulling power. It's up to you what you do with the old wheel - use it as a Frisbee if you want, but if you keep it safe, you can re-fit it later and keep your handsome new wheel for your next car.

05 With the nasty original steering wheel gone, you'll see a black disc with writing on it. This is the clock spring. Do NOT move this disc at all, or you'll wreck it.

06 Now back to the horn pad/airbag we took off at the start. Unplug the yellow connector in the centre (the airbag wiring plug), then pull off the blue and black horn wires. Remove the mini wiring loom . . .

07 . . . and plug it into the clock spring.

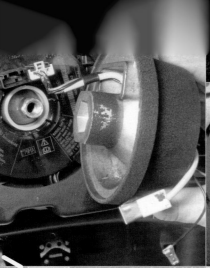

08 Thread the airbag and horn wires through the new boss. Slip the new boss into place on the splines, making sure the TOP marking is at the top (duh). If you put the boss on anything less than straight, your new wheel will also be out of line, which looks pants.

09 Slide on the horn adapter plate, then refit the steering wheel bolt.

10 Time for the first look at our very tasty Momo 'Net' wheel, which is held in place by six Allen screws - make sure they're done up tight.

11 With a wheel to hold onto, we can now torque that steering wheel bolt. 50 Nm is the magic number here. By the way, don't be lazy and let the steering lock take the strain - there's a good chance you'll bust it. Hold onto the wheel with your free hand.

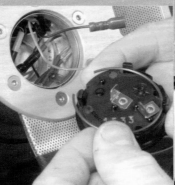

12 Our wheel comes with a cunning little airbag wiring loom. By bridging the two pins in the airbag (yellow) wiring plug, this fools the system into thinking the driver's airbag is still present, so the dash warning light works as before (comes on, goes out). The passenger airbag and seat belt tensioners will still work, too. Make your own loom with two short wires soldered to a 5 amp fuse.

13 Fit the horn spring clip to the back of the horn button (very important - without this, the horn circuit is incomplete) . . .

14 . . . then connect on the blue and black wire spade terminals to the back of the new horn button (doesn't matter which way round these go). Notice we had to fit some new big-boy spades, as the original Ford items were just too small for the new button. Size really does matter.

15 Final job is to push the horn pad home, and that's it - job done!

Pedalling your Focus

A tasty race-equipment touch to your modded machine, pedal extensions really look the part. The clutch and brake must have rubbers fitted - sensible (so your feet don't slip off them at an awkward moment) and also a legal requirement. Don't buy extensions without.

01 In keeping with our funky Momo theme, these Grand Prix pedals will look stunning in the cabin. Before we get too carried away, first job is to remove the old brake and clutch pedal rubbers. Go on - peel them off. Starting with the loud pedal first, offer the new pedal into place and mark the mounting holes.

02 Next, drill the holes. Place some wood behind the pedal to stop it sinking whilst you drill - it will also save your carpet from becoming holey if you should go too far. If you have one, use a centre punch to mark the hole so the drill won't slide about to begin with.

03 An Allen-headed bolt with nut and washer on the back will keep the pedal extension firmly in place. We removed our pedal to show you the rear view of the loud pedal. This webbed look is to strengthen the plastic, but may prove awkward when trying to fix your pedal in place. Longer bolts may be required and not supplied - check your kit before you start.

04 When fitting any aftermarket pedals, you must have a minimum distance of 50mm between each one (or at least, the gaps should be equal - check out the instructions on your kit). Common sense says if the pedals are too close together, it could be curtains - you have been warned.

05 Whilst fitting the clutch pedal, we discovered a smart way of ensuring the pedal extensions are fitted straight. Take a piece of masking tape and cover the pedal you're working on, then draw a centre-line down the pedal. When you offer the extension into place, align the pedal to the line visible through the holes - amazing! Mark and drill the mounting holes.

06 Tighten the bolts using an Allen key and spanner. And that's it - one tasty looking set of pedals. So good, you'll buzz every time your toes touch 'em!

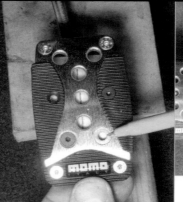

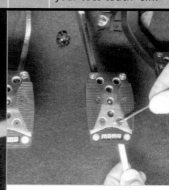

Achtung!
Check with your insurance before fitting pedal extensions. A while ago there was a big fuss after a couple of cars fitted with pedal extensions crashed.

The personal touch –
re-trimming

Okay, so you're definitely not happy with how the inside of your Focus looks, but you're not sold on any of the off-the-shelf options for tricking it up, either. You know how you want it to look, though, so get creative!

There are any number of upholsterers in Yellow Pages, who will be able to create any look you want (we got one in our own back yard, almost - Pipers of Sparkford, Somerset, and very helpful lads they are, too). If your idea of Focus heaven is an interior swathed in black and purple leather, these guys can help. Don't assume that you'll have to go to Carisma, to get a car interior re-trimmed - they might well be the daddies at this, but any upholsterer worth the name should be able to help, even if they normally only do sofas!

Of course, if you're even slightly handy with things like glue and scissors, you might be inspired to get brave and DIY. An upholsterers will still be a useful source for materials (and maybe advice too?).

Not everyone knows this, but Cobra, famous makers of wicked bucket seats, also offer trimming services. When we approached them for a pair of sexy Sidewinder seats, they offered to trim them AND our rear seats, door cards and parcel shelf in our choice of material. We thought about this for approximately two seconds, then set out in search of their factory in deepest, darkest Telford. Cobra's vast range of sports seats get exported worldwide, and are a particular favourite in Australian racing/rally driving - and with the owners of many of the feature cars you see in the magazines.

Seat removal

01 So we can start dreaming of how the new interior's going to look, the old stuff's got to come out. But those front seats of yours have seat belt tensioners in, which are linked to the airbag circuit, so you must disconnect the battery negative (earth) lead and wait for 10 minutes before going any further. If you don't, something very nasty might happen when you unplug the seat wiring later on.

02 Slide the front seat fully backwards, and remove the plastic trim cover from the outer seat runner. Undo and remove the two front seat runner bolts (big Torx bolts).

03 Slide the seat fully forwards, and remove the trim cover from the back of the seat rail - this one's held in place by Velcro, so don't be alarmed if you have to pull quite hard to release the Velcro from the carpet. Now undo and remove the two rear seat runner bolts.

04 Before you try and lift the front seat out of the car, disconnect the wiring connectors underneath. Once this has been done and the seat is free, you can lift it out.

05 For the full interior re-trim, the rear seats have to come out as well, and the rear seat cushion's first. Remove the mounting bolts (one each side), and lift the cushion out of the car. Simple.

06 Fold both halves of the rear seat backrest forwards, then remove the four seat retaining bolts – two at either end, on the outsides.

07 Next, remove the bolt in the centre section of the seats. This bolt holds a securing plate in place, which when removed allows you to separate the two parts of the backrest. Slide the retaining plate out, and you can lift the seats up to release them. Remember when re-fitting the seats that all these bolts should be done up good 'n' tight.

Seat **fitting**

We couldn't wait to get our freshly-trimmed beauties into the car, but there's still work to be done. Like fitting a Focus subframe (courtesy of Cobra) to the base of our new seats. Turn the seat
01 over and offer the subframe into place. Slide the seat runners forwards to tighten the rear bolts, then slide the runners backwards and tighten the front bolts.

Back to the old front seat now, to rob it of the seat belt assembly, wiring connectors and seat belt tensioner loom. Start by sliding back the release lug on the wiring connector,
02 then work your way round the seat unclipping the loom.

Next, remove the seat belt stalk by undoing the (big, Torx) retaining bolt. Gather the wiring loom, connector and seat belt stalk together (which
03 includes the tensioner) and lift them from the old seat.

04 Place the seat belt stalk in place on the new subframe. The old seat belt bolt can be re-used (as long as it's in good nick), but it's best to add a drop or two of thread-locking fluid to the threads before fitting. Tighten the bolts to 38 Nm, or as tight as you can.

05 Safely route the wiring for the seat belt tensioner around the subframe so it won't be fouled by any moving parts. Cable-tie the wires in place - if they get chopped accidentally, it could trigger the airbag. Not funny.

06 At last - the seat's ready to be refitted to the car. Use a little more threadlock on the seat retaining bolts (for max safety - a loose seat could be a tad inconvenient) and tighten to 28 Nm.

01 On a miserable cold morning, we set out in search of a factory in Telford. Not just any factory, we'll have you know, but the factory that makes the famous Cobra seats.

02 So, with the hello's over, it's straight into work. The trimmer that did this incredible job used to work for a very famous brand of sports car, and certainly knows his stuff. In fact, by the time we arrived, he'd already covered our new Sidewinders in a very respectable TVR-style red leather, and was hard at it preparing to cover the rear seat. Wow! We're impressed already.

Leather
seats

The first job is to get that nasty cloth off the rear seats in one piece. (We like the Focus, Henry, but you've let yourself down on the seats.) This is done by prising the material out from the base of the seat, unclipping the hog-

03 rings that hold the fabric to the foam.

So does the old cover get binned, once it's removed? Not a bit. We know it fits perfectly, so it gets 'dismantled' and used as a template for the new material. So the trimmer marks every section making up the rear seat cover with letters

04 such as F for front and so on.

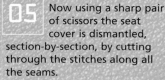

05 Now using a sharp pair of scissors the seat cover is dismantled, section-by-section, by cutting through the stitches along all the seams.

06 The seat sections are then sent to the man with the iron glove (look closely), who lays each section out onto the leather and marks out the templates.

07 An extremely sharp cutting tool is then used to cut each section out, hence the metal protective glove he wears – very sensible.

Here's some more cutting going on. Is it - foam? Virtually every section of this seat cover's going to end up being foam-backed. Why? To make the seat more comfy? Well, it does do that, but the real reason is to improve the visual effect. Any material looks too flat and lifeless without the foam backing, and it 'puffs up' the stitched sections.

08

Next the leather pieces are sent to the sewing experts. With the help of the trimmer, the sections of leather get joined to the foam, and are then pieced together based on the markings made on the original seat cover. The machinist then does her stuff - we've never seen anyone work a sewing machine so quickly before, and produce such a quality finish. Nice.

09

The final job is to fit the new cover over the old seat foam. This is quite tricky because the leather isn't as flexible as the original cloth, but it's very strong and can be pulled into place. The new cover then gets attached using new hog-rings, and locating strips removed from the old covers. That is one very nice leather interior. Cheers to all the excellent folk at Cobra.

10

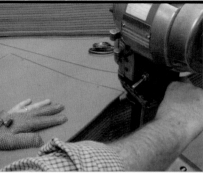

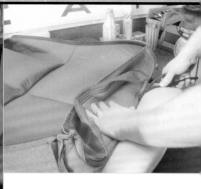

Door card trimming

01 We were well-chuffed with our seats, but just imagine our delight when Cobra offered to trim our front and rear door cards with matching cowhide as well! First job is to cut a section of leather to fit the area you're covering, leaving at least an inch overlap all the way around. Our expert trimmer did this by eye - you can always create a template.

02 Spread some strong fabric adhesive onto the underside of the leather and on the panel you're covering . . .

The next part of this is time-consuming. Using a small flat-bladed screwdriver, our skilful trimmer worked his way round the edges collecting up the material and pushing the leather down into the plastic edges of the door card. It's really important not to scratch or pierce the leather, or it ruins the look. It's a lot less easy than it sounds. Trimmer-dude, we salute you.

. . . then pop the leather into place and smooth it out over the area, so there are no trapped air bubbles that could ruin the finished effect.

03

04

05 We couldn't wait to get back to Haynes and fit our fantastic new leather interior, so this is a shot of us doing just that!

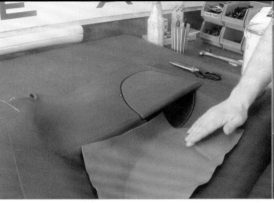

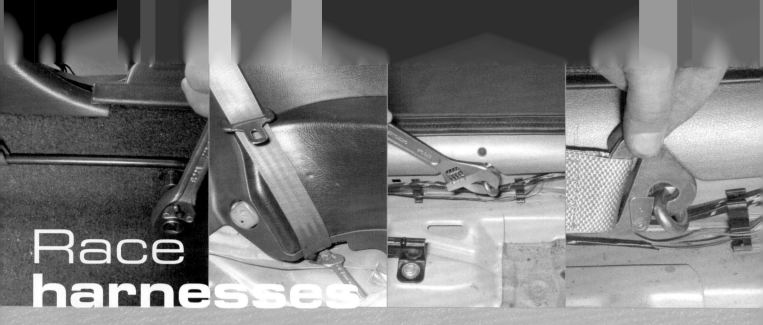

Race
harnesses

It's true that not everyone likes harnesses, but anyone like that's just boring, or should probably eat less pies. Besides, you don't fit sexy race seats and then not fit race belts, do you?

The only problem with harnesses is caused by where you have to mount them. Even with a three-point harness, you end up using one of the rear seat belt mounts, and it seriously reduces your ability to carry bodies in the back seats (webbing everywhere). The MOT crew say that, if you've got rear seats, you must have rear seat belts fitted, so you either 'double-up' on your rear belt mounts (use the same mounting bolts for your harnesses and rear belts), or you take the back seats out altogether. Removing the rear seats leaves the rear deck free for chequerplate, speakers, roll cages - whatever you like. It's just important to understand how fundamental harnesses can end up being, to the whole look of your car - there's almost no half-measures with race belts, so you've got to really want 'em.

One thing you must **not** do is to try making up your own seat belt/harness mounting points. Ford structural engineers spent plenty of time selecting mounting points and testing them for strength. Drilling your own holes and sticking bolts through is fine for mounting speakers and stuff, but you're heading for an interview with the Grim Reaper if you try it with seat belts. The forces in a big shunt are immense. We're not convinced either that the practice of slinging harnesses round a rear strut brace is kosher, from the safety angle - the poxy strut braces available are so flimsy (they're usually ally) you can bend them in your hands. Nuts to trusting my life to one of those! Finally, make sure any harnesses you buy are EC-approved, or an eagle-eyed MOT tester might make you take 'em out.

Your Haynes manual should help you to remove the old belts. After that, it's just a case of re-using the old belt mountings to fit the new harness "eyes", which the harnesses clip onto. Tighten the eyes fully down to the floor, using an adjustable spanner. Check whether your new seat subframes have proper belt mountings on them - if so, you can use these for one of the front mounts (the other one comes from the old belt's sliding rail on the floor). Don't be shy about tightening things properly, and no bodges, please - these are **safety** harnesses, after all.

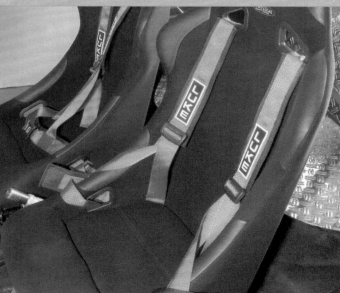

ICE
Headset

No Focus has a really nasty head unit - those old Ford days are gone. It's just that none of the standards are that great, either (and they're all huge, just to make fitting something aftermarket a bit harder - thanks, guys). Course, by the time an Focus has passed through several owners, it's pretty unlikely to still have a standard set in anyway, but if all you've got is a hole, don't feel too bad. Standard sets are fine if all you want to do is aimlessly listen to the radio with your arm out the window, but not - definitely not - if you want to impress your mates with the depth and volume of your bass.

Or, in most cases, if you want to listen to CDs. It's got to go - and there's plenty of decent headsets out there which will give you a night-and-day difference in sound quality and features. The headset is the heart of your new install - always go for the best you can afford. Ask the experts which features matter most, if you're building a full system. And don't just go for the look!

Our new Kenwood KDC-7024 headset is pretty typical of the current single-CD state of the art - decent looks, good sound, plenty of features.

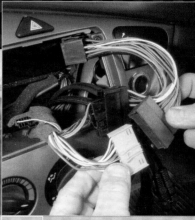

01 First, the old set's got to be shifted. Resist the urge to just crowbar the thing out of the dash - you'll be needing two of the standard radio removal tools to do the job with less damage. And you could always sell it, or keep it, to stick back in when you sell the car?

02 Another reason not to get too excited when removing the old set is that most of the wiring behind is fully 'recyclable' - ie we'll be using it again. Although the Focus doesn't have ISO plugs for power and speakers, the old wiring's still useful. As is the aerial plug, of course.

03 To get the ISO plugs to connect to our new headset, we need an adapter plug or two. These just plug into the existing Ford wiring, and give your new set instant power and speakers. They also make it dead easy to revert to the standard headset when selling-on. One bit of advice - if at first the adapter plugs don't seem to fit, keep trying. It's not always obvious how they go.

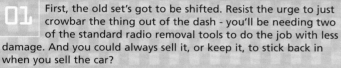

ISO plug wiring **colours**

Black plug (power/earth)	**Brown plug (speakers)**
Red - 12V permanent live	White pair - front left
Yellow - radio memory live	Grey pair - front right
Black - earth	Green pair - rear left
Blue - Remote/P-cont	Purple pair - rear right
Orange - dimmer	

As you can see, we're now pretty much there, having routed all the necessary wiring (new speaker wire, RCA lead) up to the back of the radio hole. Don't forget your autochanger lead, if you have one. Before we get too far, though, the new **04** set's cage has to go in. Make sure it's the right way up.

Those of you wanting the bling of an in-dash screen could use the space above your new headset to fit one. For the less well-minted among you, **05** clip in a ready-made blanking panel like this.

Before the set goes in, secure the cage by bending down just **06** a few (not all) of the tabs inside with a screwdriver.

07 Here we go with the wiring - but don't panic, 'cos none of it's tricky if you pay attention. First, using our new ISO plugs, we can connect up the headset's own little wiring loom.

08 If you're running amps in your system, you'll need a remote or P-cont lead, to switch them on (see the section on amps). The headset has a P-cont output wire, usually blue or blue/white. Any ordinary bit of wire will do for this - from the headset, feed it round the car to your amps. Our RCA leads each had a built-in lead, which is a neat idea. Here we're connecting both leads to the output from the headset.

09 Look at that mass of RCA leads. But our man's doing the right thing, and consulting the Kenwood manual. Well, it's a lot better than blowing up your headset.

10 Armed with the knowledge of which RCAs to connect where, our mechanic presses on. The RCA left and right channels are colour-coded, so you've no excuse for mixing them up - red is for right. I'm sure you can work out the other one…

Test that everything's working at this point, before pushing the unit right into its cage. If all's well, push the headset home until it clicks. If it gets stuck, take the set out, and un-bunch all the wiring by hand. Do not force it in, or you could end up having a very bad day. If you have trouble, removing the glovebox (see 'security') will let you reach in behind. Success? Now get out the instruction manual again, and set those levels properly. Enjoy.

Don't forget to plug in the aerial lead if you plan on listening to Hip-Hop FM. Grrrreat.

11

Lastly, plug in the other end of the set's own wiring loom to the set itself. Without it, you won't be listening to anything much.

12

13

Rear speakers

If we're talking about a set of 6x9s, rear shelf-mounting is the simplest option. If you don't want to butcher your standard shelf (always a flimsy item), either make a new one from MDF (using your stock shelf as a template), or buy a ready-made acoustic 'stealth' shelf. Either way, make hiding your new speakers a priority - tasty speakers on display in the back window could soon mean no rear window, and no speakers...

While shelf mounting has its advantages, 3-door Foci have another top spot for speakers - the rear side panels. Again, the standard Ford items are virtually 6x9s, so with just a little trimming, those standard holes can take a major speaker upgrade. We love it.

Stealth shelf 6x9s

 01 First job with a new ready-made shelf is to mark the speaker positions. Not tricky.

02 With a speaker outline marked, remove the wood from the rest of the shelf, and drill a nice big hole somewhere inside the outline... then get busy with the jigsaw.

03 Use the speaker mounts (or even the speakers themselves) as a template to drill the mounting holes . . .

04 . . . then screw on the speakers themselves. Don't forget that 6x9s can be run off the headset, to provide a little 'rear fill' - if you have them amped-up, you might find that the sound's too biased to the back of the car.

05 Remember that the length of wire to each speaker should be the same (as near as poss), or you might find the speakers run slightly out of phase. Crimp on the right terminals, and connect up your speakers. For max neatness, use P-clips screwed along the edge of the shelf. To remove the shelf more easily, fit some bullet connectors in the speaker wiring, or ask your ICE dealer for a Neutrik connector plug.

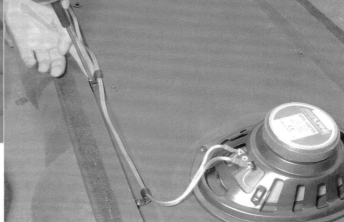

Achtung!
MDF dust is nasty stuff to breathe in. Wear a mask when you're cutting, drilling or sanding it.

Rear side panel 6x9s

01 Unclip and remove the rear side panels to get access to the rear speaker, then undo the four speaker screws . . .

02 . . . disconnect the wiring plug, and the old unit's a goner. But don't bin it, unless you're sure you'll sell the car with its ICE install intact.

03 Now for the first trial fitting of our new 6x9s. We were lucky on the front doors - they went straight in . . .

04 . . . this time, our luck ran out - the magnet wouldn't sink in far enough. Having found another use for our tin of grease (something round to mark the outline) . . .

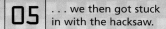

05 . . . we then got stuck in with the hacksaw.

06 After a little more trimming (using the handy paper template provided), the speaker went in sweetly. Now we need some mounting holes . . .

07 . . . and after they've been drilled, slip on a speed clip, and those self-tappers will bite first time.

08 Like the front doors, it pays to sound-deaden the back end too. A quick clean with the very fragrant meths . . .

09 . . . and a little more stick-on roofing weatherstrip went in. This stuff's so cheap, you can use several layers if you like.

10 Feed in the new speaker wire, complete with terminals, and connect up the new speaker before screwing it into place. One step closer to audio heaven.

Front
speakers

The standard items in the Focus speak volumes (hur-hur) about any car manufacturer's desire to build things down to a price - ie spend as little as poss. But for once, the news isn't all bad.

Believe it or not, Ford actually fit some passable oval speakers in the doors and rear panels, which are nearly the same size as the common 6x9. Meaning you can, with very little effort, upgrade to 6x9s in the doors. What a result. Just check your speaker depths before buying.

01 With the door trim panel off (see 'interiors'), removing the old speakers (for later burial) is easy-peas. Four screws round the edge . . .

02 . . . and a slightly-tricky plug off the back, and out comes the old speaker.

. . . then choose your material. The market leader in deadening is Dynamat - but - it comes at a price. What else is out there? Brown Bread. Sounds dead. And it's cheaper, too. Cheaper still is this stuff - adhesive flashing for roofing repairs, from a DIY store. Use the real thing, if you prefer, but this works. Besides, who'll see it? Cut **07** off a decent-size length . . .

. . . then poke it in through the speaker hole. Don't get too carried away in your quest for sonic perfection, but don't skimp on it, either. Treat the large 'floppy' areas of the door, and some round the speaker hole will help too. Two things - use it warm (warm it up with a heat gun, on a cold day), and watch your fingers on the **08** expensive stuff (the metal foil edges are sharp!).

Cut off a length of new speaker wire, long enough to reach from the speaker to your amp or headset. Actually, you want two bits of wire, the same length (one for each speaker). Attach speaker terminals to the bared ends - the large speaker terminal is **09** positive, so we're using the striped/writing wire on that.

If you want an easy life, you can re-use the Ford speaker wiring (cut the old plug off, use the Haynes manual wiring diagrams to work out which is the pos wire). But getting quality speaker wire into the doors isn't hard. With the door open, prise out the grommet at one end of the door harness flexi-tube, and make a **10** hole at the base with a sharp tool.

03 Now try your new 6x9s in the hole - with any luck, they'll go straight in (minor trimming may be required). Hold them right in the hole, then work the window up and down, to make sure there's room.

04 You'll be doing unbelievably well if your new speaker mounting holes line up with the old ones all round, but you might be able to use some of them. Mark those you need for drilling . . .

05 . . . and get busy with the cordless. Drilling through the speaker itself is only for the really brave - one slip, and your new Sony could be history.

06 Before actually mounting the speaker, sound-deaden that tin. The larger areas of the metal door panel will flex and vibrate with all the kicking power of your new sound system. Tizzing speakers we can live without. By sticking thick panels to the inside of your door inner and outer skins, you make the metal 'thicker', and vibration-free. Wind up the window, then clean up the door panel with some decent solvent . . .

Prise out this grommet on the door pillar, below the door harness, and we have access to the inside of the car. Drill a speaker wire-sized hole in the centre. Can you see where we're going now?

. . . and attach it to the door harness flexi-tube with a cable-tie. Seal up the holes in the grommets with a little silicone sealant. Looks neat, should sound even better, wasn't hard.

Last of all, mount the speaker in the door, and do the screws up tight. That's what we call a proper job.

11 **12** Feed the speaker wire through the two grommets . . . **13** **14**

Subs & boxes

No system's complete without that essential deep bass boom and rumble. Don't muck about with bass tubes - get the real thing to avoid disappointment. So you lose some of your boot space - so what? Is getting the shopping in an issue? We think not.

Most people opt for the easy life when it comes to boxes, at least until they're ready for a full-on mental install. The Focus at least has a fairly roomy boot, so standard boxes will fit easily. Making up your own box isn't hard though, especially if you were any good at maths and geometry. Oh, and woodwork. Most subs come with instructions telling you what volume of box they work best in, but ask an expert (or a mate) what they think - the standard boxes are just fine, and none are pricey. The only real reason to build your own is if you've got an odd-shaped boot (or want something that looks trick).

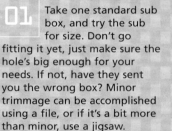

01 Take one standard sub box, and try the sub for size. Don't go fitting it yet, just make sure the hole's big enough for your needs. If not, have they sent you the wrong box? Minor trimmage can be accomplished using a file, or if it's a bit more than minor, use a jigsaw.

02 Once we're sure the sub's a good fit, it can come out again. Forgetting to wire up your sub before fitting it is a very common mistake, caused by being too keen. Most ready-made boxes come fitted with a terminal plate on the side of the box - with these, just run your speaker wire from the sub to the inside of the plate (keep the pos and neg wiring the right way round).

Make sure the sub's logo is lined up correctly (this won't affect the sound, just the pose-value), then drill through the mounting holes round the edge of the sub.

03

Once the mounting holes are made, screw the sub down tight (unless you want bass all over the place).

04

The terminal plates have either screw-type or spring-type terminals for connecting your speaker wire. You can just strip the end, twist it up and shove it in. Or you can 'tin' the end of your speaker wire, with solder, which makes it easier to fit your speaker wire, and removes the chance of any stray strands (which could touch, and blow a channel on your amp or headset). Keeping to our wiring convention, we're joining the writing-on wire to the positive (red) terminal.

05

Achtung!
You don't want a heavy sub box sliding about in your boot, so nail it down somehow. Velcro might stop it sliding on the boot carpet, but it's still a bit inadequate - how firmly is the boot carpet attached? In a bad accident, that heavy sub box could go flying - if it connected with your bonce, it'd be lights out. Try using some of those little metal corner brackets you can get from the DIY store, and really pin that box down. Might even improve the sound!

X-Box/ screen

Screen

Bored of your CDs? Nothing on the radio? We have just the thing if you and a mate get bored, stuck in a 10-mile tailback on a bank holiday. Definitely a growing trend on the ICE scene, no top modded motor's complete these days without a games console, screen, DVD - where d'you stop? Just don't get caught playing it while you're moving, that's all.

01 Won't see much without a screen, so let's do that first. The trickiest bit of all is deciding where it'll go - obviously, both front seat people have to see it, so somewhere central, but how high up? Try the screen and its bracket in place, and check it adjusts how you want it. Is it accessible from below/behind, for feeding-in the wires? We chose this spot next to the centre vents.

02 Removing one of those vents would obviously make fitting the screen much easier, so not being afraid to pull things apart, we did. Once the glovebox was out of the way (see how we fitted the auxiliary fusebox in 'security'), the vent could be 'helped' out from inside.

03 This is the mounting plate for the screen - hold this in place, and mark for drilling a hole. As this goes right into your lovely dash, check you've got it right a few times . . .

04 . . . before getting the drill out. I think this is what they call the point of no return.

05 That hole also has to be big enough to take the screen's video lead, and its plug, which is quite chunky. It's likely you'll have to supersize it with a file. Although the Focus dash is pretty solid, it makes sense to brace the mounting using a large ('panel') washer on the inside.

06 Fit the screen to the mounting bracket, then feed in the video lead and the plug. Using our large washer and the nut provided, making the screen a solid fit on the dash wasn't hard . . .

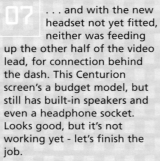

07 . . . and with the new headset not yet fitted, neither was feeding up the other half of the video lead, for connection behind the dash. This Centurion screen's a budget model, but still has built-in speakers and even a headphone socket. Looks good, but it's not working yet - let's finish the job.

08 Our screen came with an all-in-one lead containing the three-part video feed from the X-Box (or PS2/DVD), and also the power supply/earth. We'll connect up the X-Box later - for now, we want power to our screen. They give you a cigar lighter plug, but this looks a bit pants - let's wire it in properly. Chop the plug off, strip the ends, and we have skinny red and black wires.

09 The red's a live feed (you guessed it), which we're taking from our auxiliary fusebox (fitted in the 'security' section).

10 Finding an earth point for the black wire's not difficult either. Down in the driver's footwell, we drilled us a hole in the metal bodywork (mind those other wires) . . .

11 . . . then fitted a nut and bolt through, and we've got all the earth we can handle.

12 Connect the power plug in the screen's all-in-one lead, and the little green lights now tell us the screen's ready for input - let's give it some.

X-Box

To give power to your console, you need an AC inverter - ours was about £50 from Comet. What this does is take your car's 12-volt DC electrics, and turns it into mains voltage, giving you a domestic three-pin socket in your car - how cool is that? As with our screen, our inverter came with a fag lighter plug, which we dismantled. The wire we're snipping here is the earth . . .

01

. . . which we attached a ring terminal to, and bolted to an earth point we made at the back of the boot.

02

We stripped the end of the live wire, soldered it to one of the live feeds we were using for one of the amps . . .

03

. . . and then refitted it to our boot-mounted distribution block.

04

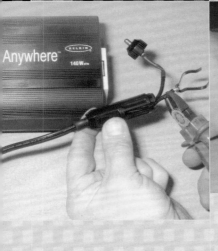

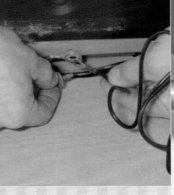

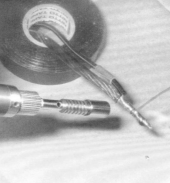

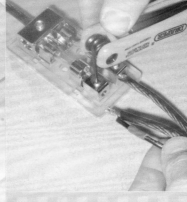

Power-wise, it's now just plug and play for our X-Box.

05

With the power on, just connect the controllers and the video lead from the screen . . .

06

. . . and it's game on! Total cost, including screen, inverter and X-Box (with free games) - less than £350. Now that's what we call a bargain - true in-car entertainment, and maximum respect. Just one last thought - we discovered the X-Box (a pretty chunky console) sits nicely in the (open) Focus glovebox. Hmmm...

07

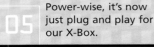

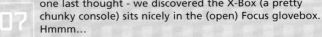

Wiring-up

For most people, this is the scariest part of an install - just the thought of masses of multi-coloured spaghetti sticking out of your dash might have you running to the experts (or a knowledgeable mate). But - if you do everything in a logical order, and observe a few simple rules, wiring-up isn't half as brain-numbing as it seems.

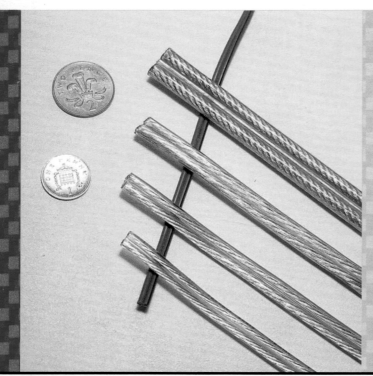

Live feeds

Although a typical head unit can be powered off the standard Ford wiring (the stock wire is good for about 15 amps, tops) running amplifiers means you'll be needing a new live feed, taken straight off the battery. Or in our case, straight off the junction box we fitted as part of our fusebox install (see 'security').

Get some decent 'eight-gauge' (quite heavy) or 'four-gauge' (getting on for battery cable thickness - serious stuff) wire, and a matching fuseholder. If you're running more than one item off this feed wire, get a distribution block too, which splits the feed up, with a separate fuse for each item - who'd have thought electrical safety can look trick too?

Pub trivia

Hands up, who knows what 'RCA' stands for? We use it every day in ICE-speak, but WHAT does it really mean? Really Clever Amplifier lead? Remote Control Acoustic lead? Well, the answer's a strange one. RCA leads and connectors are also known as 'phono' connectors in the world of TV and hi-fi, and they've been around a long, long time. How long, exactly? We're talking back in the days when you could only get radios - big suckers with valves in them, and long before anyone thought of putting one in a car. RCA actually stands for Radio Corporation of America, who hold the patent on this type of connector and lead. Not a lot of people know that.

Speaker and RCA wiring

As with all wiring, the lesson here is to be neat and orderly - or - you'll be sorry! RCA leads and speaker wires are prone to picking up interference (from just about anywhere), so the first trick to learn when running ICE wiring is to keep it away from live feeds, and also if possible, away from the car's ECUs. Another favourite way to interference-hell is to loop up your wiring, when you find you've got too much (we've all been there). Finding a way to lose any excess lengths of wire without bunching can be an art - laying it out in a zig-zag, taping it to the floor as you go, is just one solution.

Another lesson in neatness is finding out what kinds of cable clips are available, and where to use them. There's various stick-on clips which can be used as an alternative to gaffer tape on floors, and then 'P-clips', which look exactly as their name suggests, and can be screwed down (to speaker shelves, for instance). 'Looming'

your wiring is another lesson well-learned - this just means wrapping tape around, particularly on pairs of speaker wires or RCAs. As we've already said, don't loom speaker wire with power cables (or even with earths).

The last point is also about tidiness - mental tidiness. When you're dealing with speaker wiring, keep two ideas in mind - positive and negative. Each speaker has a pos (+) and neg (-) terminal. Mixing these up is not an option, so work out a system of your own, for keeping positive and negative in the right places on your headset and amp connections. Decent speaker cable is always two wires joined together - look closely, and you'll see that one wire has writing (or a stripe) on, and the other is plain. Use the wire with writing for pos connections throughout your system, and you'll never be confused again. While we're at it, RCA leads have red and white connector plugs - Red is for Right.

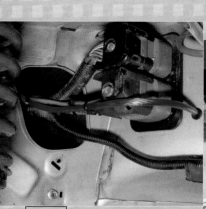

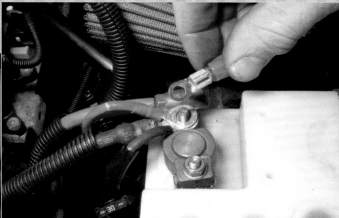

01 If you're running a live feed straight from the battery, you'll need to get it into the car at some point. Have a look at the fusebox fitting section in 'security' to see how we did the one for our fusebox. Knowing this to be an okay area, we drilled another hole next to the harness plugs in the wheelarch, and fed the new live through using a grommet. Here she is, all neatly cable-tied in place.

02 You'll also need an in-line fuseholder, containing a fuse that'll cover the total load for your system. This shouldn't be left to just flap about next to the battery - especially not when the Focus has an ideal mounting point on the air cleaner bracket. Just drill and screw.

03 With a decent ring terminal fitted (ideally, soldered) to the end of our live wire, making a good connection at the battery is a piece of... well, it's very easy. Just remember, once that wire goes onto the battery, it's live, even with the ignition off. For safety, either remove the in-line fuse, or don't let the other end touch earth, or the sparks will fly.

With the centre console removed (see 'interiors'), essential ICE wiring can be fed down the centre of the car, under the carpet. This is particularly good for the RCA leads. The alternative is routing them down the sides of the car, after unclipping the sill trim/door seal - plenty of wire can be hidden this way.

04 Keep the power feeds and speaker wires separate by running them down the other side.

Looming the wires together keeps things neat, but don't pull those cable-ties too tight - it can be useful if the wires lie flat, and bunching them up might work against you. Also, if your sill trims are secured using screws, take great care when refitting them - a screw

05 through your wiring is a good way to kill your system.

Here's where your live feed could end up - a distribution block. Split your power off to the amps as you need it - each amp gets its own fuse (downrated from the large one in the holder up front). Excellent electrical safety, trick looks. Pin the wire ends with the chunky Allen grub screws, then fit the plastic cover tight

06 (or lives will touch earths, and it's adios amigos).

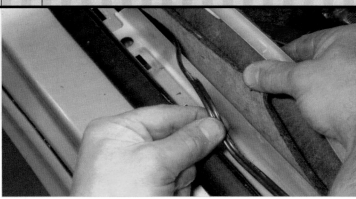

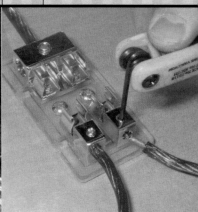

Amplifiers

Achtung!

MDF dust is nasty stuff to breathe in. Wear a mask when you're cutting, drilling or sanding it.

So, how many amps do we want in our car? One school of thought says each pair of speakers, and each sub, should have an individual amp - by setting the output from each amp separately, you can control each aspect of the sound, before you even need to think about adding a graphic equaliser. You can also better match your speakers to the level of power they need, to work best. Trouble is, running several amps means doubling-up on wiring, and you could end up drawing a monster amount of power from that battery.

Any starter system can be made to seriously kick, using just one 400W four-channel amp - choose the right one carefully (and the components to go with it), and just one will do. With a 'tri-mode' amp, you could run your front components off one pair of channels, bridge the other two for a sub, and run some 6x9s off the head unit. Don't forget that decent modern headsets chuck out fifty-per-channel now, so don't assume you'll need separate amps for everything. Ideally, in any system, the sound shouldn't all come from behind you - ears were designed to work best with sound arriving from in front (and who are we to argue?).

Decide where you'll mount the amps carefully. Any amp must be adequately cooled - don't cover it up so there's no airflow, and don't hang it upside-down from your shelf. We're keeping our back seat, which limits us for space, but we're planning on having the amps mounted either side of the sub box, in our own MDF-based boot install.

Our system set-up uses two matching Sony Xplod amps - one 1000W beast for our sub, and a 600W four-channel for the front and rear speakers. They've got the look, but how about the performance to back it up? Let's find out.

01 We're doing the earth first - and why not?. Don't use skinny wires for earths - ideally, it should be the same-thickness wire as you've used for your live feed. We've used blue wire here (well, at least it's not red). Now we need a decent earth point somewhere in the boot, to join our wire to. We used the same hole we made for our X-Box inverter. For a good earth connection, clean off any paint round the hole, and do it up tight.

05 It's not essential to use terminals on every amp connection. If you twist up the bared end of your wire first, then curl it like this so it wraps round the screw, you're sorted. Just make sure none of the bare wires can touch each other.

02 The all-important live supply is one amp connection you should really use a ring terminal on, rather than just stuffing a bare wire into the hole. And insulate any bare metal on the terminal - that live touches anything else, and the results won't be good.

03 Next up, it's the humble P-cont (remote) lead going on. This performs the vital function of carrying the 'switch-on' signal from your headset - without this, you won't hear much. The good news is, this is one time when size doesn't matter - it doesn't carry much current, so the wire can be as skinny as you like.

04 Read the amp's instruction book carefully when connecting any wires, or you might regret it, especially for bridged or tri-mode. Identify your speaker pos and neg/left and right wires with a piece of tape, and get them screwed on. As with the lives and earths, it's also vital there's no stray bits of wire left poking out.

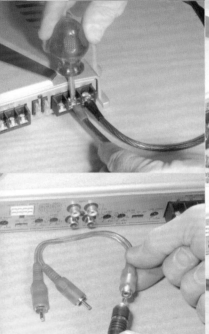

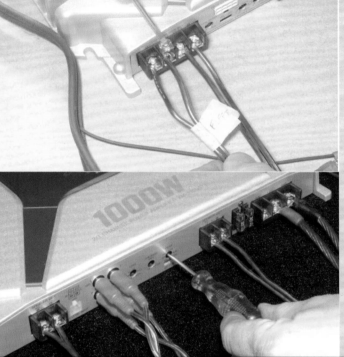

06 If you're using a four-channel amp to run front and rear speakers, you should really take a separate RCA lead from the front and rear outputs on your headset. But we're cheating, and using just one RCA, which now has to be split, using an adaptor lead known as a splitter (cunning, eh?). These plug into each end of the RCA lead, and double the number of outputs. Not all headsets offer two sets of RCA outputs (pre-outs), anyway.

07 Splitters aren't always clearly marked for left and right channels, so check what you're doing carefully - watch the red (right) and white (left) colour-coding, too. You can use splitters to run more than one amp from one RCA lead (though the 'gurus' say you shouldn't). But if the system ends up sounding great, who cares?

08 A good tip is to leave the amps loose until after you've set them up - if you can, leave good access to the gain adjustment (volume) screws after final fitting, too. Starting at normal listening volume, with the amp gain turned down, put on a kicking track, then turn the gain up until the speakers just start to distort. Turn the gain down a tad from there, and you've a good basic setting. Amp gain and headset faders can now be tweaked to give a good balanced sound - or whatever tickles your lugholes.

Tricks 'n' tips
Very few systems work 100%, first time. If the amp LEDs don't light up, for instance, are they getting power? Are the p-cont/remote wires connected properly? If the sub doesn't kick, is the amp switch set to bridged or tri-mode, not stereo? Are the low-pass switches in the correct position? RTFM.

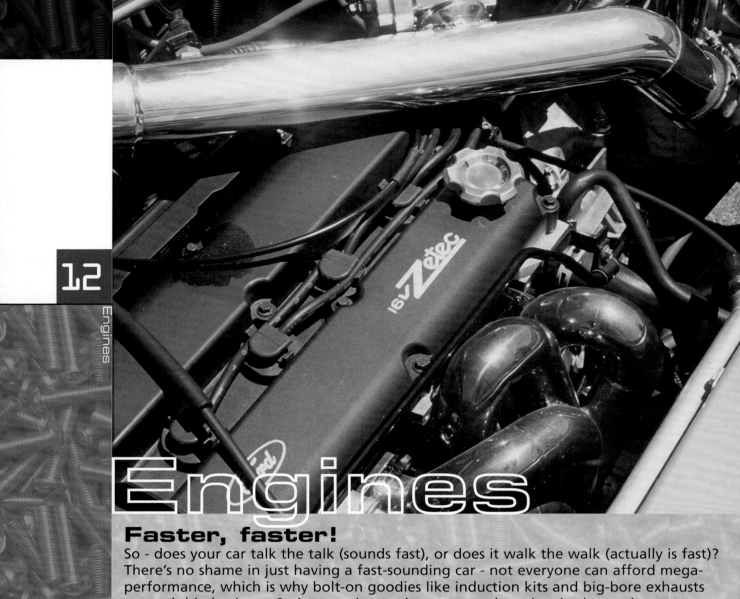

Engines

Faster, faster!

So - does your car talk the talk (sounds fast), or does it walk the walk (actually is fast)? There's no shame in just having a fast-sounding car - not everyone can afford mega-performance, which is why bolt-on goodies like induction kits and big-bore exhausts are such big business. Serious engine tuning costs, and not just in the engine parts - your insurance company will throw a wobbly at a gas-flowed head, and might refuse to cover you altogether if you go for that RS / ST170 engine conversion.

The induction kit and sports exhaust are an essential first choice, and usually it's as far as you can really go before your insurance company disowns you. Both mods help the engine to 'breathe' better, which helps when you go for the accelerator initially, improving the response you feel, while you also get a crowd-pleasing induction roar and rasp from the back box, so everyone's happy.

Now for the harsh and painful truth. On their own, an induction kit and back box may not gain you much extra 'real' power. Sorry, but it's a myth. Time and again, people fit induction kits and back boxes, expecting huge power gains, and those 'in the know' have a quiet chuckle. All these things really do is make the car sound sportier, and improve the response - accept this, and you won't be disappointed. Ask yourself why most insurance companies don't generally increase premiums for the likes of a performance rear box or induction kit. The answer is - because (on their own) they don't make enough difference!

The 'bolt-on' performance goodies have more effect as part of an engine 'makeover' package, and setting-up the engine properly after fitting these parts can make a huge difference. If you're halfway serious about increasing the go of your Focus, talk to someone with access to a rolling road, so you can prove what's been done HAS actually made a useful gain. If you've spent time and a ton of money on your car, of course you're going to think it feels faster, but is it actually making more power?

Fitting all the performance goodies in the world will be pretty pointless if the engine's already knackered, but it might not be as bad as you think. One of the best ways to start on the performance road is simply to ensure that the car's serviced properly - new spark plugs, HT leads, and an oil and filter change, are a good place to start. Correct any obvious faults, such as hoses or wiring plugs hanging off, and look for any obviously-damaged or leaking components, too.

One of the simplest items to fit, the replacement air filter element has been around for years - of course, now the induction kit's the thing to have, but a replacement element is more discreet (if you're worried about such things).

While we're at it, don't listen to your mates who tell you to simply take out the air filter completely - this is a really daft idea. The fuel system's air intake acts like a mini vacuum cleaner, sucking in air from the front of the car, and it doesn't just suck in air, but also dust, dirt and leaves. Without a filter, all this muck would quickly end up in the sensitive parts of the fuel system, and will quickly make the car undriveable. Worse, if any of it makes it into the engine, this will lead to engine wear. Remember too, that cheaper performance filters can be of very suspect quality - if your new filter disintegrates completely inside six months, it'll do wonders for the airflow, but it'll also be letting in all sorts of rubbish!

Some performance filters have to be oiled before fitting - follow the instructions provided; don't ignore this part, or the filter won't be effective. If the filter won't fit, check whether you actually have the right one - don't force it in, and don't cut it to fit, as either of these will result in gaps, which would allow unfiltered air to get in.

Air filter element

01 Before starting this procedure, make sure the ignition is switched off (take out the key). Slacken the large Jubilee clip and detach the air intake hose from the airflow sensor.

02 Unclip the airflow sensor wiring plug.

03 Remove the four screws holding the air cleaner cover to the base, and lift it away from the car.

04 Lift out the old air filter element, and depending on its state - store it for refitting later, or bin it!

05 Before fitting your new K&N panel filter, clean out the muck that has accumulated in the air box housing. Don't sweep it into the engine - either vacuum it out, or use a damp cloth to pick the worst of it up.

06 Remove the little piece of green sponge (crankcase ventilation filter) and give this a good wash too.

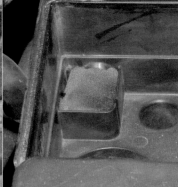

07 You're now ready to fit the new high-flow air filter. Simply pop the new filter into place - this one's supplied pre-oiled, so it couldn't be much easier. Better still, when it's old and filthy, you can buy special cleaner and fresh oil, so it can be re-used. Refit all the bits you took off, making sure that everything's well-tightened, to avoid air leaks.

Induction kit

All petrol Foci feature multi-point injection, making them ideal candidates for an induction kit. With an induction kit, the standard air filter housing and ducting are junked, and the new filter bolts directly to the airflow meter or throttle body.

Most kits also feature special air inlet ducting (hoses) to feed the new filter with the coldest possible air from the front of the car - cold air is denser, and improves engine power. Many Jap/US companies now supply 'cold air pipes', which are phat chromed tubes, shaped to direct the cool air where it's needed - again, massive power gains are claimed (and they look totally trick, which no-one's disputing). Feeding the filter with cold air is in theory good for maximum performance with a hot engine or in hot weather, but in colder conditions with a cold engine, driveability and fuel economy might suffer.

The fuelling arrangements for fuel injection are based largely on the volume of incoming air. If you start feeding the injection system an unusually large amount of air (by fitting an induction kit, for instance), the management system will compensate by throwing in more fuel. This could result in some more power - or the car will drink petrol and your exhaust emissions will be screwed up, inviting an MOT failure. We're not saying 'don't do it', just remember that power gains can be exaggerated, and that there can be pitfalls.

What no-one disputes is that an induction kit, which operates without all the standard ducting, gives the engine a real throaty roar when you go for the loud pedal. So at least it sounds fast. Pop the hood, and it looks wicked. Jubbly.

01 Remove the air filter element as described previously in this section. Unscrew two Allen screws and remove the airflow sensor from the air cleaner cover. The airflow sensor is just a bit delicate and vital to the plot, so - don't drop it on the floor.

02 Next, remove the engine breather hose fitted between the air cleaner and engine top cover by pulling it out from each end.

. . . then fit on the new induction cone mounting bracket, using the spacer, bolt and spring washer supplied with the kit. When you have done this, the bracket should look like this. Not impressed? **07** Well, that's because we haven't fitted the cone itself yet.

That's what we wanted to see - fitting the new cone filter to the airflow sensor. Don't force **08** the cone on further than the step, as this will affect the air flow.

Secure the cone filter in place using the Jubilee clip provided. Posers among you will want to hold off fully tightening that clip until you've turned the cone so the K&N logo on the front is straight. When you're satisfied, tighten the clip so the cone is tight, but be careful - if you overtighten the clip, you could **09** crush and crack the airflow sensor (it's only plastic), so take it easy.

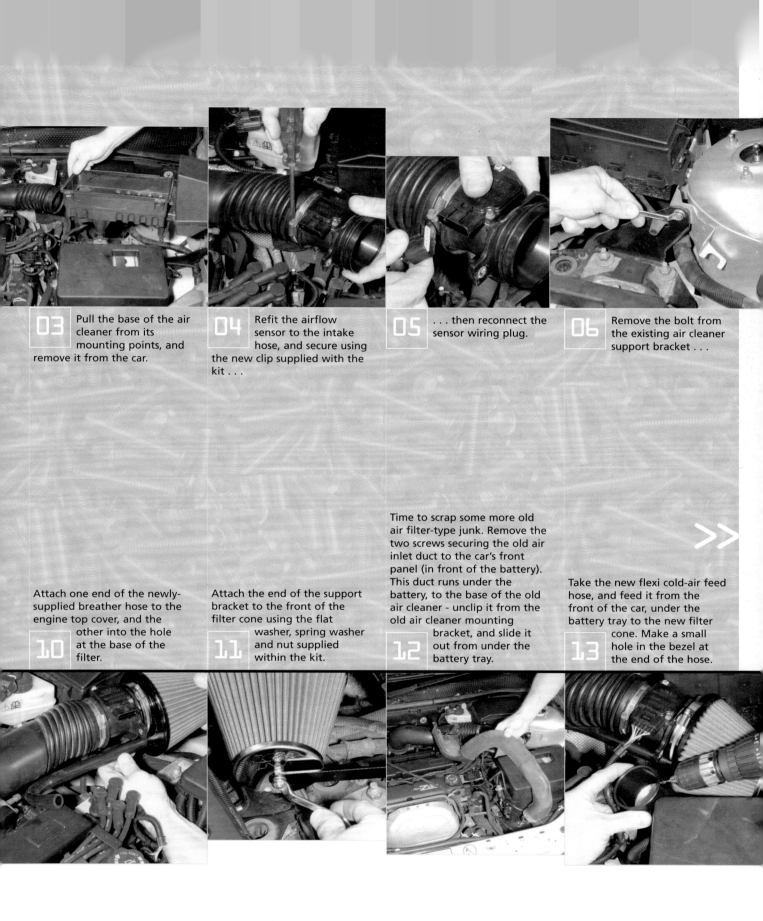

03 Pull the base of the air cleaner from its mounting points, and remove it from the car.

04 Refit the airflow sensor to the intake hose, and secure using the new clip supplied with the kit . . .

05 . . . then reconnect the sensor wiring plug.

06 Remove the bolt from the existing air cleaner support bracket . . .

10 Attach one end of the newly-supplied breather hose to the engine top cover, and the other into the hole at the base of the filter.

11 Attach the end of the support bracket to the front of the filter cone using the flat washer, spring washer and nut supplied within the kit.

12 Time to scrap some more old air filter-type junk. Remove the two screws securing the old air inlet duct to the car's front panel (in front of the battery). This duct runs under the battery, to the base of the old air cleaner - unclip it from the old air cleaner mounting bracket, and slide it out from under the battery tray.

13 Take the new flexi cold-air feed hose, and feed it from the front of the car, under the battery tray to the new filter cone. Make a small hole in the bezel at the end of the hose.

>>

Route the other end of the hose down to the front bumper. The hose must be sited where it can suck up cold air, but not so low it sucks up flood water and small furry mammals. Either use the cable-tie method to pin the hose in place, or use a DIY-store bracket like us, on our mesh-equipped new bodykit.

15

Finally...

Once you've fitted your new filter or induction kit, even if you don't take the car to a rolling road for setting up, at least take it to a garage and have the emissions checked - any minor adjustments should ensure that the engine will, if nothing else, still tick over okay, and should ensure an MOT emissions pass.

14 Position the end of the cold-air hose about 10 cm away from the filter (no closer), and secure the hose in place using the cable-tie provided. Use one of the original air cleaner mounting holes to secure the hose.

Other air filter-type mods

One old favourite, if you haven't gone for an induction kit, is drilling holes in the air filter box. Only drill the air filter box below the level where the filter element sits, or the air going into the engine won't be filtered. Making your airbox look like a Swiss cheese won't make the car faster, but it does give you the nice throaty induction roar at full throttle.

No quicker but it looks nice

Looks are just as important as performance. No hot hatch is 'finished' without making it look sweet. Details to the engine bay as well as your interior and exterior mods are an important factor, especially if you were thinking about getting your motor featured in top magazines. Every one does it, and you're next.

First up - try cleaning the engine, for flip's sake! How do you expect to emulate the show-stopping cars if your gearbox is covered in grot? Get busy with the degreaser (Gunk's a good bet), then get the hosepipe out. You can take it down to the local jetwash if you like, but remember your mobile - if you get carried away with the high-power spray, you might find the car won't start afterwards!

When it's all dry (and running again), you can start in. Get the polish to all the painted surfaces you reasonably can, and don't be afraid to unbolt a few of the simpler items to gain better access. We're assuming you've already fitted your induction kit, but if not, these nicely do away with a load of ugly plastic airbox/air cleaner and trunking, and that rusted-out exhaust manifold cover, in favour of decent-looking product. Take off the rocker cover, and paint it to match your chosen scheme (heat-

resistant paint is a must, really, such as brake caliper paint), set off with a funky oil filler cap. A strut brace is a tasty underbonnet feature, especially chromed. Braided hose covers (or coloured hose sets), ally battery covers and bottles, mirror panels - all give the underbonnet a touch of glamour.

Engine dress items are always important for creating that individual look, plus most items even claim to improve power output. Don't think we're going to get much increase in performance out of these Mega Leads, but they do look the part.

HT leads

01 To prevent the possibility of mixing the spark plug leads, change one at a time. Begin by lifting out the first HT lead.

02 Trace the wire down towards the coil, unclipping it from the wire tidy clips on the cylinder head cover.

03 Disconnect the lead from the ignition coil by pulling it off the end of the coil terminal. With the original HT lead in one hand, go through the new kit to find the lead that matches the original in length, and refit the new lead in the same way as you removed the old one. And that's it, simply repeat this process for the remaining three leads.

Braided hoses

01 Unroll your braiding, check the length against your freshly-removed hose, and trim it roughly to length - you might need something heftier than scissors for this.

02 Now expand the braiding to the right size using a suitable blunt object. Like a screwdriver handle, we mean - what were you thinking of? Once the braiding's roughly the right size, you can slip your pipe in (lovely). Smooth out the braiding round the bends, as it tends to gather up and look naff otherwise, then trim up the ends.

03 Slide a new Jubilee clip over the braiding at one end, then slip one of the coloured end fittings over the clip. Repeat this process at the other end of your chosen hose, and it'll be ready to fit back on. When you're sure the hose is fully onto its fitting, tighten the hose clip securely to avoid embarrassing leakage.

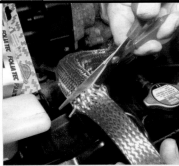

You's a hose

There are many ways to add detail and colour to otherwise boring components. Spray-painting your hoses is just one of those ways (yes, really). But, as always, you gotta use the right stuff - the red hoses you see in this pic are all done with MHW Tube-It paint, supplied by ABC Design.

01 Give the pipe a good clean to thoroughly degrease it - any oil or silicone-slippery stuff, and the paint won't stick.

01 Apply the paint in three or four light layers until pipe is evenly covered. You'll also have to wait a while (ideally, leave overnight) before that hose can go back on. Given enough time to dry, this hose paint's really good stuff - doesn't crack or flake off. But we wouldn't advise going ballistic with the pressure washer, even so.

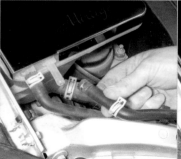

03 The lazy-boy alternative is to buy ready-made coloured replacement hoses, which usually come as a complete engine set. This is a small coolant hose we've chosen, and there was minimal water leakage - with the larger hoses, be prepared to get wet. These spring-type hose clips are a pain - arm yourself with a decent pair of pliers before starting.

04 Two things to be sure of here - have you got the right hose out of the box, and is that spring clip doing its job properly? Coolant leaks are not cool, fuel leaks could be deadly, and a kinked hose is a blocked hose - make sure all hoses are correctly fitted. They also shouldn't be touching hot or moving parts. Looking good here, though, and we've saved a huge chunk of time already.

05 If Ford fit it, it must be important. Don't ignore factory-fitted hose clips like this - your sexy new hoses mustn't wander off. If any clips don't survive the hose removal process, use cable-ties (not too tight) as a substitute. If you've lost any coolant, the system will need topping-up once you're done - you'll want a 50-50 mix of antifreeze and water, not just plain water.

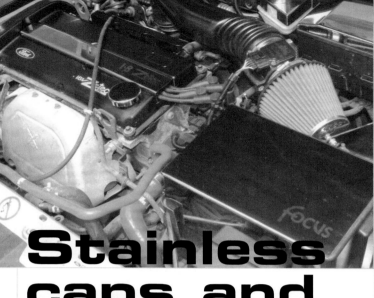

Stainless caps and bottle covers

The cool mirror finish of stainless steel. It's one of those timeless classic looks, especially under the bonnet - it's never going out of style, and it'll never look out of place. If it's a look you fancy, don't muck about with paint - it'll never look a patch on the real deal. Instead, talk to Mirage Stainless, for a top-quality, easily-fitted and good-value solution to all your stainless desires.

01 One of the largest bottles under the bonnet, and hardly very attractive, the coolant tank's crying out for the stainless treatment. But not before it gets a little love from a suitably-moistened workshop rag.

02 Flip 'er over, and inside we find several sticky pads. Once relieved of their backing, they'll ensure our new bottle cover sticks to its task.

There are caps and covers for pretty much everything under the Focus bonnet, so there's no excuse for leaving anything out. This is the power steering reservoir getting the treatment - a typically well-fitting two-part item, with a collar and cap.

Take care to line things up before committing yourself - once this stuff sticks, it's stuck. **03** Or it should be, if you did a good enough job of cleaning the bottle.

Now to make sure it doesn't move. Press down firmly and evenly, then wipe off all those **04** disgusting fingerprints, ruining the underbonnet bling.

As a final touch, get the chrome cover for the coolant bottle cap as **05** well. Slips on a treat.

06

Silicon heaven

All Foci have an engine management system with a 'computer' at its heart, known as the ECU, or Electronic Control Unit. The ECU contains several computer chips, at least one of which has programmed onto it the preferred fuel/air mixture and ignition advance setting for any given engine speed or load - this information is known as a computer 'map', and the system refers to it constantly while the car's being driven.

Obviously, with the current trend towards fuel economy and reducing harmful exhaust emissions, the values in this 'map' are set, well, conservatively, let's say (read 'boring'). With a little tweaking - like richening-up the mixture, say - the engine can be made to produce more power, or response will be improved, or both. At the expense of the environment. Whatever.

Companies like Superchips offer replacement computer chips which feature a computer map where driveability and performance are given priority over outright economy (although the company claims that, under certain conditions, even fuel economy can be better, with their products). While a chip like this does offer proven power gains on its own, it's obviously best to combine a chip with other enhancements, and to have the whole lot set up at the same time. By the time you've fitted an induction kit, four-branch manifold, big-bore pipe, and maybe even a fast-road cam, adding a chip is the icing on the cake - chipping an already-modified motor will liberate even more horses, or at least combine it with majorly-improved response. Ford tuning specialists are best placed to advise you on the most effective tuning mods.

Chipping is about the best way to extract more horses if your Focus runs on oil, not petrol. Modern turbo-diesel engine management systems control all aspects of fuelling, as you'd expect, but they also control the turbo boost. The more modern your TD is, the more there is to play with, and the more to be gained. Chipping a petrol engine can mean as little as 10 bhp, but turbo-diesels can give three times that gain, from a chip alone - and still with sensible fuel economy

Another feature programmed into the ECU is a rev limiter, which cuts the ignition (or fuel) progressively when the pre-set rev limit is reached. Most replacement chips have the rev limiter reset higher, or removed altogether. Not totally sure this is a good thing - if the engine's not maintained properly (low oil level, cambelt changes neglected), removing the rev limiter and running beyond the red line would be a quick way to kill it. But a well-maintained engine with rally cam(s) fitted could rev off the clock, if the ECU would let it, so maybe not a bad thing after all…

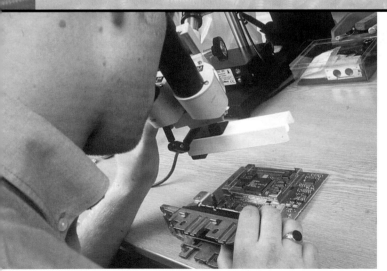

Now the bad news

Chipping is often thought of as an easy, 'no-tell' route to increased performance and driveability - after all, the ECU is well-buried inside the car, not on show under the bonnet, so who's gonna know? Needless to say, the insurance companies have been wise to this trick for a long time. A sure way to tell whether any 'performance' product does what it says on the tin is to see what it'll do to your premium - telling them you're fitting a sports ROM chip will cost. Big-time. But, in the event of a claim, if they suspect your car's been 'chipped', rest assured, they will make efforts to find out, because if you haven't told them about it, it means they save on paying out. What's an insurance assessor's salary for one day, compared to the thousands you could be claiming in case of an accident or theft? Do it by all means, but at least be honest.

Engine tuning

So you've done the filter/induction kit and exhaust box - what's next, short of going for a complete engine swap?

If you've got a sports back box, try a performance exhaust manifold up front - or better still, a full 'cat-back' system for the best gains. Your Focus is, of course, being strangled all the time you're driving. By a cat - how embarrassing is that? There's the option of a de-cat pipe, which does away with the power-sapping catalytic converter at a stroke, freeing-up as many as 10 or 15 horses on the way (but remember the car's not MOT-able with one of these fitted, so isn't strictly legal for use on the road).

A new camshaft's often a juicy way to pep up a standard motor, but the standard Focus cams are pretty good, so unless yours is/are knackered, all you'll achieve is moving the power further up the rev range. But - treat your Focus to a skimmed, gas-flowed, big-valve cylinder head (and a fast road cam or two) and it'll really start to percolate.

Engine swaps

Most young Focus owners wait 'til they've built up some no-claims bonus on their insurance, and go for a bigger Ford engine. Why throw shedloads of cash modding a weenie Ford engine, when lots less money spent on fitting a new motor could buy you the same power, with room left for tuning?

Though all the Focus petrol motors are called "Zetecs", there's two distinct flavours - the 1.4 / 1.6 are a different "family", known as the Zetec-SE. This difference means it's not quite a straight swap putting in that 1.8 or 2.0 litre lump - you'll need the 'box too, and some engineering finesse on hand. Check the internet forums for advice before diving into this kind of project.

Fitting a 2.0 litre gives you a more than 50 brake advantage over a 1.4, and a healthy dose of extra mid-range over the 1.6. If you've already got a 1.8, will a 2.0 give you much more? Probably not. Is it worth shelling out for an ST170 motor if you've got the straight 2.0 litre? Judging from the under-whelming road tests of the '170, also probably not. But if someone offers you an RS engine, box and running gear? Take it. Just remember to ask if it's legit first.

Turbocharging

Now we all know the RS is the only (petrol) Focus you could buy with a turbo, right? Well, not quite. See, it took Ford ages to bring their fast Focus out, so a company called GMD came along in 2000, and brought out a range of special Foci, all featuring Mountune-prepared turbo engines, and the sort of pukka suspension/braking kit now seen on the RS. So if you happen to spot a Focus T130, T190, T230 or T230R for sale, it'll be big money, but at least you'll know why. Turbo kits will doubtless become more widely available in time - in America, one source we know of right now is Gude, from California, who produce the 'Stinger' full turbo and intercooler kit.

Supercharging

Did we mention that the Focus is pretty big news in America? Land of the V8 and the Dodge Viper, where there "ain't no substitute for cubes"? Well, though that's still true, it seems our American cousins have learned a thing or two in recent years, and the US is certainly somewhere to look for Focus engine tuning ideas. Jackson Racing of California offer a supercharger kit for the 2.0 litre engine, offering a claimed 40% power increase. If our calculations (and their claims) are right, that's more than an ST170 puts out, with a nice beefy dollop of torque lower down. Stick a nitrous kit on top of that, and who needs an RS?

And finally

And finally tonight - the bad news. Any major engine mods means telling those nice suits who work for your insurance company, and it's likely they'll insist on a full engineer's report (these aren't especially expensive - look one up in the Yellow Pages, under 'Garage Services' or 'Vehicle Inspection').

Exhausts

It's gotta be done, hasn't it? Your rusty old exhaust lacks the girth to impress, and doesn't so much growl as miaow. Don't be a wimp and fit an exhaust trim - they'll fool nobody who really knows, and they certainly won't add to your aural pleasure (oo-er). Sort yourself out a decent back box upgrade, and even a timid 1.4 Focus can begin to cut it at the cruise.

What a back box won't do on its own is increase engine power - although it'll certainly sound like it has, provided you choose the right one, and fit it properly. Check when you're buying that it can be fitted to a standard system - you'll probably need something called a reducing sleeve for a decent fit, which is a section of pipe designed to bridge the difference between your small-diameter pipe and the larger-diameter silencer. Try and measure your standard pipe as accurately as possible, or you'll have major problems trying to get a decent seal between the old and new bits - don't assume that exhaust paste will sort everything out, because it won't.

Fashion has even entered the aftermarket exhaust scene, with different rear pipe designs going in and out of style. Everyone's done the upswept twin-pipe 'DTM' style pipes, while currently the trend in single pipes is massive Jap-style round exits, or fat oval (or twin-oval) designs. If you must have the phattest Focus on the

Know your enemy - this is what your cat looks like inside. Is it any wonder they restrict gas flow?

block, you can't beat a twin-exit system (from someone like Powerflow), even though it'll probably mean losing your spare wheel in the fitting process. Well, when was the last time you had a puncture? And what are mobiles and breakdown cover for, anyway?

You might need to slightly modify even your standard rear bodywork/bumper to accommodate a bigger rear pipe; if you're going for a bodykit later, your back box will have to come off again, so it can be poked through your rear valance/mesh.

You'll see some useful power gains if you go for the complete performance exhaust system, rather than just the back box. Like the factory-fit system, the sports silencer works best combined with the front pipe and manifold it was designed for! Performance four-branch manifolds alone can give very useful power gains. Watch what you buy, though - cheap exhaust manifolds which crack for a pastime are not unknown, and many aftermarket systems need careful fitting and fettling before you'll stop it resonating or banging away underneath. A sports rear box alone shouldn't attract an increased insurance premium, but a full system probably will.

All Foci (even the RS) are lumbered with a catalytic converter (or

'cat'), which acts like a restrictor in the exhaust, inhibiting the gas flow and sapping some engine power (maybe 5 to 10%). Various specialist exhaust companies market replacement sections which do away with the cat (a 'de-cat pipe'), and get you your power back. Unfortunately, by taking off or disabling the cat, your car won't be able to pass the emissions test at MOT time, so you'll have to 're-convert' the car every 12 months. This means the car's illegal on the road with a de-cat pipe fitted - you'd have no defence for this, if questions were asked at the roadside, and potentially no insurance if the unthinkable happens. Sorry, but we have to say it…

If your Focus has been slammed to the floor, will your big new sports system be leaving behind a trail of sparks as it scrapes along the deck? Shouldn't do, if it's been properly fitted, but will the local multi-storey be out-of-bounds for your Focus, from now on? And - pub trivia moment - you can actually be done for causing damage to the highway, if your exhaust's dragging. Well, great.

You probably couldn't give a stuff if your loud system's a very loud major public nuisance, but will that loud pipe start interfering with your sound system? If you rack up many motorway miles, you might find the constant drone of a loud pipe gets to be a real pain on a long trip, too…

Fitting a **sports back box**

01 Support the back end of the car on axle stands (see 'wheels & tyres'), then remove the rear bumper (as described in 'bodywork'). Offer up your new exhaust to the existing back box, and check that the mounting points and shape of the pipes are the same. Now you know how much work you're looking at. Our Peco Big Bore 4 looks to be a fine fit - a nice easy day for our mechanic!

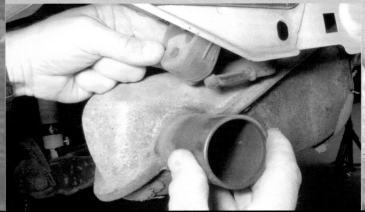

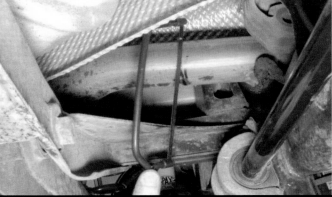

02 Begin by unhooking the back box from its rear rubber mounting, then unhook the inner mounting (just above the rear axle). Our Focus still had the original Ford system with an integral back box - so we now have to cut the pipe. An older Focus might have had a replacement box by now, in which case you just undo the clamp and slide it off. Or undo the clamp and struggle like hell, more like.

03 Hold the new back box aligned with the old box, and mark where the pipe on the new box ends on the existing pipe to the back box. Don't cut the pipe at this point, as you need extra pipe to slide into the pipe on the new box. So move back 3 inches (towards the existing back box) and cut the pipe here. Don't cut the pipe near to the inner mounting point or the anti-roll bar, or it'll be near-impossible to fit your back box.

04 Now the old box has been cut off, it's time for you to slide your new back box (and a new exhaust clamp) into position on the pipe.

05 With the exhaust resting in place, you can check that the tailpipe on the box you have chosen don't touch any part of the exhaust recess/hole in the rear bumper. If it does, you'll have to mark and trim these areas.

06 It's time to clamp the little beauty in place. You can see here the importance of not cutting your pipe in the wrong place! If you're worried about the new box blowing at the joint, slip it apart and smear on some exhaust assembly paste, then reassemble and tighten the clamp.

07 Hook the back box onto the inner and rear rubber mountings. Even without the rear bodywork fitted, it still looks pretty schweet.

Safety and tools

Safety

We all know that working on your car can be dangerous - and we're not talking about the danger of losing your street cred by fitting naff alloys or furry dice! Okay, so you'd be hard-pushed to injure yourself fitting some cool floor mats or a tax disc holder, but tackle more-serious mods, and you could be treading dangerous ground. Let's be honest - we have to put this safety section in to cover ourselves, but now it's in, it would be nice if you read it…

Burning/scalding

The only way you'll really burn yourself is if your car's just been running - avoid this, and you won't get burned. Easy, eh? Otherwise, you risk burns from any hot parts of the engine (and especially the exhaust - if you've got one, the cat runs very hot), or from spilling hot coolant if you undo the radiator hoses or filler cap, as you might when you're braiding hoses.

Fire

Sadly, there's several ways your car could catch fire, when you think about it. You've got a big tank full of fuel (and other flammable liquids about, like brake fluid), together with electrics - some of which run to very high voltages. If you smoke too, this could be even worse for your health than you thought.

a Liquid fuel is flammable. Fuel vapour can explode - don't smoke, or create any kind of spark, if there's fuel vapour (fuel smell) about.

b Letting fuel spill onto a hot engine is dangerous, but brake fluid spills go up even more readily. Respect is due with brake fluid, which also attacks paintwork and plastics - wash off with water.

c Fires can also be started by careless modding involving the electrical system. It's possible to overload (and overheat) existing wiring by tapping off too many times for new live feeds. Not insulating bare wires or connections can lead to short-circuits, and the sparks or overheated wiring which results can start a fire. Always investigate any newly-wired-in kit which stops working, or which keeps blowing fuses - those wires could already be smouldering…

Crushing

Having your car land on top of you is no laughing matter, and it's a nasty accident waiting to happen if you risk using dodgy old jacks, bricks, and other means of lifting/supporting your car. Please don't.

Your standard vehicle jack is for emergency roadside use only - a proper trolley jack and a set of axle stands won't break the overdraft, and might save broken bones. Don't buy a cheap trolley jack, and don't expect a well-used secondhand one to be perfect, either - when the hydraulic seals start to fail, a trolley jack will drop very fast; this is why you should always have decent stands in place under the car as well.

Steering, suspension & brakes

Screwing up any one of these on your car, through badly-fitted mods, could land you and others in hospital or worse. Nuff said? It's always worth getting a mate, or a friendly garage, to check over what you've just fitted (or even what you've just had fitted, in some cases - not all "pro" fitters are perfect!). Pay attention to tightening vital nuts and bolts properly - buy or borrow a torque wrench.

To be absolutely sure, take your newly-modded machine to a friendly MOT tester (if there is such a thing) - this man's your ultimate authority on safety, after all. Even if he's normally a pain once a year, he could save your life. Think it over.

Even properly-fitted mods can radically alter the car's handling - and not always for the better. Take a few days getting used to how the car feels before showing off.

Wheels

Don't take liberties fitting wheels. Make sure the wheels have the right stud/bolt hole pattern for your car, and that the wheel nuts/bolts are doing their job. Bolts which are too long might catch on your brakes (especially rear drums) - too short, and, well, the wheels are just waiting to fall off. Not nice. Also pay attention to the bolt heads or wheel nuts - some are supposed to have large tapered washers fitted, to locate properly in the wheel. If the nuts/bolts "pull through" the wheel when tightened, the wheel's gonna fall off, isn't it?

Asbestos

Only likely to be a major worry when working on, or near, your brakes. That black dust that gets all over your alloys comes from your brake pads, and it may contain asbestos. Breathing in asbestos dust can lead to a disease called asbestosis (inflammation of the lungs - very nasty indeed), so try not to inhale brake dust when you're changing your pads or discs.

Airbags

Unless you run into something at high speed, the only time an airbag will enter your life is when you change your steering wheel for something more sexy, and have to disable the airbag in the process. Pay attention to all the precautionary advice given in our text, and you'll have no problems.

One more thing - don't tap into the airbag wiring to run any extra electrical kit. Any mods to the airbag circuit could set it off unexpectedly.

Exhaust gases

Even on cars with cats, exhaust fumes are still potentially lethal. Don't work in an unventilated garage with the engine running. When fitting new exhaust bits, be sure that there's no gas leakage from the joints. When modifying in the tailgate area, note that exhaust gas can get sucked into the car through badly-fitting tailgate seals/joints (or even through your rear arches, if they've been trimmed so much there's holes into the car).

Tools

In writing this book, we've assumed you already have a selection of basic tools - screwdrivers, socket set, spanners, hammer, sharp knife, power drill. Any unusual extra tools you might need are mentioned in the relevant text. Torx and Allen screws are often found on trim panels, so a set of keys of each type is a wise purchase.

From a safety angle, always buy the best tools you can afford - or if you must use cheap ones, remember that they can break under stress or unusual usage (and we've all got the busted screwdrivers to prove it!).

DO Wear goggles when using power tools.

DO Keep loose clothing/long hair away from moving engine parts.

DO Take off watches and jewellery when working on electrics.

DO Keep the work area tidy - stops accidents and losing parts.

DON'T Rush a job, or take stupid short-cuts.

DON'T Use the wrong tools for the job, or ones which don't fit.

DON'T Let kids or pets play around your car when you're working.

DON'T Work entirely alone under a car that's been jacked up.

Legal modding?
No such thing!!

The harsh & painful truth

The minute you start down the road to a modified motor, you stand a good chance of being in trouble with the Man. It seems like there's almost nothing worthwhile you can do to your car, without breaking some sort of law. So the answer's not to do it at all, then? Well, no, but let's keep it real.

There's this bunch of vehicle-related regulations called Construction & Use. It's a huge set of books, used by the car manufacturers and the Department of Transport among others, and it sets out in black and white all the legal issues that could land you in trouble. It's the ultimate authority for modifying, in theory. But few people (and even fewer policemen) know all of it inside-out, and it's forever being updated and revised, so it's not often enforced to the letter at the roadside - just in court. Despite the existence of C & U, in trying to put together any guide to the law and modifying, it quickly becomes clear that almost everything's a "grey area", with no-one prepared to go on record and say what is okay to modify and what's not. Well, brilliant. So if there's no fixed rules (in the real world), how are you meant to live by them? In the circumstances, all we can promise to do is help to make sense of nonsense…

Avoiding roadside interviews

Why do some people get pulled all the time, and others hardly ever? It's often all about attitude. We'd all like to be free to drive around "in yer face", windows down, system full up, loud exhaust bellowing, sparks striking, tyres squealing - but - nothing is a bigger "come-on" to the boys in blue than "irresponsible" driving like this. Rest assured, if your motor's anywhere near fully sorted, the coppers will find something they can nick you for, when they pull you over - it's a dead cert. Trying not to wind them up too much before this happens (and certainly not once you're stopped) will make for an easier life. There's showing off, and then there's taking the pee. Save it for the next cruise.

The worst thing from your point of view is that, once you've been stopped, it's down to that particular copper's judgement as to whether your car's illegal. If he/she's having a bad day anyway, smart-mouthing-off isn't gonna help your case at all. If you can persuade him/her that you're at least taking on board what's being said, you might be let off with a warning. If it goes further, you'll be reported for an offence - while this doesn't mean you'll end up being prosecuted for it, it ain't good. Some defects (like worn tyres) will result in a so-called "seven-day wonder", which usually means you have to fix whatever's deemed wrong, maybe get the car inspected, and present yourself with the proof at a police station, inside seven days, or face prosecution.

If you can manage to drive reasonably sensibly when the law's about, and can ideally show that you've tried to keep your car legal when you get questioned, you stand a much better chance of enjoying your relationship with your modded beast. This guide is intended to help you steer clear of the more obvious things you could get pulled for. By reading it, you might even be able to have an informed, well-mannered discussion about things legal with the next officer of the law you meet at the side of the road. As in: "Oh really, officer? I was not aware of that. Thank you for pointing it out." Just don't argue with them, that's all…

Documents

The first thing you'll be asked to produce. If you're driving around without tax, MOT or insurance, we might as well stop now, as you won't be doing much more driving of anything after just one pull.

Okay, so you don't normally carry all your car-related documents with you - for safety, you've got them stashed carefully at home, haven't you? But carrying photocopies of your licence, MOT and insurance certificate is a good idea. While they're not legally-binding absolute proof, producing these in a roadside check might mean you don't have to produce the real things at a copshop later in the week. Shows a certain responsibility, and confidence in your own legality on the road, too. In some parts of the country, it's even said to be a good idea to carry copies of any receipts for your stereo gear - if there's any suspicion about it being stolen (surely not), some coppers have been known to confiscate it (or the car it's in) on the spot!

Number plates

One of the simplest mods, and one of the easiest to spot (and prove) if you're a copper. Nowadays, any changes made to the standard approved character font (such as italics or fancy type), spacing, or size of the plate constitutes an offence. Remember too that if you've moved the rear plate from its original spot (like from the tailgate recess, during smoothing) it still has to be properly lit at night. You're unlikely to even buy an illegal plate now, as the companies making them are also liable for prosecution if you get stopped. It's all just something else to blame on speed cameras - plates have to be easy for them to shoot, and modding yours suggests you're trying to escape a speeding conviction (well, who isn't?).

Getting pulled for an illegal plate is for suckers - you're making it too easy for them. While this offence only entails a small fine and confiscation of the plates, you're drawing unwelcome police attention to the rest of your car. Not smart. At all.

Sunstrips and tints

The sunstrip is now an essential item for any modded motor, but telling Mr Plod you had to fit one is no defence if you've gone a bit too far. The sunstrip should not be so low down the screen that it interferes with your ability to see out. Is this obvious? Apparently not. As a guide, if the strip's so low your wiper(s) touch it, it's too low. Don't try fitting short wiper blades to get round this - the police aren't as stupid as that, and you could get done for wipers that don't clear a sufficient area of the screen. Push it so far, and no further!

Window tinting is a trickier area. It seems you can have up to a 25% tint on a windscreen, and up to 30% on all other glass - but how do you measure this? Er. And what do you do if your glass is tinted to start with? Er, probably nothing. Of course you can buy window film in various "darknesses", from not-very-dark to "ambulance-black", but being able to buy it does not make it legal for road use (most companies cover themselves by saying "for show use only"). Go for just a light smoke on the side and rear glass, and you'd have to be unlucky to get done for it. If you must fit really dark tints, you're safest doing the rear side windows only.

Some forces now have a light meter to test light transmission through glass at the roadside - fail this, and it's a big on-the-spot fine.

Single wiper conversion

Not usually a problem, and certainly not worth a pull on its own, but combine a big sunstrip with a short wiper blade, and you're just asking for trouble. Insufficient view of the road ahead. There's also the question of whether it's legal to have the arm parking vertically, in the centre of the screen, as it obscures your vision. Probably not legal, then - even if it looks cool. Unfortunately, the Man doesn't do cool.

Lights

Lights of all kinds have to be one of the single biggest problem areas in modifying, and the police are depressingly well-informed. Most people make light mods a priority, whether it's Morette conversions for headlights or Lexus-style rear clusters. If they fit alright, and work, what's the problem?

First off, don't bother with any lights which aren't fully UK-legal - it's just too much hassle. Being "E-marked" only makes them legal in Europe, and most of our Euro-chums drive on the right. One of our project cars ended up with left-hand-drive rear clusters, and as a result, had no rear reflectors and a rear foglight on the wrong side (should be on the right). Getting stopped for not having rear reflectors would be a bit harsh, but why risk it, even to save a few quid?

Once you've had any headlight mods done (other than light brows) always have the beam alignment checked - it's part of the MOT, after all. The same applies to any front fogs or spots you've fitted (the various points of law involved here are too many to mention - light colour, height, spacing, operation with main/dipped headlights - ask at an MOT centre before fitting, and have them checked out after fitting).

If Plod's really having a bad day, he might even question the legality of your new blue headlight bulbs - are they too powerful? Keeping the bulb packaging in the glovebox might be a neat solution here (60/55W max).

Many modders favour spraying rear light clusters to make them look trick, as opposed to replacing them - but there's trouble in store here, too. One of the greyest of grey areas is - how much light tinting is too much? The much-talked-about but not-often-seen "common sense" comes into play here. Making your lights so dim that they're reduced to a feeble red/orange glow is pretty dim itself. If you're spraying, only use proper light-tinting spray, and not too many coats of that. Colour-coding lights with ordinary spray paint is best left to a pro sprayer or bodyshop (it can be done by mixing lots of lacquer with not much paint, for instance). Tinted lights are actually more of a problem in daylight than at night, so check yours while the sun's out.

Lastly, two words about neons. Oh, dear. It seems that neons of all kinds have now been deemed illegal for road use (and that's

interior ones as well as exteriors, which have pretty much always been a no-no). If you fit neons inside, make sure you rig in a switch so you can easily turn them off when the law arrives - or don't drive around with them on (save it for when you're parked up). Distracts other road users, apparently.

ICE

Jungle massive, or massive public nuisance? The two sides of the ICE argument in a nutshell. If you've been around the modding scene for any length of time, you'll already know stories of people who've been done for playing car stereos too loud. Seems some local authorities now have by-laws concerning "music audible from outside a vehicle", and hefty fines if you're caught. Even where this isn't the case, and assuming a dB meter isn't on hand to prove the offence of "excessive noise", the police can still prosecute for "disturbing the peace" - on the basis of one officer's judgement of the noise level. If a case is proved, you could lose your gear. Whoops. Seems we're back to "do it - but don't over-do it" again. If you really want to demo your system, pick somewhere a bit less public (like a quiet trading estate, after dark) or go for safety in numbers (at a cruise).

Big alloys/tyres

One of the first things to go on any lad's car, sexy alloys are right at the heart of car modifying. So what'll interest the law?

Well, the first thing every copper's going to wonder is - are the wheels nicked? He'd need a good reason to accuse you, but this is another instance where having copies of receipts might prove useful.

Otherwise, the wheels mustn't rub on, or stick out from, the arches - either of these will prove to be a problem if you get stopped. And you don't need to drive a modded motor to get done for having bald tyres...

Lowered suspension

Of course you have to lower your car, to have any hope of street cred. But did you know it's actually an offence to cause damage to the road surface, if your car's so low (or your mates so lardy) that it grounds out? Apparently so! Never mind what damage it might be doing to your exhaust, or the brake/fuel lines under the car - you can actually get done for risking damage to the road. Well, great. What's the answer? Once you've lowered the car, load it up with your biggest mates, and test it over roads you normally use - or else find a route into town that avoids all speed bumps. If you've got coilovers, you'll have an easier time tuning out the scraping noises.

Remember that your new big-bore exhaust or backbox must be hung up well enough that it doesn't hit the deck, even if you haven't absolutely slammed your car on the floor. At night, leaving a trail of sparks behind is a bit of a giveaway...

Exhausts

One of the easiest-to-fit performance upgrades, and another essential item if you want to be taken seriously on the street. Unless your chosen pipe/system is just too damn loud, you'd be very unlucky to get stopped for it, but if you will draw attention this way, you could be kicking yourself later.

For instance - have you in fact fitted a home-made straight-through pipe, to a car which used to have a "cat"? By drawing Plod's attention with that extra-loud system, he could then ask you to get the car's emissions tested - worse, you could get pulled for a "random" roadside emissions check. Fail this (and you surely will), and you could be right in the brown stuff. Even if you re-convert the car back to stock for the MOT, you'll be illegal on the road (and therefore without insurance) whenever your loud pipe's on. Still sound like fun, or would you be happier with just a back box?

It's also worth mentioning that your tailpipe mustn't stick out beyond the very back of the car, or in any other way which might be dangerous to pedestrians. Come on - you were a ped once!

Bodykits

The popular bodykits for the UK market have all passed the relevant tests, and are fully-approved for use on the specific vehicles they're intended for. As long as you haven't messed up fitting a standard kit, you should be fine, legally-speaking. The trouble starts when you do your own little mods and tweaks, such as bodging on that huge whale-tail spoiler or front air dam/splitter - it can be argued in some cases that these aren't appropriate on safety grounds, and you can get prosecuted. If any bodywork is fitted so it obscured your lights, or so badly attached that a strong breeze might blow it off, you can see their point. At least there's no such thing as Style Police. Not yet, anyway.

Seats and harnesses

Have to meet the UK safety standards, and must be securely bolted in. That's about it. It should be possible to fasten and release any seat belt or harness with one hand. Given that seat belts are pretty important safety features, it's understandable then that the police don't like to see flimsy alloy rear strut braces used as seat harness mounting points. Any other signs of bodging will also spell trouble. It's unlikely they'd bother with a full safety inspection at the roadside, but they could insist on a full MOT test/engineer's report inside 7 days. It's your life.

While we're on the subject of crash safety, the police also don't like to see sub boxes and amps just lying on the carpet, where the back seat used to be - if it's not anchored down, where are these items gonna end up, in a big shunt? Embedded in you, possibly?

Other mods

We'll never cover everything else here, and the law's always changing anyway, so we're fighting a losing battle in a book like this, but here goes with some other legalistic points we've noted on the way:

a It's illegal to remove side repeaters from front wings, unless they're "replaced" with Merc-style side repeater mirrors. Nice.

b All except the most prehistoric cars must have at least one rear foglight. If there's only one, it must be fitted on the right. We've never heard of anyone getting stopped for it, but you must also have a pair of rear reflectors. If your rear clusters ain't got 'em, can you get trendy ones? Er, no.

c Fuel filler caps have to be fitted so there's no danger of fuel spillage, or of excess fumes leaking from the top of the filler neck. This means using an appropriate petrol-resistant sealer (should be supplied in the kit). Oh, and not bodging the job in general seems a good idea. Unlikely to attract a pull, though.

d Front doors have to retain a manual means of opening from outside, even if they've been de-locked for remote locking. This means you can't take off the front door handles, usually. It seems that rear door handles can be removed if you like.

e Tailgates have to have some means of opening, even if it's only from inside, once the lock/handle's been removed. We think it's another safety thing - means of escape in a crash, and all that.

f You have to have at least one exterior mirror, and it must be capable of being adjusted somehow.

g If you fit new fog and spotlights, they actually have to work. No-one fits new lights just for show (or do they?), but if they stop working later when a fuse blows, relay packs up, or the wiring connectors rust up, you'd better fix 'em or remove 'em.

h Pedal extensions must have rubbers fitted on the brake and clutch pedals, and must be spaced sufficiently so there's no chance of hitting two pedals at once. This last bit sounds obvious, but lots of extension sets out there are so hard to fit that achieving this can be rather difficult. Don't get caught out.

i On cars with airbags, if you fit a sports wheel and disconnect the airbag in the process, the airbag warning light will be on permanently. Apart from being annoying, this is also illegal.

j Pace-car strobe lights (or any other flashing lights, apart from indicators) are illegal for road use. Of course.

k Anything else we didn't think of - is probably illegal too. Sorry.

Any questions? Try the MOT Helpline (0845 6005977). Yes, really.

Thanks to Andrew Dare of the Vehicle Inspectorate, Exeter, for his help in steering us through this minefield!

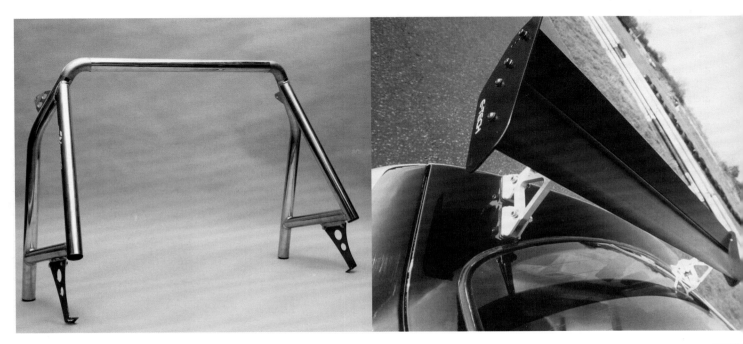

Thanks to:

We gratefully acknowledge all the help and advice offered from the following suppliers, without whom, etc, etc. Many of those credited below went way beyond the call of duty to help us produce this book - you know who you are. Cheers, guys! Roll the credits...

ABC Design Autostyling Ltd
(AutoArt & MHW)
www.abcdesignltd.com

Avon Custom
(paint and bodywork)
01934 876250
www.avoncustom.co.uk

Brown & Geeson (Momo)
01268 764411
www.brownandgeeson.com

Car Electronics Ltd
(ICE equipment)
0116 244 9847
www.cel-direct.com

Cobra Seats
01952 684020
www.cobraseats.com

Dash Dynamics
0870 127 0003
www.dashdynamics.co.uk

Demon Tweeks (accessories)
01978 664466
www.demon-tweeks.co.uk

Draper Tools (tools)
023 8026 6355
www.draper.co.uk

ESP Design Ltd
01621 869866
www.espdesign.co.uk

Eurostyling (Folia Tec)
01908 324950
www.eurostyling.com

Halfords
08457 626 625

House of Kolor (paint)
01302 341788
www.houseofkolor.com

K & N Filters
(Induction kits)
01925 636950
www.knfilters.co.uk

L.A & R.W Piper
(car trimming)
01963 441431
www.trimmers.fsnet.co.uk

Microscan Alarms
www.microscanalarms.co.uk

Mirage Stainless Styling
(engine styling)
01469 540427
www.miragestainlessstyling.co.uk

A & I Peco (exhaust box)
0151 647 6041
www.peco.co.uk

Red Dot Racing
(brake discs & pads)
020 8888 2354
www.reddotracing.co.uk

Richbrook
(sport auto accessories)
020 8543 7111
www.richbrook.co.uk

Ripspeed at Halfords
0845 609 1259

Performance 3000
(undercar neons)
01935 427554
www.performance3000.com

SPAX
01869 244771
www.spaxperformance.com

Toyo Tyres
01933 411144
www.toyo.co.uk

A special thank you to:
Bryn Musselwhite

Editorial Director	Matthew Minter
Designer	Simon Larkin
Page Build	James Robertson
Workshop	Paul Buckland Pete Trott
Editor	Ian Barnes
Project Co-ordinator	Carole Turk
Production Control	Kevin Heals

Haynes Car Manuals

Alfa Romeo Alfasud/Sprint (74 - 88) up to F * — 0292
Alfa Romeo Alfetta (73 - 87) up to E * — 0531
Audi 80, 90 & Coupe Petrol (79 - Nov 88) up to F — 0605
Audi 80, 90 & Coupe Petrol (Oct 86 - 90) D to H — 1491
Audi 100 & 200 Petrol (Oct 82 - 90) up to H — 0907
Audi 100 & A6 Petrol & Diesel (May 91 - May 97) H to P — 3504
Audi A3 Petrol & Diesel (96 - May 03) P to 03 — 4253
Audi A4 Petrol & Diesel (95 - Feb 00) M to V — 3575
Austin A35 & A40 (56 - 67) up to F * — 0118
Austin/MG/Rover Maestro 1.3 & 1.6 Petrol (83 - 95) up to M — 0922
Austin/MG Metro (80 - May 90) up to G — 0718
Austin/Rover Montego 1.3 & 1.6 Petrol (84 - 94) A to L — 1066
Austin/MG/Rover Montego 2.0 Petrol (84 - 95) A to M — 1067
Mini (59 - 69) up to H * — 0527
Mini (69 - 01) up to X — 0646
Austin/Rover 2.0 litre Diesel Engine (86 - 93) C to L — 1857
Austin Healey 100/6 & 3000 (56 - 68) up to G * — 0049
Bedford CF Petrol (69 - 87) up to E — 0163
Bedford/Vauxhall Rascal & Suzuki Supercarry (86 - Oct 94) C to M — 3015
BMW 316, 320 & 320i (4-cyl) (75 - Feb 83) up to Y * — 0276
BMW 320, 320i, 323i & 325i (6-cyl) (Oct 77 - Sept 87) up to E — 0815
BMW 3- & 5-Series Petrol (81 - 91) up to J — 1948
BMW 3-Series Petrol (Apr 91 - 96) H to N — 3210
BMW 3-Series Petrol (Sept 98 - 03) S to 53 — 4067
BMW 520i & 525e (Oct 81 - June 88) up to E — 1560
BMW 525, 528 & 528i (73 - Sept 81) up to X * — 0632
BMW 5-Series 6-cyl Petrol (April 96 - Aug 03) N to 03 — 4151
BMW 1500, 1502, 1600, 1602, 2000 & 2002 (59 - 77) up to S * — 0240
Chrysler PT Cruiser Petrol (00 - 03) W to 53 — 4058
Citroën 2CV, Ami & Dyane (67 - 90) up to H — 0196
Citroën AX Petrol & Diesel (87 - 97) D to P — 3014
Citroën Berlingo & Peugeot Partner Petrol & Diesel (96 - 05) P to 55 — 4281
Citroën BX Petrol (83 - 94) A to L — 0908
Citroën C15 Van Petrol & Diesel (89 - Oct 98) F to S — 3509
Citroën C3 Petrol & Diesel (02 - 05) 51 to 05 — 4197
Citroën CX Petrol (75 - 88) up to F — 0528
Citroën Saxo Petrol & Diesel (96 - 04) N to 54 — 3506
Citroën Saxo Petrol & Diesel (96 - 01) N to X — 3506
Citroën Visa Petrol (79 - 88) up to F — 0620
Citroën Xantia Petrol & Diesel (93 - 01) K to Y — 3082
Citroën XM Petrol & Diesel (89 - 00) G to X — 3451
Citroën Xsara Petrol & Diesel (97 - Sept 00) R to W — 3751
Citroën Xsara Picasso Petrol & Diesel (00 - 02) W to 52 — 3944
Citroën ZX Diesel (91 - 98) J to S — 1922
Citroën ZX Petrol (91 - 98) H to S — 1881
Citroën 1.7 & 1.9 litre Diesel Engine (84 - 96) A to N — 1379
Fiat 126 (73 - 87) up to E * — 0305
Fiat 500 (57 - 73) up to M * — 0090
Fiat Bravo & Brava Petrol (95 - 00) N to W — 3572
Fiat Cinquecento (93 - 98) K to R — 3501
Fiat Panda (81 - 95) up to M — 0793
Fiat Punto Petrol & Diesel (94 - Oct 99) L to V — 3251
Fiat Punto Petrol (Oct 99 - July 03) V to 03 — 4066
Fiat Regata Petrol (84 - 88) A to F — 1167
Fiat Tipo Petrol (88 - 91) E to J — 1625
Fiat Uno Petrol (83 - 95) up to M — 0923
Fiat X1/9 (74 - 89) up to G * — 0273
Ford Anglia (59 - 68) up to G * — 0001
Ford Capri II (& III) 1.6 & 2.0 (74 - 87) up to E * — 0283
Ford Capri II (& III) 2.8 & 3.0 V6 (74 - 87) up to E — 1309
Ford Cortina Mk III 1300 & 1600 (70 - 76) up to P — 0070
Ford Escort Mk I 1100 & 1300 (68 - 74) up to N * — 0171
Ford Escort Mk I Mexico, RS 1600 & RS 2000 (70 - 74) up to N * — 0139
Ford Escort Mk II Mexico, RS 1800 & RS 2000 (75 - 80) up to W * — 0735
Ford Escort (75 - Aug 80) up to V * — 0280
Ford Escort Petrol (Sept 80 - Sept 90) up to H — 0686
Ford Escort & Orion Petrol (Sept 90 - 00) H to X — 1737
Ford Escort & Orion Diesel (Sept 90 - 00) H to X — 4081
Ford Fiesta (76 - Aug 83) up to Y — 0334
Ford Fiesta Petrol (Aug 83 - Feb 89) A to F — 1030
Ford Fiesta Petrol (Feb 89 - Oct 95) F to N — 1595
Ford Fiesta Petrol & Diesel (Oct 95 - Mar 02) N to 02 — 3397
Ford Fiesta Petrol & Diesel (Apr 02 - 05) 02 to 54 — 4170
Ford Focus Petrol & Diesel (98 - 01) S to Y — 3759
Ford Focus Petrol & Diesel (Oct 01 - 04) 51 to 54 — 4167
Ford Galaxy Petrol & Diesel (95 - Aug 00) M to W — 3984
Ford Granada Petrol (Sept 77 - Feb 85) up to B * — 0481
Ford Granada & Scorpio Petrol (Mar 85 - 94) B to M — 1245
Ford Ka (96 - 02) P to 52 — 3570
Ford Mondeo Petrol (93 - Sept 00) K to X — 1923
Ford Mondeo Petrol & Diesel (Oct 00 - Jul 03) X to 03 — 3990
Ford Mondeo Diesel (93 - 96) L to N — 3465
Ford Orion Petrol (83 - Sept 90) up to H — 1009
Ford Sierra 4-cyl Petrol (82 - 93) up to K — 0903
Ford Sierra V6 Petrol (82 - 91) up to J — 0904
Ford Transit Petrol (Mk 2) (78 - Jan 86) up to C — 0719
Ford Transit Petrol (Mk 3) (Feb 86 - 89) C to G — 1468
Ford Transit Diesel (Feb 86 - 99) C to T — 3019
Ford 1.6 & 1.8 litre Diesel Engine (84 - 96) A to N — 1172
Ford 2.1, 2.3 & 2.5 litre Diesel Engine (77 - 90) up to H — 1606
Freight Rover Sherpa Petrol (74 - 87) up to E — 0463
Hillman Avenger (70 - 82) up to Y — 0037
Hillman Imp (63 - 76) up to R * — 0022
Honda Civic (Feb 84 - Oct 87) A to E — 1226
Honda Civic (Nov 91 - 96) J to N — 3199
Honda Civic Petrol (Mar 95 - 00) M to X — 4050
Hyundai Pony (85 - 94) C to M — 3398
Jaguar E Type (61 - 72) up to L * — 0140
Jaguar Mk I & II, 240 & 340 (55 - 69) up to H * — 0098
Jaguar XJ6, XJ & Sovereign; Daimler Sovereign (68 - Oct 86) up to D — 0242

Jaguar XJ6 & Sovereign (Oct 86 - Sept 94) D to M — 3261
Jaguar XJ12, XJS & Sovereign; Daimler Double Six (72 - 88) up to F — 0478
Jeep Cherokee Petrol (93 - 96) K to N — 1943
Lada 1200, 1300, 1500 & 1600 (74 - 91) up to J — 0413
Lada Samara (87 - 91) D to J — 1610
Land Rover 90, 110 & Defender Diesel (83 - 95) up to N — 3017
Land Rover Discovery Petrol & Diesel (89 - 98) G to S — 3016
Land Rover Freelander Petrol & Diesel (97 - 02) R to 52 — 3929
Land Rover Series IIA & III Diesel (58 - 85) up to C — 0529
Land Rover Series II, IIA & III 4-cyl Petrol (58 - 85) up to C — 0314
Mazda 323 (Mar 81 - Oct 89) up to G — 1608
Mazda 323 (Oct 89 - 98) G to R — 3455
Mazda 626 (May 83 - Sept 87) up to E — 0929
Mazda B1600, B1800 & B2000 Pick-up Petrol (72 - 88) up to F — 0267
Mazda RX-7 (79 - 85) up to C * — 0460
Mercedes-Benz 190, 190E & 190D Petrol & Diesel (83 - 93) A to L — 3450
Mercedes-Benz 200D, 240D, 240TD, 300D & 300TD 123 Series (Oct 76 - 85) up to C — 1114
Mercedes-Benz 250 & 280 (68 - 72) up to L * — 0346
Mercedes-Benz 250 & 280 123 Series Petrol (Oct 76 - 84) up to B * — 0677
Mercedes-Benz 124 Series Petrol & Diesel (85 - Aug 93) C to K — 3253
Mercedes-Benz C-Class Petrol & Diesel (93 - Aug 00) L to W — 3511
MGA (55 - 62) * — 0475
MGB (62 - 80) up to W — 0111
MG Midget & Austin-Healey Sprite (58 - 80) up to W * — 0265
Mini Petrol (July 01 - 05) Y to 05 — 4273
Mitsubishi Shogun & L200 Pick-Ups Petrol (83 - 94) up to M — 1944
Morris Ital 1.3 (80 - 84) up to B — 0705
Morris Minor 1000 (56 - 71) up to K — 0024
Nissan Almera Petrol (95 - Feb 00) N to V — 4053
Nissan Bluebird (May 84 - Mar 86) A to C — 1223
Nissan Bluebird Petrol (Mar 86 - 90) C to H — 1473
Nissan Cherry (Sept 82 - 86) up to D — 1031
Nissan Micra (83 - Jan 93) up to K — 0931
Nissan Micra (93 - 02) K to 52 — 3254
Nissan Micra (93 - 99) K to T — 3254
Nissan Primera Petrol (90 - Aug 99) H to T — 1851
Nissan Stanza (82 - 86) up to D — 0824
Nissan Sunny Petrol (May 82 - Oct 86) up to D — 0895
Nissan Sunny Petrol (Oct 86 - Mar 91) D to H — 1378
Nissan Sunny Petrol (Apr 91 - 95) H to N — 3219
Opel Ascona & Manta (B Series) (Sept 75 - 88) up to F * — 0316
Opel Ascona Petrol (81 - 88) — 3215
Opel Astra Petrol (Oct 91 - Feb 98) — 3156
Opel Corsa Petrol (83 - Mar 93) — 3160
Opel Corsa Petrol (Mar 93 - 97) — 3159
Opel Kadett Petrol (Nov 79 - Oct 84) up to B — 0634
Opel Kadett Petrol (Oct 84 - Oct 91) — 3196
Opel Omega & Senator Petrol (Nov 86 - 94) — 3157
Opel Rekord Petrol (Feb 78 - Oct 86) up to D — 0543
Opel Vectra Petrol (Oct 88 - Oct 95) — 3158
Peugeot 106 Petrol & Diesel (91 - 04) J to 53 — 1882
Peugeot 205 Petrol (83 - 97) A to P — 0932
Peugeot 206 Petrol & Diesel (98 - 01) S to X — 3757
Peugeot 306 Petrol & Diesel (93 - 02) K to 02 — 3073
Peugeot 307 Petrol & Diesel (01 - 04) Y to 54 — 4147
Peugeot 309 Petrol (86 - 93) C to K — 1266
Peugeot 405 Petrol (88 - 97) E to P — 1559
Peugeot 405 Diesel (88 - 97) E to P — 3198
Peugeot 406 Petrol & Diesel (96 - Mar 99) N to T — 3394
Peugeot 406 Petrol & Diesel (Mar 99 - 02) T to 52 — 3982
Peugeot 505 Petrol (79 - 89) up to G — 0762
Peugeot 1.7/1.8 & 1.9 litre Diesel Engine (82 - 96) up to N — 0950
Peugeot 2.0, 2.1, 2.3 & 2.5 litre Diesel Engines (74 - 90) up to H — 1607
Porsche 911 (65 - 85) up to C — 0264
Porsche 924 & 924 Turbo (76 - 85) up to C — 0397
Proton (89 - 97) F to P — 3255
Range Rover V8 Petrol (70 - Oct 92) up to K — 0606
Reliant Robin & Kitten (73 - 83) up to A * — 0436
Renault 4 (61 - 86) up to D * — 0072
Renault 5 Petrol (85 - 96) B to N — 1219
Renault 9 & 11 Petrol (82 - 89) up to F — 0822
Renault 18 Petrol (79 - 86) up to D — 0598
Renault 19 Petrol (89 - 96) F to N — 1646
Renault 19 Diesel (89 - 96) F to N — 1946
Renault 21 Petrol (86 - 94) C to M — 1397
Renault 25 Petrol & Diesel (84 - 92) B to K — 1228
Renault Clio Petrol (91 - May 98) H to R — 1853
Renault Clio Diesel (91 - June 96) H to N — 3031
Renault Clio Petrol & Diesel (May 98 - May 01) R to Y — 3906
Renault Clio Petrol & Diesel (June 01 - 04) Y to 54 — 4168
Renault Espace Petrol & Diesel (85 - 96) C to N — 3197
Renault Laguna Petrol & Diesel (94 - 00) L to W — 3252
Renault Mégane & Scénic Petrol & Diesel (96 - 98) N to R — 3395
Renault Mégane & Scénic Petrol & Diesel (Apr 99 - 02) T to 52 — 3916
Renault Megane Petrol & Diesel (Oct 02 - 05) 52 to 55 — 4284
Renault Scenic Petrol & Diesel (Sept 03 - 06) 53 to 06 — 4297
Rover 213 & 216 (84 - 89) A to G — 1116
Rover 214 & 414 Petrol (89 - 96) G to N — 1689
Rover 216 & 416 Petrol (89 - 96) G to N — 1830
Rover 211, 214, 216, 218 & 220 Petrol & Diesel (Dec 95 - 99) N to V — 3399
Rover 25 & MG ZR Petrol & Diesel (Oct 99 - 04) V to 54 — 4145
Rover 414, 416 & 420 Petrol & Diesel (May 95 - 98) M to N — 3453
Rover 618, 620 & 623 Petrol (93 - 97) K to P — 3257
Rover 820, 825 & 827 Petrol (86 - 95) D to N — 1380
Rover 3500 (76 - 87) up to E * — 0365
Rover Metro, 111 & 114 Petrol (May 90 - 98) G to S — 1711
Saab 95 & 96 (66 - 76) up to R * — 0198
Saab 90, 99 & 900 (79 - Oct 93) up to L — 0765

Saab 900 (Oct 93 - 98) L to R — 3512
Saab 9000 (4-cyl) (85 - 98) C to S — 1686
Saab 9-5 4-cyl Petrol (97 - 04) R to 54 — 4156
Seat Ibiza & Cordoba Petrol & Diesel (Oct 93 - Oct 99) L to V — 3571
Seat Ibiza & Malaga Petrol (85 - 92) B to K — 1609
Skoda Estelle (77 - 89) up to G — 0604
Skoda Favorit (89 - 96) F to N — 1801
Skoda Felicia Petrol & Diesel (95 - 01) M to X — 3505
Subaru 1600 & 1800 (Nov 79 - 90) up to H * — 0995
Sunbeam Alpine, Rapier & H120 (67 - 74) up to N * — 0051
Suzuki SJ Series, Samurai & Vitara (4-cyl) Petrol (82 - 97) up to P — 1942
Talbot Alpine, Solara, Minx & Rapier (75 - 86) up to D — 0337
Talbot Horizon Petrol (78 - 86) up to D — 0473
Talbot Samba (82 - 86) up to D — 0823
Toyota Carina E Petrol (May 92 - 97) J to P — 3256
Toyota Corolla (80 - 85) up to D — 0683
Toyota Corolla (Sept 83 - Sept 87) A to E — 1024
Toyota Corolla (Sept 87 - Aug 92) E to K — 1683
Toyota Corolla Petrol (Aug 92 - 97) K to P — 3259
Toyota Hi-Ace & Hi-Lux Petrol (69 - Oct 83) up to A — 0304
Toyota Yaris Petrol (99 - 05) T to 05 — 4265
Triumph GT6 & Vitesse (62 - 74) up to N * — 0112
Triumph Herald (59 - 71) up to K * — 0010
Triumph Spitfire (62 - 81) up to X — 0113
Triumph Stag (70 - 78) up to T * — 0441
Triumph TR2, TR3, TR3A, TR4 & TR4A (52 - 67) up to F * — 0028
Triumph TR5 & 6 (67 - 75) up to P * — 0031
Triumph TR7 (75 - 82) up to Y * — 0322
Vauxhall Astra Petrol (80 - Oct 84) up to B — 0635
Vauxhall Astra & Belmont Petrol (Oct 84 - Oct 91) B to J — 1136
Vauxhall Astra Petrol (Oct 91 - Feb 98) J to R — 1832
Vauxhall/Opel Astra & Zafira Petrol (Feb 98 - Apr 04) R to 04 — 3758
Vauxhall/Opel Astra & Zafira Diesel (Feb 98 - Apr 04) R to 04 — 3797
Vauxhall/Opel Calibra (90 - 98) G to S — 3502
Vauxhall Carlton Petrol (Oct 78 - Oct 86) up to D — 0480
Vauxhall Carlton & Senator Petrol (Nov 86 - 94) D to L — 1469
Vauxhall Cavalier Petrol (81 - Oct 88) up to F — 0812
Vauxhall Cavalier Petrol (Oct 88 - 95) F to N — 1570
Vauxhall Chevette (75 - 84) up to B — 0285
Vauxhall/Opel Corsa Diesel (Mar 93 - Oct 00) K to X — 4087
Vauxhall Corsa Petrol (Mar 93 - 97) K to R — 1985
Vauxhall/Opel Corsa Petrol (Apr 97 - Oct 00) P to X — 3921
Vauxhall/Opel Corsa Petrol & Diesel (Oct 00 - Sept 03) X to 53 — 4079
Vauxhall/Opel Frontera Petrol & Diesel (91 - Sept 98) J to S — 3454
Vauxhall/Opel Nova Petrol (83 - 93) up to K — 0909
Vauxhall/Opel Omega Petrol (94 - 99) L to T — 3510
Vauxhall/Opel Vectra Petrol & Diesel (95 - Feb 99) N to S — 3396
Vauxhall/Opel Vectra Petrol & Diesel (Mar 99 - May 02) T to 02 — 3930
Vauxhall/Opel 1.5, 1.6 & 1.7 litre Diesel Engine (82 - 96) up to N — 1222
Volkswagen 411 & 412 (68 - 75) up to P * — 0091
Volkswagen Beetle 1200 (54 - 77) up to S — 0036
Volkswagen Beetle 1300 & 1500 (65 - 75) up to P — 0039
Volkswagen Beetle 1302 & 1302S (70 - 72) up to L * — 0110
Volkswagen Beetle 1303, 1303S & GT (72 - 75) up to P — 0159
Volkswagen Beetle Petrol & Diesel (Apr 99 - 01) T to 51 — 3798
Volkswagen Golf & Bora Petrol & Diesel (April 98 - 00) R to X — 3727
Volkswagen Golf & Jetta Mk 1 Petrol 1.1 & 1.3 (74 - 84) up to A — 0716
Volkswagen Golf, Jetta & Scirocco Mk 1 Petrol 1.5, 1.6 & 1.8 (74 - 84) up to A — 0726
Volkswagen Golf & Jetta Mk 1 Diesel (78 - 84) up to A — 0451
Volkswagen Golf & Jetta Mk 2 Petrol (Mar 84 - Feb 92) A to J — 1081
Volkswagen Golf & Vento Petrol & Diesel (Feb 92 - Mar 98) J to R — 3097
Volkswagen Golf & Bora 4-cyl Petrol & Diesel (01 - 03) X to 53 — 4169
Volkswagen LT Petrol Vans & Light Trucks (76 - 87) up to E — 0637
Volkswagen Passat & Santana Petrol (Sept 81 - May 88) up to E — 0814
Volkswagen Passat 4-cyl Petrol & Diesel (May 88 - 96) E to P — 3498
Volkswagen Passat 4-cyl Petrol & Diesel (Dec 96 - Nov 00) P to X — 3917
VW Passat Petrol & Diesel (Dec 00 - May 05) X to 05 — 4279
Volkswagen Polo & Derby (76 - Jan 82) up to X — 0335
Volkswagen Polo (82 - Oct 90) up to H — 0813
Volkswagen Polo Petrol (Nov 90 - Aug 94) H to L — 3245
Volkswagen Polo Hatchback Petrol & Diesel (94 - 99) M to S — 3500
Volkswagen Polo Hatchback Petrol & Diesel (00 - Jan 02) V to 51 — 4150
Volkswagen Scirocco (82 - 90) up to H — 1224
Volkswagen Transporter 1600 (68 - 79) up to V — 0082
Volkswagen Transporter 1700, 1800 & 2000 (72 - 79) up to V * — 0226
Volkswagen Transporter (air-cooled) Petrol (79 - 82) up to Y * — 0638
Volkswagen Transporter (water-cooled) Petrol (82 - 90) up to H — 3452
Volkswagen Type 3 (63 - 73) up to M * — 0084
Volvo 120 & 130 Series (& P1800) (61 - 73) up to M * — 0203
Volvo 142, 144 & 145 (66 - 74) up to N * — 0129
Volvo 240 Series Petrol (74 - 93) up to K — 0270
Volvo 262, 264 & 260/265 (75 - 85) up to C * — 0400
Volvo 340, 343, 345 & 360 (76 - 91) up to J — 0715
Volvo 440, 460 & 480 Petrol (87 - 97) D to P — 1691
Volvo 740 & 760 Petrol (82 - 91) up to J — 1258
Volvo 850 Petrol (92 - 96) J to P — 3260
Volvo 940 Petrol (90 - 96) H to N — 3249
Volvo S40 & V40 Petrol (96 - Mar 04) N to 04 — 3569
Volvo S70, V70 & C70 Petrol (96 - 99) P to V — 3573
Volvo V70 / S80 Petrol & Diesel (98 - 05) S to 55 — 4263

* = Classic Reprints